Places of Power

About The Author

❖

Photo by Brian Kemsley

KATHLEEN KEMSLEY grew up in the suburbs of California, and spent vacations at the family cabin in Yosemite. During summer breaks from college, she worked at Yellowstone and Grand Canyon National Parks. Upon graduation from the University of California, Berkeley in 1980, Kathleen moved to the Grand Canyon, where she worked for the concessioner, and later the National Park Service. She went to Denali National Park, Alaska, in 1984 to work as a Park Technician. Kathleen now resides with her husband on the Kenai Peninsula, Alaska, where she works as a 911 dispatcher. Her hobbies include hiking, canoeing, cross country skiing, and photography.

A Decade of Living in National Parks

PLACES
OF
POWER

Kathleen R. Kemsley

Cover art by Nanci Tuttle Grzesiak

Library of Congress Catalog Card Number: 91-50961

ISBN: 0-923568-20-4

Maps and photos by the author

Typesetting by
LaserText Typesetting / 3886 Sheldrake Avenue / Okemos, Michigan 48864

LIBRARY OF CONGRESS CATALOGING-IN-PUBLICATION DATA

Kemsley, Kathleen R. (Kathleen Robinson), 1958 –
    Places of power : a decade of living in national parks / Kathleen R. Kemsley.
        p.   cm.
    ISBN 0-923568-20-4
    1. Kemsley, Kathleen R. (Kathleen Robinson), 1958 –   .
    2. National parks and reserves—West (U.S.) 3. United States.
    National Park Service—Officials and employees—Biography.
    I. Title.
SB481.6.K46A3   1991
508.73—dc20   90-50961
                                                                          CIP

PUBLISHED BY

Wilderness Adventure Books
320 Garden Lane
Box 968
Fowlerville, Michigan 48836

Manufactured in the United States of America

This book is dedicated to
Jack and Lois Robinson, with love.

Companion to the hushed rustling
Of the sugar pine bough,
I come alone
Almost silently
The wild peaceful beauty becomes
A part of me
And I of it
An evening grosbeak
Calmly stares me down and goes about its business
Gold on brown
And I know
That cars and cities do exist
But this is real
Only this is real.

—*Kathleen R. Kemsley*

Contents

Acknowledgements

Writing a book is a solitary pursuit. But in working on the manuscript for this book, many people have come into my mind. Some I have not seen in years, while others remain close friends today. I would like to acknowledge the contributions of a few of the people who have helped me along the way to getting this book written.

Douglas Powell and Roger Byrne were both influential professors in the Geography Department at the University of California, Berkeley. Larry Van Slyke, Curtis Sauer, and Thomas Griffiths, all park service rangers, believed in my potential enough to hire me for some exciting jobs. Co-parkies Kimmie Johnson, Brad Blomquist, Jennifer Lawton, Ruthann Murray, Kim Crumbo, T. R. Anaya, Clare and Ken Curtis, Debbie Frauson, Steve and Marie Pickle, Jan Goggins, Dennis Haskew, Rick Scharf, Jeff Barbour, Lulu Santamaria: though I don't know where most of you are today, thanks for sharing in part of my life.

The following people, family and extended family, have been a part of my experiences in the parks, accompanying me on adventures and keeping in touch with me over the years: Jack and Lois Robinson, Christie and Dave White, Abel Robinson, Randy Latta, Rob and Jean Russell, Louise Schultz, Isaac and Jed Kemsley.

And for their patience and encouragement during the three years I have been working on this book, I would like to give a special thanks to Margi Ulvestad, Patricia Miley, Darrell and Georgia Knackstadt, Ann Mercer, Mary Casebeer, Jim Cassidy, Larry James, Leah Vienna, O. B. Cully, Bill Kemsley, William Maloney, Jaime Rodriguez, Susan Van Schoor, Diane Bullock, Lin Lusnia, Lisa Schmitter, and the rest of you; you know who you are.

Finally, to Brian Kemsley, for putting up with my moods, for continually sounding the voice of encouragement, and for believing in me when I didn't believe in myself, my heartfelt gratitude.

1

❖❖❖

Wawona

One of my earliest childhood memories was of watching the firefalls off Glacier Point. I was only about five years old when Mom and Dad bundled us up in sweatshirts and drove us down to the valley after dinner to see the spectacle.

We stood in a crowd of people on the grass, tilting our heads way back to see to the top of sheer granite walls sculpted by glaciers. It seemed that I waited an eternity before the ball of fire appeared. It flared, hanging on the lip of a rock, suspended in darkness high above my head. And then it spilled over and tumbled down the cliff, throwing off sparks and illuminating the polished stone face of the granite.

That was the last summer the park put on a firefall display in Yosemite Valley. It was one of those entertainment extravaganzas, like Hopi Indians performing rain dances and bleachers built around garbage dumps from which to view feeding bears, which was quietly abandoned by the parks as cultural and environmental consciousness was raised in the 1960s. Still, as a young child I was impressed by the visual impact of a ball of fire being hurtled off a granite cliff into the summer night.

The *ooohs* and *ahhhs* of the tourists in the crowd reminded me of the sound effects associated with a pyrotechnics display on the fourth of July. The moon, almost full and rising like an Ansel Adams photograph over Half Dome, was temporarily up-staged by the human creation of fire tumbling from Glacier Point.

I attributed my fascination with national parks to the fact that I spent part of every childhood summer at Yosemite. My family owned a large, dorm-like two story cabin in Fish Camp, just outside the south entrance to the park. Because my father's job kept our family moving from place to place every couple of years while I was growing up, visits to the cabin were the constant in my life. I thought of the cabin as home; it was more like home than any of the tract houses we inhabited in suburban California.

The original cabin owned by Dad's family had been located near Wawona in the southern end of the park. My grandparents, along with Dad and his sisters, often journeyed to Yosemite to escape the heat of the San Joaquin Valley summer. Many of the people who owned cabins near theirs were also their neighbors in Merced.

Dad's childhood, like mine, was intertwined with Yosemite. He recalled a great flood in 1939 which overnight transformed the South Fork of the Merced River from a sedate river flowing smoothly over highly polished granite slabs to a boulder-choked torrent of melted snow. He said the sound of rocks and trees being torn from the banks by the force of the river water, swollen by spring melt off, could be heard several miles away. That cabin met its demise in 1948. Dad and some of his teen-age friends had come up from Merced one winter weekend, to ski the slopes at Badger Pass. Somehow, a stray ember escaped from the stone fireplace while they were gone skiing. When they returned from Badger that evening, the cabin had burned to the ground.

After the cabin burned, my grandfather sold the land behind the Wawona Hotel and decided not to rebuild. Four years later, when the grandchildren began to arrive, he reconsidered. He purchased three adjoining lots in Fish Camp, five miles south of the park entrance, for the use of his children's families. I suppose I was in diapers the first time I traveled to Fish Camp. I could not recall a summer ever during my childhood which did not include at least a couple weeks spent at the cabin.

Fish Camp in the early 1960s had a permanent population of 13 people. The town consisted of a general store, the Silvertip Lodge, and a pond which was stocked with trout. Our cabin was built on a hill about a mile up behind the store. From the cabin, a spider web of logging roads led far back into the mountains of the Sierra National Forest. Those roads provided me and John, my brother, and Christie, my sister, with numerous hiking routes to explore on the days we did not pile into the car and drive to Wawona.

It seemed when I was young that the drive from Fish Camp to the river took hours. In fact it was only about ten miles, but the twisting road and the summer tourist traffic slowed us down considerably. The consensus among us kids was that Dad took the curves fast enough to make for a thrilling ride.

"I've been driving this road since I was twelve years old," he protested when anyone complained about his speed. We kids joined right in when he lost patience with the tourist drivers. Every time a camper ahead of us braked on a curve or crawled along at 20 miles per hour, we would shriek, "Use a turnout, buddy!" just as we had heard Dad do.

We always considered the South Fork of the Merced River above Wawona to be our own territory. Certainly in the earlier years it was our exclusive domain. We packed a lunch in Mom's wicker basket, loaded the dog into the car, and drove up to the Wawona Hotel. There, an unmarked turn off the main road led to a rutted dirt route not wide enough for two cars. We drove past the site of the original cabin where Dad had spent his summers as a boy. At the end of the road we parked and walked upriver until we found a place with room enough to spread out, and commenced to spend the day frolicking by the water.

Things for a child to do at the river were endless. We floated the rapids in inner tubes in July and August, when the water level was low enough to render the current tame. We discovered enormous colonies of ladybugs on the rocks at river's edge. The population of spotted bugs was so thick that, when viewed from a distance, the river bank appeared to be as orange as rust. We fished for trout and learned how to skip flat rocks. One day Mom and I saw a black bear ambling along the far side of the river; in those days the South Fork Merced River was a fairly remote section of Yosemite National Park.

Once when I was about nine years old, the river almost took me. We were on the lazy day agenda, eating a picnic lunch sprawled out on the granite slab only a quarter mile upriver from where we had parked the car. I walked down to the river's edge, barefoot, to retrieve a chilled can of orange soda from the icy water. In early June the water was much too cold and swift for swimming, but it functioned well as a refrigerator for our pop.

As I leaned over to grab the can, my bare feet slid on the glassy surface of water-polished granite. Instantly I was in the river and swept away downstream. Screams inadvertently escaped from my throat when I hit the icy water, alerting my kin to my plight; but I was already moving swiftly down the river and out of their sight around the bend.

After a moment or two of struggle, I gave up fighting the current and tried to concentrate on flowing with it. I could not touch the bottom of the swift river. After I dog paddled my way around the bend, the river channel became clogged with large boulders. They were the ones Dad had described, which had been placed during the flood of 1939.

The icy water threw me into one large gray rock, then into another. I began to feel weak. My head cracked against a third rock. For the first time since I had fallen, I began to get scared. Though I was confident of my swimming ability, I was becoming cold and numb. Perhaps 90 seconds had passed since I went in.

Finally the water steered me toward an eddy. Hardly able to feel my legs because of the cold river, I tested for bottom and my unsteady feet found it. Out of the icy river I dragged myself. I had just enough strength to pull myself completely out of the water; then I collapsed on the rocky bank.

I did not know how long I lay there, absorbing the healing warmth of sunlight. Startled to consciousness by the sound of footsteps, I looked up to see Mom running toward me.

"Oh, Kitty, we thought you were gone," she said between gasps of breath. "What happened?"

"I slipped on the granite and fell in," I told her. "Then I found a place to get out, and I did it." I did not tell her about getting slammed into the boulders. I was safe, and that was all that mattered.

Mom helped me up. "Can you walk? Listen, let me tell you something. Never turn your back on the ocean, you know what I mean? You have to respect the water—respect all of nature— for it can be very powerful. You must watch your own step, Kitty. Nature doesn't make exceptions, even for little girls like you."

"O.K., Mom. I'll be careful," I promised. The rash promise of a nine year old. . . . I never forgot that wild ride down the rapids. There were to be many more experiences for me in the wilderness, on its own terms, before I ever truly came to understand the meaning of her words.

Besides the natural wonders and the natural hazards of my river world, there beneath the yellow pine "puzzlewood" trees and spotless blue sky, I became interested in some of the more ancient inhabitants of the Yosemite region. I first became aware of previous occupants along the South Fork of the Merced River after Dad had an accident. Losing his footing during a hike in the woods, he tore a three-inch gash in his ankle. He was on crutches for the rest of the vacation and unable to swim in the river with the rest of us because of his stitches. When we were all down by the river one day, he hobbled off alone toward some cliffs overlooking the river. Returning a couple hours later, he brought with him a tiny, perfect arrowhead crafted out of obsidian, which he had found up on the hillside.

I got the fever after seeing that arrowhead, and I began to search for more of them. My technique was a combination of serendipity and an ability to walk around gravel washes bent double, eyes glued to the ground, for long periods of time, while the sun beat down on my back, turning it a rich shade of brown.

Besides arrowheads, we picked up the chips and flakes of obsidian we found. Obsidian was not indigenous to the area. To get it, the native people traded with Mono Indians on the east side of the Sierra Nevada. Skillfully they chipped the soft, slick black volcanic rock until it formed a tiny point, suitable for hunting birds and fish. As far as I knew, no one else was aware of the existence of the artifacts of that gone civilization, scattered across the gravel washes above the river. We shamelessly collected every piece of obsidian and every arrowhead we found.

My family never had a run-in with the Park Service over that one. We were either unaware or unconcerned about park regulations prohibiting the removal of artifacts. I did not learn about the retribution for that crime until years later. We rationalized at that time that almost no one ever went to the places where we found our arrowheads, so they would never know the difference if we removed a few of them.

By the time I was a teenager, our privacy along the South Fork of the Merced River was challenged. We no longer went to Yosemite Valley at all by 1970, because the crowded conditions and a layer of orange smog visible at dusk reminded us too much of Southern California. Shuttle buses hauled the tourists around the Valley; Ticketron began taking reservations for the Valley campgrounds. Around that time, too, other people began driving up the one-lane rutted dirt road to the river. When our private space began to fill up with tourists, we responded by moving upriver, farther into the headwaters of the South Fork Merced River.

One of our favorite destinations, several miles up the river, we named "Double Falls." There, the river split into two currents and splashed over the smooth granite in twin cascades 20 feet high. A big old tree had fallen across the top of one of those falls. We spent many exuberant hours leaping and diving from the log into an emerald green pool of water so clear that we could see right to the bottom, fifteen feet down.

A few times, we even found people at Double Falls—nudists and hippies who thought they were in the wilderness and had not counted on the presence of our noisy clan up there. Mom begged us to avert our eyes; Dad took movies of them and later spliced them into our family home movies, after which a hastily scrawled title would appear: "Oops, wrong subject!"

Even as other people began to move into our territory on the upper river, we had never in all the years on the Merced River seen a representative of the National Park Service, a ranger. One day in 1973, however, even a ranger made it up into the sacred haven of water-polished granite and obsidian fields. On a hot July day, he appeared at the brink of the steep bank above our picnic spot, dressed in a heavy green shirt, wool pants and a broad-brimmed Smokey-the-Bear hat.

Down on the flats, none of us saw him approaching. Dad

was drinking beer and Mom was lying out in the sun with her bathing suit unhooked in the back. Christie was reading a book, and John and I were busy throwing rocks at an empty pop can. As the pop can bobbed in an eddy close to shore, we heaved grapefruit sized stones at it, taking turns trying to sink the can.

Down the steep bank marched the ranger. He walked up behind Dad. "Excuse me, sir," he said, and cleared his throat.

John and I stopped throwing rocks and stared over at him. He looked ridiculously overdressed next to Dad, who was clad only in bathing trunks.

"I must ask you to tell your children to stop throwing rocks," the ranger said.

"What are you talking about?" Dad asked sharply, standing up.

The ranger cleared his throat again. "Well, sir, if people throw rocks into the river, it damages the ecosystem, you see. It upsets the balance of nature. This is a national park. They can't do that."

Dad looked over at us and laughed out loud. I began to laugh too, for we were standing in a virtual rock garden—acres and acres of small round boulders, deposited by years of spring flooding. The rock carpet extended down around the bend and out as far as I could see, lining the river channel. Apparently Dad had noticed the same thing. "See all those rocks the kids are standing on? They cover the whole river bottom. Throwing them ten feet is not going to change anything. They get pushed around every year when the snow melts.

"I've been coming here since before you were born, Sonny," Dad continued. "If you want to know about the balance of nature, let me tell you about the flood of '39. Now here's a story about nature. It changes, it doesn't stand still. I was up at the cabin one day, and I suddenly heard a roar. . . ."

Dad kept the ranger captive for 15 minutes repeating the story we had all heard a thousand times before. While Dad talked, I whispered to John that he had better get the pop can. He waded out and grabbed it, and acted like he was drinking out of it, so that the ranger would not leap to the conclusion that we were littering as well as upsetting Mother Nature.

Finally Dad finished his story, "...so you can't tell me about changing the river ecology. I've seen it firsthand!"

"Even so, please keep an eye on those kids," the ranger said. Already he was backing up. "Have a good day, sir. Hope you have a fine day."

After the ranger left, we all had a good laugh. "The Balance of Nature" became a standing joke in the family, and if anything we threw rocks and sank cans more vigorously after that. But always with a glance first over the shoulder ... our river paradise had grown more crowded, and thus more regulated, over the years.

I wondered about that ranger later on. Where did he live, and what did he do during his free time? Certainly he did not spend his weekends bombing cans with river rocks. But he must have occupied his time away from the job with some sort of interesting activity. Surely, living in the park, that ranger was never bored.

I had noticed the concession employees too. They lived in a dorm behind the Wawona Hotel, and often as we drove past the dorm on the way up to the river I saw them lounging on the porch or feeding the deer whose fear of people had long ago been dissolved by a taste for human junk food. Almost tame, the deer came right up to the side of the dorm and posed for pictures in exchange for a handout.

The hotel employees were young, cheerful looking men and women. They sat in groups on the dorm porch drinking beer and laughing. When we stopped at the hotel on the way to the river to visit with one of Dad's relatives who managed the place, I peered curiously at the employees I saw. Dressed in spotless, identical uniforms, they walked by quickly, not looking at me.

There was a bounce to their steps.

Who were these parkie people working at the Wawona Hotel? Who were the good-looking young people inside the ranger suits? Where did they come from, and where did they go at the end of the season? Did they have parties, did they fall in love? Did they like their jobs and the tourists, or did they just tolerate those things in exchange for the beauty of their surroundings? Their existence intrigued me at a very young age. It seemed to me that working in a park like Yosemite would be a great way to spend a summer. Idly, I wondered how I might go about getting a job in a national park when I got to be old enough.

Eventually, I learned the answers to all those questions, for I became a parkie person myself. My relationship with parks and park people began on those childhood forays on the South Fork of the Merced River in Yosemite Park. And it did not end until many years later, in the wilderness of Alaska.

Through all that time, the parks loved me well.

2

❖

Mammoth Hot Springs

Sometime between midterms and final exams during my first quarter of college in San Diego, the mental picture of the dorm behind the Wawona Hotel in Yosemite returned to me. With no plans for the following summer, and little enthusiasm about the prospect of spending those three months in Los Angeles at my parents' house, I began taking steps to find out how I could get a job for the summer in a national park.

I wrote to the National Park Service headquarters in Washington, D.C., to obtain a pamphlet listing the addresses of concessionaires who hired summer help in the parks. Once I received the list, I chose 15 parks which looked intriguing and sent to them for more information. By return mail I received piles of application forms. Every one of the forms I filled out by hand. I sent them in, then settled back to await the results.

By April I had received three job offers, from Sequoia, Grand Canyon, and Yellowstone National Parks. The one I decided to take was the position in Yellowstone.

Yellowstone National Park

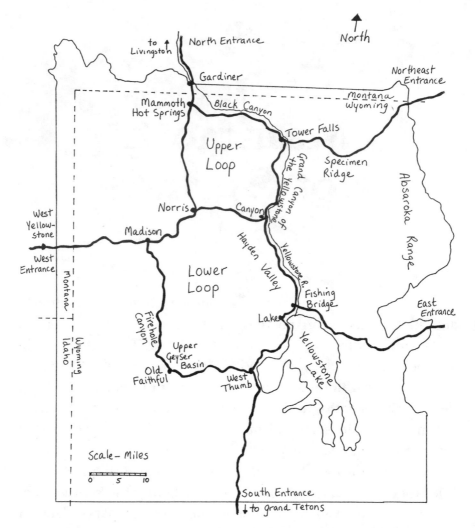

"Why Yellowstone?" my roommate asked me when I told her of my plans.

"Simple," I said, laughing. "It's the farthest away from here. I've never been to Wyoming. Don't you think it's exciting?"

Apparently I was the only one of my college friends who did think it sounded exciting. I tried to entice some of them into applying with me for park jobs, but none were interested. So I went by myself, eager to get away from the stuffy intellectuals at college and the fog-shrouded coast of California.

I traveled to Yellowstone in the company of my friend Randy, his sister Julie, and my brother John. In Randy's parents' camper, we drove through Utah's canyon country and the benign pastures of southern Idaho for a week on the way to Yellowstone.

We arrived at Mammoth Hot Springs, Yellowstone National Park, at noon. Randy and the others helped me offload my two boxes full of clothes and personal gear, and soon after that they left. I stood by the hotel watching the camper until it disappeared around the curve of the road. I was alone in Yellowstone. Turning my back on the road, I walked into the hotel and approached the desk clerk.

"I'm here," I said.

Mammoth Hot Springs was situated at the far northern end of Yellowstone National Park, just five miles from the park entrance and the Montana state line. It was off the beaten track in comparison to the more famous features of Yellowstone such as Old Faithful and the Grand Canyon of the Yellowstone River. Many tourists making the quick loop through the park missed Mammoth completely. Those travelers arriving from Glacier Park and those who had allotted two or more days to see the park were the ones who stopped in Mammoth Hot Springs.

The main thermal attraction in my area was a series of travertine limestone ledges bubbling and steaming with hot water which flowed from the bowels of the earth. During my first week in Mammoth, I walked up to the terraces half a mile from the hotel to give myself a self-guided tour. I picked up a pamphlet at the parking lot which described each spring and interpreted for novice geologists the highlights of the terraces.

The Mammoth Hot Springs Hotel,
viewed from Minerva Terrace

A plank trail led from the parking lot across the fragile calcium deposits, carefully marking the route so that tourist feet could not impact the delicate ecosystem of water and bright algae and slippery folds of lime.

I learned from the pamphlet that, while the amount of water or steam being emitted from any one part of the terrace area could vary hourly, the total volume of water expended by the hot springs remained constant. The booklet also told me that all the colors I saw brightening the hot pools in each spring indicated the presence of different species of algae. Various types of the algae grew in each spring, depending on its temperature, so that by looking at the color of any given hot pool, I could tell approximately how warm it was.

Just as interesting to me as the natural features of the hot spring terrace was the parade of people I saw on my tour. I peered with great humor from behind my sunglasses at "Mabel and George," the hundreds of tourists who tramped through, took pictures of each other, and hurried away to their next destination.

I paused in my walk to sit on a bench strategically located to overlook the Mammoth Hot Springs Hotel. Beyond the bright colors of the hot spring terraces, the hotel rested in the middle of a huge, freshly mowed lawn. It looked like it had been planted there at the beginning of time and had just grown along with the trees until it had reached a mellow maturity. The hotel was neither obnoxiously fancy nor sadly neglected. The adjective which came to my mind as I sat on the bench, looking down at it, was "grand." It was a hotel built in an era that had passed; when it was new, people arrived at Yellowstone in Model A's, wore bobbed hair and still talked about the World War, unaware that there would one day be a need to number the world wars. The Mammoth Hot Springs Hotel had aged gracefully, appearing just as comfortable and unobtrusive as it must have looked sixty years before.

I turned my attention to the procession of people passing by me. A man with a huge belly waddled by, dressed in an orange tie-dyed sleeveless vest and a green pair of those polyester pants branded with a permanent crease. He was talking to a buddy on a walkie-talkie. I looked around but could not see his friend nearby. The absent man's voice sailed over the airwaves as Orange Vest moved past me: "Say, Joe, did you hear the one about the Montana bull shipper?"

Next came two thirtyish women who herded five children between them. One woman was reading from the pamphlet: " 'The raw material here is limestone. Over 4,000 pounds of material is produced by the springs each day, and some of the terraces grow as much as two feet each year.' Are you listening to me, kids?" She lined them all up for a photo, and several of the kids made faces at the camera. The other woman spoke sharply to a little girl who was leaning over the edge of the plank trail, trying to touch the boiling water of a hot pool.

I thought, as the two women hustled their brood along down the path, that I bet this trip had sounded like a good idea when the two women talked about it over coffee in their kitchen back in Ohio. But I also was certain that they were having second thoughts about it now.

Two older women walked past me going the other way. I overheard a snatch of their conversation:

"*Oooh,*" one complained, "my legs still hurt."

"That's what happens when you carouse around all day, acting so frisky. At your age!"

Calcium carbonate material makes up
the hot spring terraces of Mammoth.

The people moved past and disappeared around a curve in the trail. And the hot springs paid them no heed. In a quiet lull between the clumps of tourists, I watched the water bubble and flow over the terraces. The steam rose silently into the sky and disappeared. It delighted me to know that the steam kept rising, whether anyone was there to make comments about it or not.

Wandering by foot around the Mammoth Hot Springs area, I discovered other places, not public like the terraces, where I could go to be alone with the open expansive land of the Yellowstone region. One such place was a small hill directly north of the Mammoth complex. A 20 minute hike took me to the apex of the hill. From there I could look one way and see the settlement built around the hot spring terraces; turning my back on that, I could gaze over an endless series of hills and valleys, through which the Yellowstone River flowed north into Montana and ultimately to the Mississippi River and the Louisiana delta.

Once when I went up there, I stumbled across a couple of grave markers. One was etched with the name of a man who died in 1886 at the age of 25; the other bore the name of a woman who passed away three years earlier, when she was 35. The graves were still distinguishable from the surrounding rolling hills and long grasses, for the perimeter had been marked off from the wilderness by white rocks.

I spent many hours in my first few weeks at Mammoth perched on top of that minor unnamed mountain north of the hotel in the company of the two departed pioneers. Sitting on a rock in the wind, I found some of the serenity which I had come all the way from southern California to seek.

The moments of solitude and peace, however, became scarcer as the summer progressed. For, after the first few weeks of memorizing names and learning my job, I became a participant. I joined forces with the locals and became immersed in the parkie culture that existed at Mammoth Hot Springs. It was everything I had imagined it would be when I had stared at employees lounging on the dorm porch behind the Wawona Hotel years earlier. It was more than I had imagined. The parkies and the tourists and the spectacular scenery eased their way into my heart and lodged there. And once clamped, the elements of the Yellowstone experience never loosened their grip. I never had a chance to fight back, nor did I try to fight. I surrendered to the power of the place.

The hot springs never commented. Their steam just rose into the clear air and disappeared, as it had for thousands of years before I ever arrived on the scene.

Another day off, during the early weeks of my sojourn in Mammoth Hot Springs, was spent hiking the six mile Beaver Pond Trail. The route started at the fringe of the Mammoth hotel complex and wound back through the woods to the northwest, following the contours of the land.

I took the hike by myself. I had made some friends already among the parkie people with whom I worked, but that day I was craving the solitude offered by the Yellowstone wilds. I carried water, lunch, camera, notebook and bear bells. When I had sat through the orientation program given by Park Service interpreters the day I arrived, they put on a little skit about bears. Beyond the silliness of their routine ("This is what you do when a bear chases you . . . *Eeeekk!*"), the message came through that the best way to avoid a confrontation with a bear in the wild was to warn it of your approach and let it identify, through your sounds, exactly what you were.

I bought some bear bells at the convenience store immediately. Though I did not take them when hiking with others, figuring that our voices would provide a satisfactory warning, I did tie them on to my day pack when I went solo hiking. In addition, I sang as loudly as I could, in rhythm to my steps, to insure that I would scare the bears away. I was not a gifted singer, but I belted out tunes like "The Night They Drove Old Dixie Down" with gusto, all the same, so that the bears would know I was moving in their direction.

I was especially wary of bears on the hike that day because the word had gone around the park that a couple weeks earlier a man had been mauled by a bear. He was a biologist who had been studying bear behavior. If anyone should have known how to avoid bear attacks, he should have. He was alone, hiking in the middle of the day, when he surprised a sow with three cubs. She attacked him savagely. He was airlifted to a hospital in Salt Lake City and was said to be in critical condition.

The country surrounding the Beaver Ponds Trail
is prime bear habitat.

With the thought of the biologist lurking in the back of my mind, my mood was guarded for the first couple miles of trail. Gradually, the serenity of the woods soothed me and my fears dissipated like the steam of the hot springs into the clear summer air.

I paused at one of the beaver ponds along the route to eat lunch. The sun was shining and a warm breeze slid through the tall grass. Leaves of aspen shimmered and whispered against a perfect sky. Hours earlier I had left behind the last painted sign, "Do Not Step Off The Marked Paths." I stepped, and basked in the swatches of sunshine and wind.

I emerged from a reverie to sense movement on the far side of the beaver pond. Without moving a muscle, I stared at the tall grass and presently saw a black shape moving slowly through it.

My heart pounded. A bear! It was a lone black bear, no larger than those I had seen in Yosemite, perhaps 200 pounds. The bear did not appear to be aware of my presence, so I sat very still and watched it.

Thoughts flew through my mind like swallows. I recalled the instructions given to me during the orientation skit about shouting and waving at a bear. "Hello, Bear, how's it going?" I nearly laughed aloud at the thought of this ludicrous one-sided conversation. Then I considered taking pictures, but quickly shelved that idea. I had heard too many stories about people found dead after being mauled by a bear, while in their cameras were photos of the bear approaching closer and closer.

After watching it move among the grasses for a few minutes, I began to enjoy spying on the bear in spite of my fears. The creature moved with surprising agility for its size. Somehow, I had acquired a mental image of bears as lumbering, heavy-footed animals, but the one I watched appeared to be comfortable and even graceful as it rambled through the woods near the pond, searching without too much effort for an afternoon snack.

The wind moved through the bear's coat like fingers. It looked to me to be completely at ease in its home territory with neither fences nor civilization to restrict its movements.

Presently, the bear wandered out of my field of vision and moved off toward a stand of aspen beyond the lake. I understood that was my cue to make an exit from the bear's domain. Rather than continue along the trail, I decided to retrace the route along which I had come. At the moment, it made sense to me that, since I had not seen any bears on the hike in, I would more likely avoid them by going out the same way.

Once out of earshot of the black bear, I resumed the off-key singing and watched more closely for telltale signs of bears on the trail. I saw no steaming scat piles nor any six inch wide paw prints, and the walk back to Mammoth was uneventful as far as bear sightings were concerned.

My thoughts were filled with bears. It used to be that bears and Yellowstone were synonymous. As recently as ten years before I had arrived at Yellowstone, bears were a common sight along the park road. Park Service workers, as yet unenlightened about bear management, had condoned the dumping of garbage in open pits, and even at one time had set up bleachers at a garbage dump to provide tourists with a comfortable vantage point from which to view the feeding bears. As visitation to the park increased, so did the incidents of "bear jams"—places along the road where tourists parked four deep to feed the animals which shamelessly approached their vehicles begging for food.

In that zoo-like atmosphere, the frequency of maulings and bear vandalism increased. The bears of Yellowstone had learned that humans equaled handouts, and the tantrums they threw when they did not get their expected meal were devastating. Tents and trailers were destroyed and several people were mauled by bears that did not understand the word "no."

Horror stories circulated in the park about tourists who had failed to grasp that the bears were not tame. The one told most often, because it was so outrageous, was about a woman who smeared honey on her three year old daughter's face and then took pictures as a bear licked it off.

Finally, beginning in the late 1960s, park management adopted a different philosophy toward the bears. The creatures were wild animals, so rangers decided that they should be placed back in the wild. One by one, the bears which hung around near dumps and campgrounds were sedated and moved to the most remote areas of the park.

Unfortunately, no one told the bears that they needed to change their foraging habits. Many a bear, transferred to Hayden Valley or Republic Pass, found its way back to the lucrative feeding grounds near the concentrated human populations. The rule followed by park officials was that a "problem" bear, that is, one that could not read its script from the bear management plan, had three chances. If it was shipped out to the back woods and insisted on returning to civilization three times, it was destroyed.

The Park Service public relations people stated that problem bears were sent to a zoo. That was what we were supposed to tell the bleeding heart A.S.P.C.A. members disguised as curious Yellowstone tourists. But I knew that the expense of shipping a live bear to a zoo—let alone finding a zoo willing to take yet another bear—was prohibitive. So most of the time, those bears which had been taught by their mothers and grandmothers that humans represented a free meal were punished with the death penalty.

I had the opportunity to see one of the so-called problem bears firsthand. Early one morning the head cook, arriving to open the restaurant kitchen, discovered that the back door had been forced open and the kitchen gone through by a bear. His first reaction was to accuse wayward employees of having thrown a party in the kitchen the night before, because the pots and pans were knocked over, cans were off the shelves, and furniture had been overturned. But teeth marks in the sides of cans in the pantry quickly revealed the true identity of the intruder into the kitchen.

Park Service biologists arrived the next night and set up a bear trap outside the kitchen door. The trap was a cylindrical metal contraption which resembled a couple of 55 gallon drums which had been welded together. A steak was placed in the trap as bait.

Darkness fell. About midnight, a loud, metallic clang like a jail door being slammed was heard all over the employee dorm complex. I joined several others on the porch of the girls dorm with a flashlight, to see if the bear had been caught.

Cautiously, someone walked up to the trap and shined a light inside. Looking out of the cylinder was a very irate black bear. The flashlight in its eyes fueled its fury. It went into a rage, roaring and leaping at the cage door with remarkable strength. But the cage was built stoutly and the bear was unable to make its jailbreak.

Presently, the Park Service people arrived and took the cylinder and bear away. I later learned that the bear they caught behind the Mammoth kitchen had committed strike two by breaking into the restaurant. It had been transported to a remote area of the park near Madison, with the stipulation that if it returned once more it would not be given another chance to rehabilitate. Nobody read that contract to the bear. I did not find out if that particular bear ever did return to civilization, but I hoped it would be gone long enough to forget its association between people and food. I understood what the park people were trying to do. Truly I valued the glimpse of a bear in the wild far more highly than a full view of it propped up on hind legs outside my car window. But the mistake had been made by unenlightened park managers and anthropomorphic Yogi Bear fans. The present generation of bears was paying for the mistake with their lives.

Even more than the scapegoat role assigned by the Park Service to the Yellowstone bears, I resented the ignorance of tourists who, even in 1977, were genuinely disappointed that they could not see bears on the road. Many of this variety of park visitor had never so much as set foot in the wilderness, and their comments about Yogi and Boo-Boo infuriated me. Over and over I tried to educate them—"Bears are wild animals, Ma'am"—but the faces kept changing daily and the attitude stayed the same. Finally I began to make sarcastic jokes about the bears, suggesting to the most obnoxious that they leave their coolers open and sleep with fresh fish lining their sleeping bags.

Maulings were still common enough that a statement such as that brought most of them to their senses. A few, however, disappeared into the park, driving south from Mammoth, with the same television-inspired ideas with which they had arrived. Unable to change them, all I could do was shake my head at them, and try to laugh.

The woman who smeared honey on her child's face, I was certain, must have been one of those.

3

❖❖

Waitressing

Originally, I was hired in Yellowstone to be a "kitchen helper." The pay was $2.00 per hour. After the cost of room and board was deducted from my check, I cleared about $50.00 per week, hardly a prosperous wage. But I was not there solely for the money. In all the years I worked in the parks, I never once was accused of being motivated by financial ambition.

I worked for Yellowstone Park Company during the last two seasons they ran the concession in Yellowstone. From what I saw of their management practices, I was not surprised when I heard that they lost the contract in 1979.

Kitchen helper, I quickly discovered, was a euphemism for low woman on the totem pole. I rotated in the kitchen between the employees' cafeteria (ladling slop), the pantry (making salads 55 gallons at a time in a plastic trash can), and the dishwasher (flinging plates into the ancient dishwasher). The worst duty by far was the one at which I was required to stand at a deep sink for eight hours scrubbing pots and pans. At one point, bolstered by boldness borne of sheer exhaustion, I approached my supervisor and suggested we split shifts on the pots and pans, so that each kitchen helper might have to spend merely four hours at a stretch leaning over the soapy water, armed only with a Brillo pad.

His response to my suggestion was cold hearted: "Don't complain to me about those pots. I've had to stand back there for eight hours before! Get back to work."

Often, the management would assign the dishwashing chore to someone as punishment for arriving to work late or hung over. Perhaps that explained why, when the health department sprang a surprise inspection on the Mammoth kitchen one morning, they were appalled. Running a finger over the inside of a large pot, the inspectors found residue of grease a quarter inch thick.

The inspectors found many more things to criticize about the sanitation practices in the Mammoth Hot Springs Hotel kitchen. I myself could have told them horror stories, if they had only asked me. I saw waitresses in a hurry drop English muffins on the floor, and, without missing a beat, retrieve them and take them out to customers. And I saw a girl with a Band-Aid over a cut on her finger reach her arms into a trash can to toss the salad—only to discover, after she finished tossing, that the Band-Aid had disappeared. It later showed up in a chef's salad that was served to a horrified customer in the dining room.

The main problem the Yellowstone Park Company faced was the quality of employees they hired. As a group, we were unstable and inexperienced. Every week several people quit and new ones were literally hired off the street. There was one guy who worked there in the kitchen for several weeks. Then he quit abruptly, stole some money from a co-worker and left the park in a stolen car. Later we learned that he was wanted in five states for armed robbery.

To be fair, most of us were not felony types. The people who came to work at Mammoth were as varied as the tourists who visited it. Quite a few were college students like me, from every

state in the Union. Others were drifters, street people away from
their city streets who had somehow managed to end up broke at
the Montana state line. They hired on for as long as it took to
gather money enough to stake their next leg of travel.

We spanned a broad spectrum of categories, as far as mo-
tives for spending the summer in the nation's most famous national park were concerned. Among us were Campus Crusaders,
carrying a Christian message into the parks. There were young
women in Mammoth alone, away for the first time from their
boyfriends or their overprotective families. Some were serious
students of geology or resource management, who intended to
use their summer making contacts in the Park Service. And
there were those whose main interest was attendance at the
endless floating party.

But, above all, most of us were there primarily because we
fell in love with Yellowstone. The menial labor and double
shifts and six day work weeks were a necessary evil. That was
the price we paid to experience the park and a summer away
from home.

I stayed at my job out of a stubborn unwillingness to quit
and go home, and because I so greatly enjoyed my time off. After three weeks as a kitchen helper, I was promoted to busperson in the restaurant. A month later, I was moved up to a waitress position. The second year, when I returned to work at
Mammoth Hot Springs, again beginning as a kitchen helper, I
was working as a waitress in the coffee shop within three weeks
of my arrival.

On the surface, waitressing appeared even less lucrative fi-
nancially than washing pots. We made $1.35 per hour, and
once the room and board charges were deducted, we ended up
with a paycheck of ten or twenty dollars. Once, when I had to
take a couple of sick days, for which I was not paid, I received,
instead of a paycheck, a bill for $8.85 from the Yellowstone
Park Company.

Preparing for another day as a waitress
at the Mammoth coffee shop.

But the waitresses, or waitrii, as we called ourselves to avoid using sexist job titles, made a fairly decent living from our tips. In the coffee shop, $20.00 was the average take. Once promoted to the dining room, where steaks and seafood were featured on the menu, a hustling waitrii could make 50 to 60 dollars each night.

I had a love-hate relationship with the tourists from the beginning. A disdainful attitude had been bred into me through years of dodging "Mabel and George" on the South Fork of the Merced River. When I considered them en masse, the park visitors were an inconvenience and a bore.

The restaurant opened at 6:00 A.M. Before we threw back the doors, we sat at a table while the coffee brewed, snacking on fruit cups and sweet rolls and discussing the previous night's parties. Then one of the waitrii would announce ceremoniously that the entire Japanese army was lined up outside the door. We pasted on our smiles along with our name tags and steeled ourselves for the onslaught. I did not enjoy serving mass-produced meals to patrons who spoke little English and certainly would not be eating memorable cuisine. During the busiest hours, the faces and personalities and dinner orders of all the tourists flowed together in my mind into an endless progression of hungry humans.

Between the peak meal hours, however, there were lulls when the restaurant was not overflowing with humanity. At those times I had a chance to talk to the people at my tables and get to know them a bit. I was not only motivated by a desire to make a good tip, I also found that many of them were interesting individuals. I came to value the glimpses I got into a slice of their lives.

I loved to hear people's descriptions of their travels—when they were enjoying themselves. Sometimes the people at my tables compared everything they had seen on their journey with their home town, which could do no wrong. I could not stand to hear Yellowstone judged second to any place else. I had a hard time understanding how people could even make a comparison between Yellowstone and some ironworker's town back east. Those were the people who brought their home comforts with them. I had seen them down in the campground, generators roaring in the moonlight, trying to tune in Billings on their portable televisions. I sincerely wondered why they had bothered to come to Yellowstone in the first place.

But for every one of those folks, there was another who enjoyed experiencing the unfamiliar. With a little practice, I learned to pick those people out by the way they answered my standard opening line, "Where are you from?"

I savored the good travelogues. One couple from Pennsylvania described their journey west to me like this:

"It's incredible to watch the transformation of the landscape as you drive through it. In South Dakota, the land is completely flat. You can actually see the rainstorms approaching: It's raining there and it's clear over here. Then as you continue west the mountains rise up suddenly off that plain. We don't have mountains like that in Pennsylvania. The most wonderful part of the trip for us was traveling through land that was totally undeveloped, all the way to the horizon. The more we experience of this country, the more we realize what riches it has to offer."

I asked them what parts of Yellowstone they had seen. They said they had been out backpacking at Grizzly Lake.

"We went the day after a man was mauled by a black bear out there," the woman said. "We had the lake to ourselves."

"I heard about that," I replied, "and it sounded to me like the man practically asked to be mauled. I heard that he did not store his food properly, and the bear came looking for an easy meal."

The man said, "Yes, we heard that too. When we got our backcountry permits, the rangers told us how to hang our food in the trees. We didn't have a problem with any bears at all. And we caught some trout out there that were really tasty."

"We caught some in Yellowstone Lake, too," the woman added. "One of the fish I caught was 15 inches long, and I had to throw it back. We were told we couldn't keep anything bigger than 13 inches."

"That's odd," I commented. "Why is that?"

"That's so the larger fish in the lake can eat the smaller pest fish, keeping a balance ecologically. We met one man out there who had caught 65 fish, and he was only able to keep four of them. He was having a great time, though. As we were. It has been a wonderful trip."

Another woman whose favorable comments about Yellowstone struck a familiar chord with me sat in my section one morning for a late breakfast. I estimated her age to be about 50; she had weather-roughened skin and was clad in worn blue jeans. She looked like an outdoorswoman to me, but she said she was from the city of Denver. "So many people have moved to Denver in the past few years," she told me, "that it has become overcrowded, noisy and polluted."

"I'm from Los Angeles," I said. "I can relate."

She continued, "The smog settles into a pocket over Denver and never moves out. I'm staying in one of those cabins out behind the hotel. It was so quiet up here that I had to turn the radio on the first night, just to get to sleep.

"When I awoke, I heard birds singing. In Denver, the birds cough."

Amidst the frantic rush to take dinner orders and fill coffee cups and satisfy the tourists' desire to know what a California native was doing waiting tables in Wyoming, there were moments which stood out, moments which brought a smile of pure joy to my face. One such moment occurred on a Sunday morning. As part of my side duties, I was in the bathroom, cleaning the mirror with a rag when a woman walked into the room.

"Thank you for doing that," she said.

"What?" I said, unsure whether she was speaking sincerely or cynically.

"I said, thank you," she repeated. "I appreciate people keeping the rest rooms clean."

I turned around to look at her. She had long, thick brown hair and was very attractive—and very pregnant.

"When are you expecting, if you don't mind my asking?" I said.

"Next month. It will be my first child. I can feel it kicking almost all the time now. Would you like to feel it?"

"I would," I said. I put the rag down and walked to her, reaching my hand out shyly. She placed my palm on her large belly. I stood perfectly still. Within a few seconds I felt the surge of movement which betrayed a baby beginning to get anxious about making its appearance in the world. I asked her if she was hoping for a boy or a girl.

"I don't care," she responded, smiling. "I just want it to be healthy."

"Well, it feels pretty healthy to me," I said. "Thank you for sharing it with me."

As I watched her walk out of the restaurant and disappear into the morning sunshine, I found myself hoping that her baby would be not only healthy, but as beautiful and full of joy as its mother was.

My career as a waitress had its difficult moments. I nearly died of embarrassment one morning when I fetched a cup of hot chocolate out of the machine. I never found out if the culprit had been in the cup or in the machine itself, but the result was that I placed in front of a sleepy-eyed man a cup of steaming chocolate garnished with a dead fly. Jokes from my co-workers about "waiter, there's a fly in my soup" trailed me for weeks after that episode.

Every waitrii who stayed at the job for any length of time had a story to tell about spilling food. Fortunately, my experience with that particular hazard of the trade occurred just a couple weeks after I was promoted to waitrii, so my inexperience could be used as an excuse. Our system of serving food involved balancing plates on a circular tray about three feet in diameter. Once plates were stacked onto the tray, we used a bent-knee technique to hoist the tray to one shoulder. Then, moving swiftly through two doorways and attempting not to jostle the load or collide with anyone else, we slid out to the section we were serving. With the free hand, we grabbed a tray stand and carried the food to the table. The tray stand was then unfolded, and the heavy tray was brought to rest on top of it.

That was the theory. What happened to me one day, I was not sure; it all happened too fast. At the height of the busy dinner hour, I was bringing six hamburgers out to a family in my section. I loaded my tray and lifted with my knees, as I had been taught. Through both doorways I moved with the tray balanced on my shoulder blade. As I approached the table, I felt the load on the tray begin to shift. Once it started to go, there was no way for me to stop it. Right in front of those hungry people's eyes, their dinner went tumbling to the floor. They did not take the mishap with a sense of humor. I fled the room, leaving the mess for my busperson to clean up. Quickly, I went back to the cooks and ordered six more hamburgers. One of the waitrii who had witnessed the mishap offered to take the second order of burgers out for me. She suggested I take a break, and I followed her suggestion. I was not expecting a tip from that table anyway.

Three grubby looking young men came into the coffee shop one day, just before the dinner hour. I went over to take their order.

"What will you have?" I asked.

"Nothing, we have nothing," a blonde man with missing teeth and a strong foreign accent said. The other two grinned at me.

"You're not eating?" I queried them. "Where are you guys from?"

"From Copenhagen," said the blonde man. "We have no money. In restaurant we eat what they give us. We like to finish what is in others' dinners."

"Let me get this straight. You want to eat the leftovers from other people's dinners?"

"Yes, yes," he said, nodding vigorously. "You Americans, you waste so much. We make use of your waste. Yes?"

I looked around. My supervisor was on her dinner break, and no one else was paying attention to my customers. "As far as I'm concerned, it's all right with me. You can move over there." I indicated an adjacent table, which had not yet been cleared of its dirty dishes.

"Thank you much," said the blonde man. Without further discussion, the three moved to the table piled with dirty dishes and rapidly consumed the crusts, bites of salad, and lettuce on the plates. They even ate the parsley.

The three stayed in my section for more than an hour. Each time a group left the restaurant, the three quietly moved to the vacant table, finishing off the scraps abandoned by the previous occupants. When they had finally eaten their fill, they asked me for a check. I wrote them up for a cup of coffee each. They gave me a dollar tip, paid for their coffee, and disappeared out the door of the restaurant. I had a sneaking suspicion that the health department would not have approved of that episode, but I never mentioned it to anyone. In my opinion, those three Danes did me and my busperson a favor by cleaning the plates. I thought theirs was an ingenious method of obtaining a free dinner.

I was amazed at the people who showed up at the tables I waited in the Mammoth Hot Springs restaurant. My aunt, uncle and two of my cousins, who happened to be touring Yellowstone unbeknown to me, turned up one busy evening. They ordered hamburgers like everyone else and informed me of some family gossip. Another time, a discussion with a young woman during a slow afternoon in the coffee shop revealed the fact that she was the same person I had gone to third grade with in California. Her mother and my mother had been co-leaders of our Girl Scout troop.

It was a small world in the Mammoth restaurant, and a friendly one. I got lost in my work while I was on shift there, and once I got the routine of carrying trays and making small talk figured out, I looked forward to my job. At the moments when I made a personal connection with a customer, sharing a joke or a hometown or an experience, I did not feel I was being cheated by the Yellowstone Park Company. I worked cheerfully and with great enthusiasm for my $1.35 per hour. Satisfied at the end of a busy shift, I felt I had attained a major achievement in my life, on my own. I was proud to say that I was a waitress in Yellowstone National Park.

4

❖❖

Specimen Ridge

I met a young man named Rodney who was in Yellowstone working as a busperson in the restaurant. His origin, which was Kansas, made me pause momentarily before agreeing to go hiking with him on a day off. The terrain was quite flat in Kansas, and I wondered what he could possibly know about climbing mountains. But one bright July day I agreed to go with him anyway, because I was eager to explore the northeast section of the park.

Our destination was Specimen Ridge. We drove out toward the park's northeast entrance from Mammoth, parking the car in a pullout next to the Lamar River. It was still early in the day, the sun was shining and the aspens quivered in a slight breeze. The day was perfect for hiking. I carried in my day pack my usual mandatory items: the camera and notebook, water, and a lunch. Rodney had his lunch, a pair of binoculars and a sweater.

We crossed the swift Lamar River on a fallen log and set out across the broad river valley toward a ridge several miles distant. We had been told that a trail existed, but we were unable to find it. Undaunted, we moved through knee-high sagebrush with energy and ease, taking our bearings from the ridge ahead of us.

As we walked, we got acquainted. Rodney said that this was the first time he had lived anywhere besides Kansas. "I do like it here," he said. "I never imagined mountains could be this big. In Kansas, that," he pointed, indicating a low knoll to our left, "would be called a mountain."

"I've seen mountains at least this high in California," I told him. "The Sierra Nevada contains the second largest mountain in North America."

"Why would anyone from California leave to come up here? I mean," Rodney explained hastily, making amends to Yellowstone, "I'm the first to acknowledge the beauty of this place. But California—isn't that kind of like heaven?"

"There are men to match the mountains there," I said. "Too many of them. I used to go hiking in the Yosemite area, but I had to hike a long distance to get away from the people. You know, now that backpacking has become so popular, all the city people go up to Yosemite on vacation. You see them with their brand new North Face tents and Vibram-soled boots, crawling like a string of ants up the switchbacks on Friday afternoons.

"Look around you." We were hiking across the river valley which stretched in both directions as far as we could see. "Do you see anybody else here? That's why I came—one of the reasons, anyway. It's real wilderness. That's what I have been looking for. It's what I crave."

Rodney was silent for a couple minutes. Then he said, "Somehow, that surprises me. Now I come from a small town, and I don't know much about people. I came here to learn about getting along with people, making friends. I am sort of a loner. It seems like you came to Yellowstone to get away from people, and I came to get closer to them."

"And here we are, doing both!" I laughed. "But you must have met some people in—where did you say you went to school?"

"The University of Kansas. But I have kept my head in a book most of the time."

"Don't you live in the dorms?"

"No, I live at home," Rodney said. "My folks don't mind and neither do I. We don't bother each other too much. It was kind of a big deal for them when I decided to come out west this summer. I'm their youngest, the final child to leave the nest, the baby, you know. But I'm twenty years old. It's about time I started to find out what the world is about."

"What's your major in college?" I asked.

"Archaeology. But I'm also interested in literature. Medieval poetry and history, to be exact."

"You mean like, *Canterbury Tales* and King Arthur and all that?"

Rodney looked embarrassed. "Well—yes. That's it. I'm afraid I don't know much about the twentieth century."

"Well, I like literature too," I told him. "But I admit I like the modern authors better—Pinchot and Robbins and Kerouac. That's my taste. I am majoring in communications right now."

"Communications? What will you do with that?"

"I don't know," I said honestly. "I had thought I would be a journalist, originally. But I don't think there is much call for big-time journalists in places like Yellowstone. That is something I have been puzzling over lately. I guess there must be some way to make a living while not leaving the parks."

"You could be a ranger," he suggested.

I answered immediately, for I had already considered that option. "It is really difficult to get into the Park Service. You have to be related to God, or at least have a last name like Albright. I could change my name, I guess," I laughed.

"But seriously, Rodney, I guess I've got plenty of time to

figure it out. All I know is that this one summer will not satiate my desire for the parkie life. I'm going to have to do it more."

Presently we reached the far end of the valley. The sagebrush disappeared, replaced by tall yellow pine and lodgepole pine forests and a steep uphill climb. We stopped talking, concentrating on making our way to the top of the hill. From there we saw several more parallel hills spreading out before us like overgrown caterpillars.

"Are you sure you know where we are going?" I asked him, trying to sound playful instead of worried.

"Sure," he said. "I looked at a map yesterday. We go over that next rise, and then follow the valley up to a ridge top."

"O.K.," I said doubtfully. I wished I had looked at the map myself, but I had just assumed we would be following a trail. I did not expect to be bushwhacking.

Another hour's worth of hard hiking brought us over the next ridge and into the trough beyond. We had traversed some rough areas strewn with rocks as well as woods densely populated by tall, slim trees. We had clambered over hundreds of fallen logs. Each time we reached a clearing, Rodney would shout, "This way!" and head off briskly in another direction.

I just kept following him, although I was trying to look for landmarks too, so that I would be able to assert myself about the direction of travel on our way back. I suddenly thought of Hansel and Gretel, and wondered if I should have brought along some white pebbles. I was confident, however. I was an experienced hiker who had been on many long treks before. To be sure, none had been cross-country hikes, but I did not figure this was any different than anything I had done in the past.

We followed the trough to the west for awhile, then climbed up a very steep slope to reach a peak which appeared to tower above the rest of the mountain tops. The view from the peak was spectacular, and Rodney and I both stood staring at it for a long time, until we had caught our breaths.

View of the Lamar River Valley from Specimen Ridge

We were at the pinnacle of the ridge we had seen from the car. The entire Lamar River valley was spread out below us like a painting, except that the flash of sun reflected off the river was more dazzling than any painting I had ever seen. From that height, the river looked like a shiny wire running through a green carpet of sagebrush. On the far side of the valley we could see the thin strip of gray which was the road.

A strange noise broke the silence. Rodney heard it too. "What was that?" he asked.

"My stomach," I told him. "I am starving. Let's eat, huh?"

"Good idea," he agreed. "How about if we sit over here on these rocks?"

We sat in the sun and thoroughly enjoyed devouring our

lunches. They were box lunches, made up in our own Mammoth kitchen. Since the price of three meals a day was automatically taken out of our paychecks, the Yellowstone Park Company gave us the option of taking along a lunch if we were going to be away from Mammoth for a day. Each box lunch contained two sandwiches, potato chips, chocolate chip cookies and an apple. In addition, I had brought along some of my favorite Mystic Mint cookies. I offered one to Rodney.

"What are these?" he asked as he took the cookie.

"They're Mystic Mints," I told him. "Do you like them?"

"Never had them before."

"Really?" I was amazed. "I absolutely love them. They come in a green box which says, 'for people who love the taste of chocolate' on the front. That's me. I love chocolate."

"I'm not crazy about chocolate," he said. "I can take it or leave it. I would just as soon have oatmeal cookies."

"Boy, you and I sure are different," I observed. "I guess we are lucky we haven't killed each other yet, considering how little we have in common."

"Hey, I like you," he said. "Perhaps there's something to that saying about opposites attracting."

I did not like the way he was looking at me. I had only come along on the hike for the adventure of it. Not wanting to encourage him to keep talking in the same vein, I changed the subject.

"What about the specimens, Rodney? We are on top of Specimen Ridge, right? Where do we find them?"

He put his lunch box and garbage back into his pack. "I think they're not far. Let's try down here." He indicated a wash that sloped steeply down the back side of the ridge.

Down the wash we slid on loose chips of gray rock. When we got about half way down, Rodney stopped sliding and bent over, looking intently at something on the ground.

"So what is it we are looking for?" I asked.

"This," he announced, holding out a rock for me to look at.

I took it from him and examined it. It was heavy for its size, cylindrical in shape, about eight inches long and four inches across. The coloring was a myriad of variations on the theme of orange and brown.

"What is it?" I asked. "It sure is pretty."

"This is where my knowledge of the past comes in handy," Rodney said. He took a stance of self-importance, resembling a professor at a lectern. He cleared his throat and adjusted his glasses.

"That, my friend, is petrified wood. Once, many thousands of years ago, it was a tree. The elements and time have transformed it into stone. Look closely. You can see the concentric tree rings on the ends of that piece."

I looked. "Oh yeah, I see them," I acknowledged.

"Here's another," he continued. "This one is not brown, for it has actually petrified into quartz. You can still see the shape of the wood here, but different elements and different conditions have made this tree into a completely different type of rock."

Fascinated, I began picking up the rocks on the slope and showing them to Rodney. Quartz chunks, brilliantly colored rocks, and all sizes and shapes of petrified wood were scattered over the whole hillside. Time slipped by unheeded as we ranged over the area, searching out the specimens.

"Do you know how this happens? Petrified wood, I mean."

"I read up on it," Rodney said. "Here on the ridge, there was a forest growing when a volcano erupted over in the area of the Absaroka range. Volcanic ash buried the forest alive. During later rainfalls, water seeped into the buried trees of the forest and deposited material from the ash. The color of the stone comes, of course, from iron oxide."

"What about all the quartz?"

"Again, that is the result of water mixing with volcanic material. I'm not exactly sure how that works, but the presence of quartz indicates volcanic action.

"Apparently this series of events—a forest growing, a volcano erupting, and then ash and water turning the trees to stone
—happened 27 different times on this ridge," Rodney went on.
"According to what I read, there are actually whole forests, still
standing, petrified into stone. Perhaps we'll find them around
here somewhere."

Both of us picked up souvenirs of the most brilliantly colored or perfectly shaped petrified tree chunks as we shuffled
along. We also collected interesting looking colored rocks for
later examination and identification.

Soon my day pack was heavy with rocks I had gathered.
Slowly we made our way back up to the top of the ridge, oblivious to the time in our fascination with the specimens we were
retrieving.

When we reached the place where we had eaten lunch, the
sun was low in the sky. I had not realized how late it was getting. I said so to Rodney, and suggested that we ought to head
back down the mountain.

He looked back the way we had come. "It sure took us a
long time to get up here," he observed. "Maybe instead of going
back that way, we could try going down the face of the ridge."

"I don't know," I said doubtfully. "It looked really steep. I
think we would be better off just following the route we know."

"No, it's faster this way," he insisted. "Come on. I'll go
first."

The distance to the river valley from the top of the ridge
appeared hopelessly vast. I was uneasy about taking a new
route, but conceded to myself that we needed to consider the
time element, and the shortest route between two points was, in
fact, the straight line down the front of the ridge. I hefted my
day pack, which weighed close to 30 pounds, on my shoulders
and followed Rodney over the precipice.

Immediately the descent became steep. Rodney slipped and
slid on the loose rocks and petrified wood chunks, and above

him I slid too, dislodging an occasional rock that rolled down the hill past him harmlessly.

I picked up momentum moving down the slope. Overtaking and passing Rodney, who was struggling around a large, jagged boulder, I went on ahead careening downward.

When I was about halfway down, I began to slide. Quickly the situation got out of control; I was sliding much too fast for safety. Ahead of me a cliff suddenly loomed. My movement down the slope had loosened some rock, which gathered speed and preceded my free-falling body down the slope. As I was propelled toward the cliff, I watched with horror as those rocks sliding ahead of me bounced off the cliff and sailed out into the air.

I attempted to halt my forward movement. Desperately, I grabbed at a tiny pine tree which was growing out of the lip of the cliff. The tree was only a couple feet tall, but its roots held and it stopped my slide. I came to rest just inches from the edge of the cliff. Placing a shaky hand on a large chunk of petrified wood for support, I leaned over and peered down. What I saw was a sheer vertical drop of several hundred feet. Had I been unable to catch the little pine tree, or had it not held, I would have been catapulted to certain death on the rocks below.

My terror at the proximity of my own death turned to anger. It was he who had led me down here! "Hey," I shouted at Rodney, who was still cautiously picking his way down the slope.

"There's a cliff here—we can't go this way," I yelled. "We've got to turn around."

He stopped and leaned against a boulder. "What?" he shouted back. "I can't hear you."

"*Stay there!*" I slowly backed up until I found solid footing a yard back from the cliff. My legs were shaking and my heart pounding. I took several deep breaths and then turned and climbed back up to where Rodney stood.

"What happened?" he asked.

"Listen, I told you this was a bad idea. I almost went off that cliff. Damn it," my voice was getting louder. Fear gave force to my words. "Now listen to me. First we get rid of these rocks we have in our packs. This is crazy, carrying all this weight. Then, you follow me. I'm going up to the top of the ridge again, and we are descending the same way we came up. We gotta get out of here. I am not going to die up here. It's about time you learned something, quick, about the wilderness."

"I hate to get rid of all the rocks," he complained.

"Keep one, then, if you must. Not me. You know, someone in the kitchen told me that a curse falls on people who get greedy with souvenirs from a national park. I don't want to chance it." With that I emptied my pack of all the petrified wood; then, reconsidering, I picked one small piece up and tucked it quickly back into the pack. We then began the long, laborious task of crawling up the slope.

When we got to the top of the ridge, it was dusk. Without pausing, I plunged down the hill toward the forest. "Come on," I urged. Rodney looked exhausted. But there was no time to waste.

After darkness fell, I began to feel cold and hungry. I had not brought a jacket, and we had eaten our lunches hours ago. I did not mention any of my discomfort to Rodney, however. He was not making any effort to communicate, except for an occasional whimper or plea to stop.

I did not heed his pleas. On and on we crashed through the woods, stumbling and cursing. I knew we had to keep up the swift pace or there would be no tomorrow.

Finally Rodney stopped and sat down on a fallen log. "I can't go any farther," he said. His voice quivered as if he was about to break into tears. We were in big trouble, I thought.

"We've got to," I said forcefully. "If we stay, we are dead kids. You got matches? A flashlight, shelter, a map? A rifle to shoot the bears that are going to find us? What are you going to do, lie down and die?"

"I just can't go on," he moaned. "I'm too tired."

"Rodney, come on now," I said. I went over to where he was sitting. I could barely see him in the heavy darkness of the woods. He reached out and pulled me to him. I could feel his body shaking with fear and cold. Impatience surged through my weary body. I tried to pull away but he only clutched at me tighter.

"I don't like the woods," he said. "I'm scared. This isn't what I had in mind for a hike. I want to go home!"

My impatience with him dissolved. I saw that he was simply scared to death, panicky and completely out of his element. As the lady said, he was realizing that he was not in Kansas any more. His history books had not prepared him for the real, wild world that did not give anyone a break.

"Now listen to me," I said softly, still holding him. "My mom used to tell me never to turn my back on the ocean. The natural world allows us to participate only on its own terms, and that's what we've got to do.

"This is survival. The real thing, life or death. Forget about Canterbury for now, Rodney, and think only of these dark woods. Come on, hold my hand. Take a step . . . I'll show you the way." I pulled on his hand and he stood up. I felt as if I were talking to a child.

"Are you O.K. now?" I asked.

"I . . . I guess so," he said.

"All right. Now let's keep moving," I said.

Slowly we made our way through the forest. Finally, after what seemed like hours, we literally stumbled on a wooden fence which led us to the edge of the forest abutting the river valley and flat ground. At that precise moment, the full moon began to rise from behind the hills to the east. The pale lunar glow illuminated the valley like a floodlight. We both stopped walking.

"Wow," I gasped.

"Thank you, God," Rodney said.

We stood in silence as the moon rose. Presently the cool night air seeped through our sweat-soaked clothing; the chill prodded us to move across the valley. We dragged our feet, shivering and moving very slowly, but the goal finally was within reach.

There was still one more obstacle. When we reached the bank of the Lamar River, we were unable to locate the log we had used as a bridge to cross it earlier in the day. Was it really the same day, I thought incredulously. It seemed like we had been hiking for weeks.

"We're almost to the car," I said to Rodney. "I say we just ford that river." He had no energy left to argue; in fact he was beyond even speaking in complete sentences. "You first," he said. Then, "O.K. Then me."

So I plunged in and fought my way across the swift, waist deep water of the river. Safe on the far shore, I stood and encouraged Rodney until he too made the crossing. After that it took us only ten minutes to get back to his car. The time was 1:30 A.M.

"You feel like driving?" I asked.

"N-n-no," he said, teeth chattering. "Heater, turn the heater on."

Rodney climbed into the car and wrapped himself in a blanket he kept in the back seat. Curled up in a fetal position, he fell asleep immediately. I removed my wet jeans and slid into the front seat to drive the empty highway back toward Mammoth.

A great warmth washed over me as the healing power of the car's heater took hold. The full moon illuminated the land. I seized the time and silence as I drove to reflect on the day.

It had been a mistake to trust the instincts of a man who knew nothing of the ways of the wilderness. But my own experience had brought us through. Experience, plus—was it luck? Reaching with desperate fingers for that pine tree on the edge of the cliff, I had not been relying on luck. Awash in the brilliant moonlight, I whispered a thank you to whatever power had given me the strength to survive.

I reached into my day pack and pulled out the rough chunk of petrified wood I had hauled down the mountain. As I held it, it grew warm in my hand. I had a piece of that ridge, I thought, and it had a piece of me, too. I did not soon forget the lessons I learned at Specimen Ridge. The rock warmed me all the way home.

5

❖

Hitchhiking

I did not own a car during my two summers in Yellowstone National Park. Soon after arriving, I realized that I would need some sort of transportation in order to see the entire area. The park was larger than the state of Rhode Island. A road consisting of two loops approximating a figure eight took visitors past most of the well-known geyser basins and other natural features of the park. Mammoth was located at the very top of the upper loop. Therefore, devising a method to travel through the rest of the park was essential.

Yellowstone Park Company did run buses within the park, but that particular mode of transportation had several disadvantages. Since the area they covered was so large, buses left each location only once or twice a day. Park employees were allowed to ride the tour buses for free, on a space-available basis. This policy translated into a frustrating system whereby employees stood in the hotel lobby like hungry mongrels, hoping a tourist booked for the ride would not show up. At the very last moment we were either given the go-ahead or told to come back tomorrow because the seats had been filled by paying passengers.

The main disadvantage of traveling via the Yellowstone Park Company buses was that the rides on those buses were not billed as transportation, they were advertised as tours. That meant putting up with several hours of tour guide chatter. The tour guides, I learned, received tips from the paying passengers, so they were motivated to give witty and fascinating monologues. To my ears, their spiels resembled the pitches of carnival hawkers, but the tour patrons loved the show. I was disgusted by the phony brightness of the guides and the stupid questions asked by the passengers. The tour bus routine was a combination of show and tell and amateur hour, and I did not care for it at all.

For example, I got on a tour bus one evening which went up to the town of Gardner, just north of the Yellowstone Park boundary, and back to Mammoth. While driving past the Gardner River, the tour guide gave some fascinating tidbits about the mountain range on the far side of the river. One of the passengers interrupted him.

"Excuse me, sir. Ellie and I have a bet going here. Can you tell me, how much does a mountain weigh?"

With barely a pause, the tour driver shot back, "That depends. Do you mean with the trees or without?"

I stopped trying to catch the Yellowstone Park Company bus after that excursion. With no other options available, and with the encouragement of several of my co-workers at the restaurant, I decided to try hitchhiking my way around the park.

I was a little afraid at first to try it. I had never hitchhiked anywhere in Los Angeles. Following the advice of my more experienced friends, I wrote the words PARK EMPLOYEE in block letters on the back cover of my notebook. When I stood on the shoulder of the road and held up the sign, I easily caught rides with tourists who were curious to hear what life was like for a Yellowstone employee.

I was as shameless, in my own way, as the tour bus drivers.

In exchange for the free ride, I had a spiel of my own to give. I told them about the bright spots in my summer.

The questions I was asked most often were these: How do you get a job like this? Have you seen any bears? Where is the best place to swim, hike, fish, eat, or camp? Where are you from? What do you do in the winter? I gave opinions and told stories cheerfully, relishing my role as a park expert. And I arrived at my destination faster and in better spirits than I ever would have on a tour bus.

The voyeurism was mutual during the hours I spent in other people's cars. I peeped into the lives of the people who picked me up on the road as curiously as they queried me about my life as a park employee. Their disparate perceptions of the same place never ceased to amaze me. I enjoyed riding with people who were inspired by the park landscape. People like the couple from Indiana who picked me up on a trip from Canyon to Yellowstone Lake, however, appeared too absorbed in their own concerns to be affected by the magic of the park.

The Indiana people drove the loop road slowly. At every turnout they stopped, exited the car, and walked to the edge of the pavement. Into a bubbling cauldron or an algae-brightened hot pool they peered for five or ten seconds. Then they returned to the car and resumed driving toward the next red dot on their map.

The woman, Martha, did not want to fish, or to camp, or to do anything but eat. She played head games with Mike, her husband, manipulating him by playing the "dumb broad" opposite his "most macho Hoosier" stance.

She told me about a salmon her husband had caught: "Just like a man, he put it in the freezer whole, without ever wrapping it. I opened the freezer and there were these fish eyes staring at me. I didn't touch it for a year—it was too horrid looking."

Mike asked me how I got a job in the park. He said that he

had wanted to major in forestry in college, but his father told him to go to Notre Dame and major in business. That was what he ended up doing, but, he said, he regretted the decision.

"Well, was your Dad paying?" Martha interrupted.

"Yes, dear," Mike said.

"I guess he could call the shots then," she said triumphantly. Then she said to me, "I'm too old now to go back to college."

"How old are you—if you don't mind my asking?" I said. "Twenty nine," she announced, throwing Mike a flirtatious smile and fluttering her eyelashes. I rolled my eyeballs, but neither of them noticed.

Presently, Mike pulled over to the road's shoulder and pointed toward a meadow. Half a mile away, a moose stood ankle-deep in swamp water, eating the succulent green shoots of summer vegetation.

"It's the same moose we saw yesterday," he announced seriously, as he whipped out the binoculars.

I tried to keep my mouth shut, unsuccessfully. "I wouldn't know," I blurted out. "They all look the same to me."

I was certain that my PARK EMPLOYEE sign would protect me from trouble, and most of the time it did. Only once did I ever feel threatened. I caught a ride from Norris Geyser Basin to Mammoth with an older man who was driving a Continental. Moments after I stepped into his car, he put his hand on my knee and made some lewd suggestions. I fought him off as best I could, and when he stopped the car I leapt out and ran into the woods. He did not follow me. After he drove off, I went out to the road again. Still miles away from Mammoth, I had no choice but to hitch another ride.

I was picked up by a school teacher from Billings, Montana. Her pleasant company more than compensated for the dirty old man. She said she had been to Yellowstone years before, and was interested in stopping at some landmarks she remembered from her previous trip. I was more than willing to play tourist with her, as long as she did not threaten me. Shortly after she picked me up, she turned into a wide pullout to look for a spring which bubbled with carbonated water. She found the spring quickly, hidden in the trees at the edge of the pullout.

"It's every bit as good as club soda," she said, handing me a paper cup full.

Another place she paused was in front of a mountain which she said was called Roaring Mountain.

"It was so named because of the volcanic activity in the area," she told me. "When this mountain was active and emitting ash, it also made a tremendous noise. After the 1920 earthquake, the mountain became dormant, and only the name is left to remind us of its previous eruptions."

We talked about schools, solar heating, and good fishing spots in Yellowstone. She told me about the diet of elk—they were, she asserted, unable to eat the abundant sagebrush of the Yellowstone region. A discussion of sagebrush led to her sharing more fascinating information, such as the fact that sagebrush was often called "iceberg plant" because, although it only grew to be about a foot tall, its roots reached 20 to 50 feet beneath the surface of the soil, in search of water. From sagebrush the conversation moved to Douglas Fir trees. I learned from my chauffeur that those trees had unusually thick bark, which protected them from fire. Therefore they were the biggest and oldest trees in Yellowstone. The only thing that could destroy the fir trees, she told me, was a tiny moth which ate away the tree's buds in the spring.

I thoroughly enjoyed the conversation and companionship of the school teacher from Montana. By the time I got back to Mammoth, my faith in the thumb as a mode of transportation, temporarily shattered by the man in the Continental, was restored.

Hitchhiking provided me with an opportunity to learn

things about the people visiting the park which I might never have discovered if I had lived next door to them or worked with them in an office. There was something intimate about sharing a ride in a car with a total stranger; for a few minutes or a few hours, people tended to let down their guard and tell me their most secret feelings and dreams. I came to anticipate the opportunities I received, while bumming a ride, to glimpse a slice of people's lives.

Attempting to get to a popular swimming hole at the Firehole River one day, I obtained two successive rides. The first car contained a 15 year old girl from Nebraska whose parents were both deaf. Her father was driving, and as I sat in the back seat of the old Nova with the girl, she told me of her dreams.

"I want to be an actress," she said. "After I get out of high school, I am going to go to California. I can wait on tables until I get an acting job. That's what a lot of the actresses do. I read about them in a magazine."

"California is a long way from Nebraska," I answered. "Don't you think you will miss your home? I do miss my home, even though it is beautiful here in Yellowstone. Sometimes, when I'm lying in the sun, I imagine that I'm back home on the beach. When I open my eyes and see pine trees, it surprises me."

The girl paused thoughtfully, as if she had never before considered the possibility that she might get homesick. "Well, I will miss my family," she conceded. "I don't know how Mom and Dad could get along without me. I do all their interpretation. I talk for them. But," she added quickly, "I know I won't miss Nebraska. Three years ago we had a tornado there. It hit our house and destroyed all our possessions. We were lucky to live through that experience. My mom says I should follow my dreams. My dream is to be in the movies, so I guess I could put up with the loneliness that comes along with it. I have learned that I might have to give up one thing in order to get something else."

My next ride was with a man from Washington who had two sons, ages 8 and 17. They were touring the country in an old station wagon. The older boy was navigating.

"It looks like the road forks up ahead, Dad," he said, studying a tattered map spread on his lap.

"Do you like being the one to say which way to go?" I asked him.

"Well, I've never done it before," he said. "Mom used to do it when we went on vacation, but she . . . she passed away last winter. So, I inherited the job."

"And a fine job you're doing too, son," the father said. The look on his face showed both pride in his son and profound sadness for the reason his son had to grow up so quickly.

The geysers at Norris Geyser Basin
evoke an eerie, other-worldly feeling.

I never knew what to expect from my volunteer chauffeurs; that was at least half the fun of hitchhiking alone. One morning I went out to the road in front of the hotel on my day off, with no clear idea in mind of where I wanted to go. I was almost immediately picked up by a couple who recognized me. I had waited on them in the restaurant the night before.

Ron was a student of environmental design at the University of Georgia in Athens. His wife Julie worked in a law firm. They had been married for five years and still appeared to be very much in love. A small woman with fine brown hair and a homely face which softened into a smile frequently, Julie was very outspoken. She was the type of woman who spoke to complete strangers as if they were her next door neighbors. Ron, a tall man with a handsome visage and thick, curly brown hair, was not put off by Julie's forwardness. He was just as interested in the world around him as she was, although he spoke very softly and hesitated, as if gathering his thoughts, between sentences. They liked to listen to each other and never seemed to be bored with each other's company.

At first I tried to keep them entertained with my "park employee" routine, but as the day went on I relaxed in their pleasant company. They did not expect a show from me. Rather, they wanted to experience the park for themselves, and they made it clear that I was invited along to share their discovery mission.

We stopped at the Norris Geyser Basin and spent a couple of hours walking through it. The falling rain did not slow Ron and Julie down. Their enthusiasm for seeing every one of the geysers in the basin was contagious.

"So, it rains. So, we get wet. No problem!" Julie said. I thought she might have made a good leader for a Boy Scout troop.

In their appreciative company, I marveled at the Little Whirligig geyser, a miniature geyser that popped and gurgled and spurted a perfect little eruption only a foot high. I stood with them at the edge of Echinus geyser for the better part of an hour, waiting for it to put on its show. We were richly rewarded for our patience when it finally let loose with a powerful explosion of water that originated beneath the earth's crust. After it erupted in a spectacular burst of steam and super-heated water, the cavern from which the geyser's steam emerged drained out quickly, revealing a hole lined with big, rough rocks the color of dried blood. We agreed that the whole routine looked and sounded exactly like a toilet being flushed.

The Yellowstone River plunges into a rhyolite canyon.

On the path back to the parking lot, we stopped to look into a cauldron, filled with steaming murky liquid which bubbled and boiled. Julie commented that it looked like clam chowder, which reminded us that we were all quite hungry.

We left Norris and drove over toward Canyon. Twice along the way Ron stopped the car—once to see Virginia Cascades and the other time so he could take a picture of the snow that had fallen on the mountains the night before.

"They'll never believe back home that it snowed in August if we don't take pictures of it," he explained to me.

Once at Canyon, we went for lunch at the cafeteria. As usual, the Yellowstone Park Company's substandard fare tasted wonderful because we were so famished. As we devoured too-dry fried chicken and waterlogged peas, I told my new friends about the company's conspiracy to place eating establishments so far away from one another that a hungry patron had no choice but to think that the food they served was delicious. Even okra, I told them, would taste good for dinner if you had not eaten since dawn. After lunch we went out to look at the Canyon. The Grand Canyon of the Yellowstone River was the inspiration for early explorers of the park area to give the region the name of Yellowstone.

The bright gold color of the canyon walls, we learned from the interpretive signs posted near a viewpoint, was lent by rhyolite, which formed from cooled lava after a volcanic eruption. The rhyolite was soft and easily eroded by the rushing waters of the river which flowed out of Yellowstone Lake. The result of time, water and several ice ages was a steep, craggy "V" of yellow canyon, through which the Yellowstone River roared. At two places the river careened off a precipice in a thunderous waterfall, filling the air with mist. The canyon was indeed a spectacular sight, and would likely have merited national park status for the region even if geysers had not been present.

With Julie and Ron, I followed paths down to the canyon's

rim and viewed it from Inspiration Point, Artist's Point, Lookout Point, every imaginable point. Yet looking at the canyon so much did not become redundant because their tireless enthusiasm was infectious. They seemed to sense the same humility I felt, standing on the rim of the vast canyon.

"There is the canyon," Julie said to me as we stood looking at the green waterfall sliding over golden rocks. "And there it will be after we have left, oblivious to you and me."

Ron added, "I could never draw a blueprint for this design. I don't need to. God has done a wonderful job. I feel small." He looked over at me. "Thanks for sharing the day with us, Kitty."

"Thank you," I replied. "Through your eyes, the park has become new again. Today I have been reminded why I am here. It has been wonderful to share your travels."

Julie pulled a scrap of paper out of her backpack. She scribbled an address on it and handed it to me. "If you're ever in Georgia, look us up," she said. Impulsively she reached out to me, and I heartily returned her hug.

Reluctantly, I left Ron and Julie in the late afternoon and started on the long trip back to Mammoth. My ride from Canyon to Tower Falls was with a couple who was not everything that Ron and Julie had been. They were full of complaints. It was too cold, their hotel bed had been lumpy, the food tasted like cardboard. I tried unsuccessfully to point out some of the good points of my beloved Yellowstone, or at least to raise in them a sense of humor about shared atrocities such as the company food, but they would not budge from their grumpy outlook. Finally I gave up and rode the rest of the way to Tower in silence, staring out the window into the gathering dusk.

The final ride from Tower to Mammoth was with a tall Texan driving a pickup truck. He was divorced and had been injured on the job, so had taken a medical retirement. He was traveling for a month in the company of his ten year old son. The kid was intelligent and interested in everything. The miles went by fast. I discovered that the two of them had spent much of their trip singing old folk songs, and soon we were doing three part harmony and improvising verses to "Oh Susannah."

An hour after dark, I was safely back to Mammoth. What a wonderful day it had been! And despite all the complaining I did about my job, I was high that evening on the Yellowstone experience. I could not think of a place in the world that I would rather be than right there in the Big Sky country.

Yellowstone was seducing me with its magical powers of steam and sunlight and warm wind. I was making no protest. I surrendered to its magic without regrets, for I was receiving far more than I gave of my love.

6

❖❖

The Dorms

Some of the girls who worked at Mammoth complained that they outnumbered the guys by a ridiculously large margin. It was true that there were more females than males working at the restaurant and hotel, however I did not particularly find the ratio to be a problem to my social life.

An old boys and a girls dorm stood behind the restaurant. The boys dorm had only sixteen rooms, while the two-story girls dorm contained twice as many. Both buildings were ancient, as old as the hotel, so obviously the uneven ratio of males to females had persisted for quite a number of years. When I returned for my second year of employment at Mammoth, the company had constructed and opened a new dorm down the road from the old structures. The modern dorm, furnished with new beds and dressers like the dorms at college, was coed.

Secretly I was pleased that I was assigned to a room in the old girls dorm. The old place, with its lumpy mattresses and stained carpets and screenless windows, reminded me of the dorms behind the Wawona Hotel in Yosemite. The old building had character. A day room furnished with a couple of ancient couches provided a good place to drink Diet Pepsi and have heart-to-heart talks with friends. The sagging front porch over-looked the employees entrance to the kitchen and the boys dorm. The sun shone on it just right in the afternoon. We sat out there to drink beer after work and catch up on the local gossip. Relaxing in the sun, I enjoyed watching and discussing the comings and goings of the other employees.

There was one woman—in her mid-twenties, quite a bit more mature than most of us workers—whose job it was to be "dorm mother." She was supposed to solve problems such as lost room keys and broken clothes dryers, as well as enforce dormitory rules. Fortunately, the woman was lax about the letter of the law, which stated that all men had to be out of the girls dorm by midnight. The boys dorm had a similar rule, which was similarly ignored. I soon learned that as long as I did not set my room on fire or disturb my neighbors on either side, no one much cared what went on in the room I shared with Jan, another Californian who worked as a cook in the Mammoth kitchen.

I felt at home both in my dorm and in the employee commu-nity. We Mammoth employees were too numerous to be a tight-knit group; however, we generally did not socialize with either the tourists or the Park Service employees. I did not even spend much time getting to know the people who worked as maids, bellhops, and tour bus drivers over at the hotel, except to say hello to them in the bathroom or in the staff cafeteria. The peo-ple I worked with, other waitrii, buspeople, cooks, and kitchen helpers, were also the people I played with. As a group, we were alternately called the Food and Beverage Department, or the Mammoth Morons, depending on who was doing the name call-ing. We were 50 to 70 people whose constitution changed al-most daily, as people quit their jobs and others moved in to take their places throughout the summer. Our overriding concern was to have fun. We came from all parts of the country, and most of us had never been to Yellowstone before. We went on excursions, hikes, rafting trips, shopping sprees in Bozeman, and out to dinner in groups of three or four. We formed a softball team and a basketball team which played teams of employees from Canyon, Lake, West Thumb, Tower, and Old Faithful. We went drinking at the Gardner bars together, and we came back together, eight or ten of us jammed like sardines into the back of someone's truck.

Often we made a detour on the way home from the bars to soak in the hot pots along the Gardner River. Many a night was spent down at the place where the mineral-rich water of the Mammoth Hot Springs emptied into the river. At night, nobody wore bathing suits in the hot pots. The hotpots were, in effect, a private employees' lounge down in the dark Gardner River canyon, where all the aches and pains of working on our feet serving tourists all day could be soaked away, while we socialized as much or as little as we pleased.

The unwritten rule was that no one mentioned the goings on in the hot pots while we were at work. Nobody wanted the rangers coming down to shine their flashlights in our faces. Nobody wanted tourists showing up at our private hideaway. Several years after I left Yellowstone, someone told me that they had been to Mammoth for a vacation. They described some public hot springs, complete with a sign directing tourists to the "Boiling River." When I asked my friend to describe where the tourist attraction was located, I realized that it was the same place where we employees used to go. I was sorry to hear that the Gardner River hotpots had become public knowledge, but while I lived there they were still, as the saying goes, the best kept secret in the park.

Parkie life at Mammoth was, in general, carefree. Our meals were provided and we did not have to worry about paying for utilities or calling a plumber when the pipes leaked or the toilet clogged. The only responsibility any of us had was to get to work on time. Sometimes, after a long night of partying and hotpotting, this requirement was met by doing without sleep. I dragged myself into the restaurant many times, bleary eyed at 6:00 in the morning, struggling to dredge up reserves of energy enough to face an onslaught of the Japanese army. But going without sleep was not seen by my co-workers as a hardship, particularly; it was simply part of the lifestyle.

I thought, after spending two summers at Mammoth, that I knew the place by heart. I knew who lived in each dorm room, where they were from, and whether or not they liked their job. I partied in many of the rooms or had long, meaningful conversations in them until the wee hours of the morning. By sitting often on the porch of the girls dorm on sunny afternoons, and by sitting next to the screenless window of dorm room number 10 late at night, I came to know most of the relevant gossip from the Mammoth kitchen.

Near the end of my second summer in Mammoth I learned of the existence of a part of Mammoth off limits to both tourists and concession employees. Somehow, though, the secret of its presence was leaked to my friend Jeff, who in turn shared it with me.

We were drinking beer in the employees' pub one night, when I complained that I was bored.

"Do you," I asked Jeff, "know of anything we can do for excitement? I don't mean hotpotting or the bars in Gardner. I mean something new, that we haven't done before."

If anyone would have an idea, Jeff would, I thought. He was one of my running buddies that summer, and could always be counted on for fresh ideas. He had an adventurous spirit. Jeff told wild stories about his life as a gang member on the streets of Pittsburgh, and about a year he spent living off the land in the Canadian Rockies. I was attracted to his energy and zest for the moment at hand.

"I've got a great idea," Jeff said. He was not going to disappoint me. "Have you ever been in the Bowels of Mammoth?"

"The what?"

"The Bowels of Mammoth. Come on, I'll take you there. But you've got to keep this quiet. We aren't supposed to know about this. O.K.?"

"O.K.," I agreed. "Let's go." I followed him outside. The night was warm and the sky full of stars.

"Come over to my car for a second," Jeff said. We walked down to the boys dorm where his old white Impala was parked. He opened the trunk and took out a bottle.

"Where did this come from?" I asked as he handed it to me.

"Rotgut—careful!" he laughed as I choked on the cheap whiskey. "I found a whole warehouse full of it. Look."

He shined a flashlight into the trunk long enough for me to see a couple cases of bottles.

"You found it?" I asked suspiciously.

"That's right. Now I know you will keep your mouth shut about this. I don't want any rangers coming around asking questions."

"Oh, of course, Jeff," I said sincerely. "You know I think the world of you. I like your little secrets and surprises. Speaking of which, what about the innards or whatever you called them?"

"The Bowels," Jeff said. "You carry this bottle. I'll show the way. Follow me now, stay close."

We went around to the back of the boys dorm, where the weeds grew hip-high. I trailed Jeff along the back side of the building. He was shining the flashlight along the outer wall of the dorm. Suddenly he stopped.

"Here it is," he whispered dramatically.

I looked where the beam was pointing, and saw a piece of plywood that appeared to be nailed over a crawlspace on the wall of the building.

"Hold the flash." Jeff handed me the light and picked up a flat rock. He worked the plywood with it until the nails which held it in place began to loosen. As I stood holding the light, sounds from the employee pub drifted to my ears; I heard laughter and music and the shouts of a couple of guys who had had too much to drink.

"O.K.," Jeff said. "Ladies first. Watch your step."

The opening behind the plywood was three feet square. I got down on hands and knees and crawled through the hole. When I got inside, I found myself crouched on a dirt floor in a cave-like hole. There was not even room to stand up.

Jeff crawled in behind me. "Look—" he pointed at one corner. "There's the ladder."

I shined the flashlight and saw where he was pointing. Still on hands and knees, I moved to the ladder and descended six or seven steps to a cement floor.

A light burned near the ladder, illuminating a hallway. The ceiling of the hall was lined with pipes—all sizes of pipes, lined up next to each other like so many railroad tracks.

Jeff came down the ladder and stood beside me. "Welcome to the Bowels of Mammoth," he said grandly.

"Where are we?"

"We are underneath the boys dorm. These tunnels go all over Mammoth—under the hotel, under the girls dorm—I've heard there is even a passage that leads down to the campground, a mile from here."

He took the bottle from my hand and swallowed a swig. "Well, dear, would you like a tour?"

"You bet!"

"Keep your voice low," he warned. "People might freak out if they hear us making noise below their feet. Now then—let's go!"

Jeff and I walked through a maze of hallways, all lined with pipes which hissed and gurgled like geysers preparing to erupt. He said it was the plumbing system for the whole settlement of Mammoth Hot Springs.

"Some maintenance guy comes down here sometimes. He turns the water on and off and makes repairs. Even he doesn't look around much, though. Some of this stuff has been down here, forgotten, for decades."

Jeff seemed to know where he was going; my sense of direction failed me after the first two or three turns. Presently, we came to the end of a hallway which opened out into a big room. Off the room, which was as large as the restaurant coffee shop, were several smaller rooms lined with shelves. I followed Jeff into one of them.

"Old hotel furniture," he told me. I looked around the dimly lit chamber and saw some sagging old beds, a couple scratched up wooden dressers, and a pile of bedspreads.

"Who brought this stuff down here? It looks like it's been here forever."

"I don't know—there must be some other way to get in to the Bowels. From the hotel, maybe. Whoever brought this stuff down here is long gone, though," Jeff said.

We left that room and entered another. The second room contained shelves and shelves of large, heavy leather-bound books. I selected one at random and opened it up.

I gasped. "Hey, Jeff, have you seen these?"

"It's all right there, isn't it?" he answered. "I thought you would be interested in looking at them."

In my hands I held a ledger for the Mammoth Hot Springs hotel for the year 1923. Written laboriously by hand were pages full of columns of numbers.

"Twelve dollars for three nights' lodging, and two dollars and sixty cents for two dinners for Mr. and Mrs. Joseph Edgerton," I read.

I turned a few pages. "Income from gift shop, June 23—$41.07. Wow."

I stopped reading and looked up at the rows of shelves holding books identical to the one I had.

"Is this all of the hotel records?" I asked Jeff.

"All of the early ones. They are dated from 1914 through the 1930s. A whole history could be written just from the information in those books—if one was so inclined."

"I'm going to take this one. Do you think anyone would notice?"

"Frankly," Jeff replied, "I don't think anyone even remembers these are here."

I tucked the heavy book under my arm, and handed the whiskey bottle to Jeff. "I can't carry both of these," I said. Already I was feeling light headed from the rotgut.

"Tell you what," Jeff said. "There's more where this came from. It's an old Indian superstition that when you take something, you must leave something in exchange. You know, if you pick a flower, you spit out your peach pit on the spot. So, we'll leave this bottle here. Then if anyone else ever does find this place, and discovers that 1923 is missing from the Bowels, they will have a good stiff drink waiting for them to temper the shock."

We laughed until I nearly cried. Leaving the records room, we went back out into the main room that connected to the maze of hallways.

Suddenly Jeff stopped walking. "Listen!" he commanded. I distinctly heard the sound of distant footsteps on the cement floor.

"We better get out of here now," Jeff whispered. "Someone's coming. We got to run, now."

I clutched the ledger to my chest and followed Jeff around this hall and that. I was sure we were hopelessly lost in the Bowels, and that the maintenance man would discover us at any time. But miraculously, Jeff found his way back to the ladder.

"Give me the book," he commanded. "Now, you go up, and I will hand it to you."

After he handed it up, I went out the crawlspace. Jeff was

right behind me. When we were out into the fresh night air again, he immediately replaced the plywood over the hole in the wall and pounded the nails back in with a rock.

Once finished with that task, Jeff stopped and turned to look at me. Impulsively, he hugged me and my ledger.

"Well, now you've seen the Bowels. Keep a secret?"

"Sure enough! Let's get rid of the evidence."

"Be nonchalant. Walk slow. We're just out for a stroll in the midnight air."

Out of the weeds we sauntered arm in arm, and walked to the Impala. Casually, Jeff opened the trunk and I placed the ledger inside, next to the stolen rotgut whiskey.

Jeff removed another bottle. Closing the trunk of the Impala, he took the cap off the bottle and threw it away.

"How about a toast," he said. Dramatically, he held up the bottle. "Here's to the Bowels of Mammoth."

Our laughter floated out past the dorms and disappeared into the starswept sky.

7

❖

A Visit From Christie

My sister Christie completed her last year at college in Santa Barbara and was taking the summer off before starting a new job. During the second summer I was at Mammoth, she called to ask if I would mind if she came up to Yellowstone for a visit.

"Of course I wouldn't mind!" I told her. "I'd love to show you the park. There isn't much happening in Los Angeles, is there?"

"No," she said. "I've been hanging around the house, but I haven't much to do here. It is uncomfortable to come back home once you've lived on your own, you know?"

"I know exactly what you mean."

"Well, so I'm planning to ride up on the Greyhound bus. I am looking forward to this trip. I need a break from California."

Christie and I had become close friends, especially since we had both gone to college and grown out of the petty sibling jealousy which had been present while both of us had attended the same high school. The paths our lives were taking were diverging; still, we understood each other because so much of our early lives had included common ground. I too was anticipating her visit.

I borrowed my roommate's truck to pick Christie up at the bus station in Livingston, Montana. On the drive back to Mammoth, we stopped in Gardner to eat a pizza in one of the bars. A bunch of people I knew from work were there, dancing and drinking pitchers of beer. I said hello to them, but Christie and I sat across the room at a different table. I asked her if she wanted to meet my friends, perhaps play a game of pool and socialize.

"They look like they're having fun," I said, glancing over at the group wistfully.

"Not today," Christie said. "Really, that kind of stuff doesn't interest me much. It seems so childish, like college freshmen their first time away from home."

"Did you do much partying at school?" I asked. Though I had been up to visit her several times in Santa Barbara, I really did not know how she spent most of her time.

"Not much. I prefer close friends who know me well. People I can really talk to."

"Oh." I wondered if she thought the coffee shop crowd was shallow. All style and no substance . . . I considered that as I watched one of them stand up and demonstrate to the others a few steps of the New York Hustle. I decided to change the subject. "How are things at home?"

"Oh, you know, the usual. It was not very exciting there. Mom and Dad are working long hours and John spends most of his time out of the house, with his teenage friends, I suppose. He's almost never there, and I don't know what to say to him anyway. I didn't feel like I fit in there any more. There is nothing for me to do."

"Well, there is plenty to do here. I am looking forward to showing you the park. There's just one thing," I looked at

Christie carefully. "Do you mind if we hitchhike to get around? That's really the only viable mode of transportation, and I have found it to be one hundred percent safe."

Christie took a bite of the pepperoni pizza. "I guess that would be all right. As long as we stick together. I've never done that before. Are you sure it is safe?"

I laughed. "You'll see. We'll have a blast. I'll show you how much fun it is. You meet the most interesting people. There's nothing to be afraid of."

Christie sighed. "It's not that I'm afraid. It's just that you are more adventurous than me. I guess I always felt responsible, being the oldest of us kids."

"And I always looked up to you," I answered. "You were the mature one, the sensible one, the one who could play poker with the grownups after the rest of us were sent to bed." Impulsively, I grasped Christie's hand across the table. "Well, maybe this is a good time for us to get past these stupid big sister/little sister roles, and become buddies. Let's have some fun together while you are here, O.K.?"

"O.K.," Christie agreed. "I can't wait to see the park."

I had the next day off, so we hitchhiked together from Mammoth all the way down to Old Faithful, on the south end of the lower loop of road. We got a series of rides from a wide variety of people; all, fortunately, were benign and my sister really forgot her fears and began to enjoy the show as much as I did.

The first ride was with a very fat lady from Spokane in a Honda who was taking two ten year olds on an "adventure." She said she had never done anything like that by herself before. She drove with one hand and consumed an entire bag of potato chips with the other hand, swerving every time she reached for another handful.

Next was an old man in a Winnebago, who came up from Denver each year to sell genuine imitation Indian jewelry to the gift shops in the park. Then we got a ride from some Yellowstone Lake Hotel employees, and a man from Casper, Wyoming who had driven up to the park for the day.

We made good time to Old Faithful. The last ride let us off right near the park's most famous thermal feature, which was scheduled to erupt within a few minutes of our arrival. People were milling around the parking lot like ants flooded out of an anthill. We joined the crowd as it moved toward the geyser.

"Look at all these tourists," Christie exclaimed. "There must be four hundred people here!"

"See the bleachers over there?" I pointed to several rows of wooden seats lined up along one side of a boardwalk which encircled Old Faithful. "Those seats are full every day of the summer."

"This reminds me of Yosemite Valley in July. What a zoo," she said.

"Since we are here, we might as well watch it erupt," I suggested. "Then we can walk out on the geyser basin to get away from most of the turkeys."

"O.K. But let's stand over there, where we can see the geyser without getting crushed by the crowd."

The curious thing about Old Faithful was that it was neither the largest, the highest, nor the most regularly erupting geyser in the park. Yet it was the most famous and most often seen of all the thermal features. At least part of the reason for its popularity was that it was accessible. The Old Faithful Hotel was built within view of the geyser, so that almost no effort needed to be exerted by tourists in order to see the geyser go off.

An information booth near Old Faithful posted the estimated time of the next explosion of hot water from the geyser, further simplifying the task of "doing Old Faithful" for the tourists. By performing a series of calculations, park rangers could closely pinpoint the time of the next eruption, even though the frequency of the eruptions varied from 33 to 120 minutes apart.

Christie and I moved into the ring of spectators just as the geyser began to gurgle and spurt. After a couple of false starts, it suddenly came to life and shot a stream of hot water about 130 feet into the air. In spite of ourselves, we gasped along with the crowd. I had already seen Old Faithful erupt many times in previous trips to the south end of the park; still, the inspiring show of power from the depths of the earth continued to hold me spellbound.

As the gushing water and steam died down, I noticed a little boy standing next to us. He pulled on his mother's sleeve. "Look at the smoke coming out," he said. "That's almost as good as a fire hydrant, Mom!"

"Let's get out of here," I whispered to Christie.

We made our way around the crowds of people now walking back toward the parking lot, and followed one of the boardwalks which lead out to the Upper Geyser Basin. We paused at every thermal feature along the boardwalk, watching and listening as each geyser and each pool and each fumarole showed off for us. We marvelled at the deep blue coloration of Morning Glory pool, more brilliant than a chlorinated swimming pool in the midday sun; we laughed at the shape of the calcium towers of Grotto Geyser which reminded Christie of toadstools. She was captivated by the endless variety of thermal attractions in the geyser basin, and I enjoyed acting as tour guide for her. I discovered the incredible beauty for the umpteenth time by seeing it through her fascinated eyes.

By the time we reached the Firehole River, we had walked far enough to be rid of most of the tourists. I consulted the Guide to the Upper Geyser Basin pamphlet.

"Right across the river here is the Riverside Geyser," I told Christie. "It is more faithful than Faithful, erupting every six hours as regular as clockwork. It says here that this is the most picturesque geyser in the park. But it will not be going off for another hour. Do you want to wait?"

"Sure," Christie said. "Let's eat lunch." We sat down on the grassy river bank and made short work of the sandwiches we were carrying. They were the same old box lunches from the kitchen back at Mammoth, but as usual, because we were so hungry, the food tasted great.

After we finished eating, we both lay back on the grass and closed our eyes. The hot Wyoming sun warmed us like a blanket. The only sound was the gentle murmuring of water as the Firehole River slid by.

Christie was the first to speak. "This is wonderful," she said, sighing contentedly. "I can't think of anywhere I would rather be right now."

"Me neither," I agreed. "You know, I am so glad I came up here. I've fallen in love with Yellowstone—and with wilderness. I don't think I will ever stop working in the parks."

"I like it too," Christie answered, "but generally I am not the traveling kind. I would rather stay in one place for awhile, and have a home and a place to invite people over for dinner. I like to have friends that I don't have to leave behind.

"Mom wants me to go out in the world more, I think because she wants me to gain more experience. But I already know what I want."

"And what is that?" I asked. I was curious, because I had never talked to Christie about what she would do after she finished college. "Everyone thought you were going to marry Rob, but that didn't work out."

"We went our separate ways," Christie said thoughtfully. "And then I met Dave when I was working at the dorm cafeteria. There was something about him that attracted me right away."

"Well, I like Dave. Remember the night I walked in on you when he was kissing you? You made me promise not to tell anyone. I'm glad you found him. He's solid, stable, kind. Your type of person, I always thought."

"Dave wants to marry me," Christie said. She rolled over and looked at me. "We talked about it right before I came up here."

I reached out and grabbed her arm. "Christie, that's wonderful! I'm so happy for you. Does anyone else know?"

"Not yet. That's part of the reason I came up here. I wanted to think it over. And I wanted to tell you first. What do you think? You know Dave better than the rest of the family does."

"I'm honored that you told me first. I promise I will keep my mouth shut. And in my opinion, I think you are making a good choice. Dave is a good man."

"I am so glad you feel that way," Christie said with a sigh. "So do I. I love him, Kitty, and he loves me. We want to have a big family."

A rainbow forms when Riverside Geyser erupts along the Firehole River.

Just then we were interrupted by a long, loud noise that sounded like a burp. Startled, we sat up and looked through the bright sunlight to the far bank of the Firehole River. The Riverside Geyser was erupting right on schedule. With a hiss, it began spurting hot water in a steep arch 75 feet into the air. The stream cascaded gracefully into the river, and across the base of the arch a brilliant double rainbow formed.

Christie and I stared, unable to put our awe into words. Riverside Geyser continued to spew its water for a full fifteen minutes before slowly running down. We sat on the bank until long after the geyser's activities had ceased. On the far bank of the Firehole River, a small herd of elk wandered into view, nonchalantly grazing on the indigenous grasses of the geyser lowlands. The lukewarm water of the river flowed past sedately.

Elk feed on grasses in the Upper Geyser Basin at Old Faithful.

Finally I made a move to get up. "Guess we better head back," I said. I reached out my hand to Christie and pulled her to her feet. "This has been a great day in paradise."

"It has," Christie agreed.

We stayed overnight in one of the rooms at the Old Faithful employees' dorm. The next morning, after eating pancakes in the staff cafeteria and obtaining a couple more box lunches, we started back toward Mammoth.

Hot pots near Yellowstone Lake are hot enough to boil an egg.

We got a ride immediately near the Old Faithful cloverleaf, which took us to a spot along the Firehole River several miles below Old Faithful. There we hiked down to a place where the super-heated water of the geyser basins, combined with the cool river water, spread out to form a bathtub-warm swimming hole. It was another of those places known only by park employees, a hot spring just the right temperature for bathing. The code of honor among park employees dictated that the location of hot-pots was not given to tourists. I did not think of Christie as a tourist, though, since she, like me, had grown up with a healthy disdain for them during our summers in Yosemite.

We soaked in the hotpot for an hour. The water was 110 degrees, and like a steam bath, it relaxed and mellowed us both. As we soaked, she asked me if all the hot pools could be used as jacuzzis, like the one we were in.

"No way," I said. "Most of them are much too hot. Only a few are suitable for human habitation. The secret is guarded, not only to keep the tourists away, but because the Park Service frowns on anyone getting into the hotpots at all."

"Why?" Christie asked. "I wouldn't think they'd care. Unless, of course, they think bodies in the water upset the balance of nature."

We both laughed. "Actually, it can be dangerous. If someone gets in the wrong pot, they could die. In fact, I heard a story about that happening one time, up by Madison. This guy accidentally jumped into one that was 350 degrees. He was boiled just like a chicken."

Christie shivered in the hot pool. "Ick. I'm glad you know which ones are habitable."

"Me too. And I keep it quiet. I don't want to be responsible for someone else getting in the wrong pool. Can't you see the headlines: *Yellowstone Waitress Leads Tourist to Bubbly Death*; *Bears Dine on Poached Human*. The tourists ask about it a lot, but I just tell them I don't know of any hot pots. I think it is best to keep it a secret."

"Are there any up by Mammoth?"

"A few," I answered. "One in particular where we all go after the bars close." I caught her look, which said I don't want to hear about this.

I cleared my throat. "Speaking of Mammoth, we better be getting out to the road again and head back home. Have you had enough of the hotpots for now?"

"Sure, let's go," she said.

From the hotpots, we caught a ride as far as Norris in the back of a pickup truck piloted by three guys from Montana. They wore Stetsons and talked to us on a public address system rigged to the top of their truck. They kept us laughing with their comments about the tourists over their P.A. system. As we passed Gibbon Falls, tourists were leaning over the railing to get a better view of the falls. Much to our delight and embarrassment, the three men broadcast a graphic commentary on the shape of the tourists' backsides as we drove by.

The cowboys left us at Norris. Christie eyed the gathering thunderclouds as we stood at the junction with our thumbs out.

"I think it's going to rain," she said nervously.

"It's O.K.," I answered cheerfully. "We'll get a ride soon."

Raindrops were just beginning to fall when we got a ride from two young women from Switzerland who were driving an old station wagon. They did not speak much English, so Christie and I sat in the back seat just staring out the windows into the lightning and pouring rain.

Finally we arrived back in Mammoth. After showering and cleaning up, Christie and I settled into my dorm room. She sat on my roommate's bed, reading her Bible, while I, in the opposite corner, recorded the day's activities in my journal. My roommate, Jan, came in awhile later on a break from her job as a cook in the kitchen. She said hello to Christie, then proceeded to catch me up on the latest happenings at work. Four of the people in the kitchen failed to show up for work, two of the cooks quit, and they were making her work overtime. She sighed.

"I'm tired, but I'll do it. You wouldn't have believed Al. You know, the cook?"

"Yeah," I said, "what did he do?"

"The little dummy came into the kitchen this morning all messed up on drugs, and we were so shorthanded that no one made him leave. He was totally useless."

"Jeez, what a pain. Is he still there?"

"No, he finally went home. Thank God. To do more drugs, probably. It looked like he hadn't slept in three days. Say, did you have fun at Old Faithful?"

"Yes, we had a great time down there," I answered.

"I long for a day off," Jan sighed.

"Well, hang in there, and try to have a good evening. I may come in and get a burger from you later."

After she left, Christie stopped reading and looked up at me. "I don't think I want to know what your friends are doing," she said.

"You're right," I answered. "Just let it lie."

We were so different, I thought, as Christie went back to her reading. It surely seemed implausible that we could have come from the same family. There were some things that I guessed we would never be able to share. Still, I had enjoyed letting her into my world. During the days we spent together traveling around the park, she had not once donned an air of superiority. She had seemed more like an appreciative friend than an older sister. Despite our differences, or perhaps because we had finally accepted them, we had, in Yellowstone, finally been able to cross an invisible line. For the first time, I felt that Christie and I had formed a friendship.

8

❖

The Lake And The Canyon

I hitched a ride down to Old Faithful one July morning to visit with my friend Jean, who worked at the restaurant in Old Faithful Lodge. I had lived with Jean for part of the year in San Diego. After hearing my stories about the first summer I had spent in Yellowstone, she decided to take a quarter off from school and go to work in Yellowstone herself. She had arrived at Old Faithful in April, and when I got back to Mammoth that June I was eager to visit her and learn whether she was enjoying the park as much as I was.

Jean was working when I arrived at Old Faithful, so I left my backpack in her dorm room and went for a hike in the Upper Geyser Basin, promising to return and meet her when she got off shift. I ran into her again during the dinner hour in the staff cafeteria. Easy to spot in a crowd, Jean was a tall, athletic blonde woman with a booming laugh. She was sitting at a table with another woman and a couple of guys I did not know. I loaded up my tray with roast beef slices on toast and broccoli, and plopped down at her table.

"Hey, look who's here! Kitty, this is my roommate Sheila, and this is Bob, who lives down the hall from me. And here—" she indicated the other man, "is Rusty. He's from Wisconsin. He's here visiting Sheila."

"A tourist?" I asked, raising my eyebrow. "You know, you're surrounded by anti-tourists here, Rusty."

"Don't hold it against me, please," Rusty said. His blue eyes twinkled behind the black frames of his glasses. "I didn't bring a camera with me. I don't even own a pair of Bermuda shorts. I've been here a week, and I have not sent one postcard. Have I earned my chair at this table of locals?"

"Sure enough," I laughed. "Now, Jeannie, what shall we do this evening?"

We decided to go over to the Bear Pit bar, in Old Faithful Inn, to have a few drinks. There we stayed for several hours, telling stories about Yellowstone. It was good to see Jean's familiar face again and share some laughs with my jolly friend.

Rusty and Sheila got into an argument after we had been in the bar for awhile. I did not hear what the fight was about, but Sheila got up abruptly and left the table. Rusty followed her out, then came back alone a few minutes later. Jean saw his angry look.

"What's up?" she asked him, pushing a beer toward him.

Rusty drank half of the beer in one swallow. "I don't know. She doesn't want me around. She says she's got her own life now, and I am not a part of it."

"Have you known her long?" I asked Rusty.

"I knew her before I went into the Navy. I guess things change a lot in a couple years. I came out here to find out if things were still happening between us. I suppose I got my answer."

"Hey, you guys, let's go out and watch Old Faithful go off!" Jean was trying to shake the pall off the conversation. I too was uncomfortable with the turn of events; Jean's suggestion sounded good to me, and I said so.

Out we went into the night. Old Faithful was going to erupt, according to the Park Service sign, at 9:44 P.M. No lights flooded the boardwalk which led to the geyser; nobody was waiting on the bleachers for the event. The four of us sat close together, waiting in the darkness. And then it happened, just as it happened on sunny days when the crowds were thick: Old Faithful belched and snorted and began to spray steam and hot water from the depths of the earth.

Only at 9:44 P.M., the show was entirely for us. There was a luminous quality to the steam, apparent only when the black sky was the backdrop for the eruption. Bob said some type of chemical in the hot water created the illusion that the geyser was glowing in the dark. After five minutes of intense eruption, the geyser's activity ceased. Still we sat on the bleachers for a long time, with a million stars overhead and no one else around. It was totally quiet, except for the gurgling of the water winding its way through an unseen underground path. Finally, we left the geyser and went back to the dorm to sleep.

The next morning, Rusty asked if anyone wanted to accompany him on a horseback ride out of West Yellowstone. Jean and Bob had to work, but I had another day off. So, not in a hurry to return to Mammoth, I volunteered to accompany him. Rusty had an ancient blue car which appeared too decrepit to go another mile, but once he got it started, he assured me that his trusty car would make the journey with no problem. "It got me here from Wisconsin, didn't it?" he asked rhetorically.

On the way to West Yellowstone, we picked up five hitch-hikers: two Old Faithful employees going to one of the hot pots; two English girls trying to get back to the Greyhound bus station; and a Japanese guy whose backpack had been stolen in Jackson. I gave him some food from my box lunch before we dropped him off in the town of West Yellowstone.

The place where we rented horses was about six miles outside of West Yellowstone, in the state of Idaho. There we obtained two horses after assuring the ranch owner that we both knew how to ride. The owner told us we could take the horses anywhere we wanted to go, as long as we promised not to run them too hard and cooled them for half an hour before returning to the ranch. He gave us directions to several trails in the area, and said goodbye.

Off we went on horseback up a gravel road which soon turned on to a logging road. The logging road wound uphill through grove after grove of aspen trees, over the rolling Idaho hills. Rusty and I urged our mounts off the road and steered them to the top of a hill. At the summit there were no trees, as the area had burned a couple years earlier. Long strands of green grass grew abundantly, however, and we tethered the horses, allowing them to graze.

The view from the top was stupendous. We could see a lake below, and Montana mountains beyond it. The other way, we could see from the flat valley of the Madison River all the way to the Grand Canyon of the Yellowstone River. The blue sky was spotted with white clouds and, farther out over the mountains, thunder clouds were building up like stacks of wood in October.

Presently, Rusty and I decided to go down to the lake. As we rode down the hill, a stiff breeze arose. The lake was farther away than it had looked, but eventually we arrived there. A natural cove of the lake, protected by trees, provided an ideal swimming hole. Though rain drops were beginning to fall, the lake itself was warm. We wasted no time peeling off our dirty clothes and plunging into the water.

Rusty and I swam and splashed each other, and our laughter echoed across the hillsides as the rain came down in sheets. Later, after we tired of swimming, we sat on the grassy lake shore under a tree whose spreading branches shielded us from most of the raindrops. In the distance, thunder crackled across the sky. Rusty produced some bread, a hunk of cheese and some sausage from his horse's saddlebag.

"So you came up here to look for your past," I said as I ate. "Are you glad that you settled things with Sheila?"

"I am, really. Even though it didn't turn out the way I had wanted it to, I felt like I had to see her again. Now that I know Sheila doesn't want me around, I can go on to other things. And other people. This trip west has freed me in a way I never expected it to.

"And I met you. You are as much a part of Yellowstone to me as the hot springs," Rusty said. He took off his glasses and wiped them on his shirt. "Are you really going to leave here at the end of the summer and return to California? I don't see how you could. I have only been here a week, but already I am falling in love with this park."

"I have thought about staying," I answered. "The Old Faithful Lodge is open in the winter, and I suppose I could get a job working there. But I have two more years of college to do, and other parks are calling me, too. I don't know."

I paused, thinking. The silence was filled with the sound of rain hitting the lake surface and the distant roll of thunder.

"I guess the thing is that I want more. When I first came up here, last year, I felt I had reached the ultimate goal; I was a waitress in Yellowstone National Park, and that was enough."

"And now that's not enough?" Rusty asked.

"No. In some way I want to contribute to the park, fight for it, share it. In my dreams I imagine myself writing management plans for the forests or giving guided tours through the geyser basins. I couldn't tell you exactly what my goals are. All I know is that I have not had enough of national parks."

"I know what you mean," Rusty agreed. "It seems that we shed our old ideas like snake skins when we grow out of them. I'm shedding the idea that I was going to marry Sheila, and it is painful. Yet I am actually looking forward to the changes that will be coming. We have to stay in the present tense."

"And the present is pleasant!" I cried. "As a friend of mine once said, 'So it rains, so we get wet. No big deal.' You know? The main thing is that we appreciate what we have today."

Finally we got back on the horses and left the lake. The rain ended and in the warm after-storm afternoon sunshine, we walked the horses all the way back to the ranch. After returning the horses, we drove to West Yellowstone, and bought pizza at one of the restaurants. On the trip back to Old Faithful from West Yellowstone, we spotted a lone bison crossing the plain below the Midway Geyser Basin in the gathering dusk. I was tired but completely content in Rusty's company.

I had to go back to Mammoth and to work the next morning. Rusty promised that he would come by and see me on his way back to Wisconsin. And, true to his word, he did show up at Mammoth a couple days later. We went hot potting and then stayed up talking in my room until 1:30 A.M., at which time he announced that he had to leave.

"I'm going out the park's northeast entrance. If I leave now, I will be in the Bear Tooth Mountains at sunrise. I have to be back to Wisconsin by Friday to go to work. So this is it, Kitty. I've got to get moving now."

I watched him put on his hat and those funny glasses that broke up his face. Then he sat back down on the edge of the bed next to me and put an arm around my shoulders in his casual, familiar way.

"You've shared with me an important time in my life," Rusty said quietly. "I'm not sure what to say to you."

"How about see you later," I answered. "I hate to say goodbye to anyone. We can leave it open . . ."

Rusty got up, pulled his sweater on and walked to the door. In the dim light I could only see his silhouette. There was no moon outside.

"The French have a word for it," he said. *"Au revoir."*

"What does that mean?"

His hand was on the door knob. "Until we meet again," he whispered. And then he disappeared into the darkness of the summer night. He was heading toward the sunrise, and I hoped he would not lose it again once he got there. Though I never saw him again, I treasured the moments I had spent with the tourist from Wisconsin.

By August I needed a break. The Mammoth experience, so special to me the first year I was there, was degenerating fast as the end of my second summer approached. The endless stream of tourists had taken its toll on my attitude, and I recognized a need to escape from the microcosm of the compound where I worked. All the tourists were beginning to look the same; I was no longer interested in where they were from or how they liked the park. When I heard myself telling one particularly obnoxious group in the coffee shop that I wished they would go back where they came from, I realized that I needed to take action to remind myself what I was doing in Yellowstone.

The opportunity arose when Joel, one of the waitrii in the dining room, invited me to accompany him on an overnight hike through the Black Canyon of the Yellowstone River. Although I had become friendly with Joel on one of those slow afternoons in the kitchen, I did not know him very well and was not certain he would be good company for my sour state of mind. Desperate to get out of Mammoth for a couple days, though, I decided to take him up on his offer.

Almost as soon as he steered his truck out onto the highway and headed toward Tower Falls, I relaxed. The day was another hot, dry specimen of the waning summer. The road led out across a broad, high plateau of sagebrush; when we turned off the highway to follow a side road, dust kicked up behind the truck like a blizzard.

The trail to the Black Canyon of the Yellowstone River

We parked the truck at a pullout on Blacktail Deer Plateau and started down the trail with Joel in the lead. A very tall man with a long stride, he outpaced me and soon was quite a distance ahead of me. We had not spoken much during the ride out to the trailhead; he was apparently a man of few words, and I was so hungry for the serenity I knew could be found in the wilderness that I was not overly eager to talk to him, either.

Joel and I stayed in our own separate worlds the whole distance in to camp. After a couple hours of traversing the plateau, we reached the bank of the Yellowstone River. Joel helped me to ford across it, and then we located a nice campsite on the far side of the river. I collected firewood while he set up a tent. Beneath the trees we cooked a dinner of trail stew together and brought the pan over to the bank of the river. We shared the meal and made some coffee, all the while not speaking more than we needed to in order to communicate about the tasks we were completing.

We continued to sit there long after we finished eating. I watched the water flow slick and swift, the color of pea soup. That part of the Yellowstone River appeared relatively tame, considering that it had traveled over the two great falls at the Canyon before it arrived where we were sitting. Downstream from us, the river again plunged into a canyon, before joining forces with the Gardner River near the north boundary of Yellowstone Park.

Finally, Joel broke the silence. "It sure is peaceful here, isn't it?"

"Yes," I said, keeping my eyes on the moving water. "I really needed to get out in the fresh air again, you know what I mean? I am starting to feel really burned out on everything that has to do with Mammoth, Yellowstone, the tourists. Sometimes, I get to wondering what I'm doing here. Do you ever feel that way?"

"Not much," Joel said. "This is my first year here. I spend as much time as I can out on the trails and in the woods. I go hiking almost every weekend. I wasn't sure, to be honest with you, whether to ask you to come with me or not. My private world, where I can communicate with God and nature, is really important to me. I don't share it with most people."

"Who do you share it with? I mean, don't you go around with Jackie a lot?"

When he did not answer my question immediately, I thought that perhaps I had stepped beyond my boundaries. "I'm sorry. I didn't mean to pry. But you know, Mammoth is a small town."

"Yes, it is. It drives me crazy sometimes, the way the gossip goes around there. But it's probably good for me to talk about what happened with Jackie. You see, she and I were as close as two people could be. We had even made some plans about getting married. She and I and Rob, my best friend—the three of us went everywhere together. And then, one day, I caught Jackie in bed with Rob."

"Oh, that's awful," I sympathized. "You must have wanted to kill him."

"I wanted to, but I am not that kind of person. I saw all the violence I need for a lifetime when I was in Vietnam. So, I just walked back out of the room; I haven't spoken to either of them since then. I haven't talked to anyone else about it, either, until now. That girl broke my heart, and it is not yet mended. I still cannot look Jackie in the eyes, because I loved her.

"But you don't want to hear about my problems. Anyway, I have to be where I am now. Watching the sun go down on a river bank in the Yellowstone backcountry with my new friend from California. So, tell me about yourself, Kitty. What are you doing with your life after you leave here next month?"

The awkwardness of not knowing what to say to each other was dissolved by Joel's telling of the story of the demise of his relationship with Jackie. Trusting the man next to me on the river bank, I told him about some of my experiences in the park that summer and the summer before. I was not ready to give up on the parks yet, I told him; far from it. Though I might not return to Mammoth again, I was certainly planning to spend the next summer in a national park, perhaps in the desert or on the East Coast.

After the sun went down, the canyon into which the Yellowstone River was plunging turned to shadows. The whistling of the wind through the bends of the river was superimposed on the sound of water sliding over rock. Pine trees lining the river bank bent gently to the unseen music of the wind; and the milky way appeared, one star at a time, to spread slowly like spilled honey all the way across the sky.

Presently, Joel spoke to break the comfortable quiet which had settled around us. "Look at those stars, the openness of the sky. When you see all this, you can't doubt that someone made it all. It could not have just happened by accident. In spite of all the strange things we people do to mess things up, I know there is Someone up there who made it all and who watches over me. I was taken care of in the jungles, and I am taken care of today. I am always aware of the power of my God and the beauty of His creation, and every day I try to remember to thank Him for it."

"Yes, I agree with you, this earth is pretty incredible. Especially this part, in Yellowstone. I guess people's greed and hate are the monkey wrenches in the system. But still, perhaps each of us can do something to help straighten it out. To be honest, Joel, I see my God, or whatever you want to call it, in the woods and the stars and the water. I don't read the Bible. But I can feel it, here."

Joel sighed. "I don't read it either, because I cannot read. Still, there is a God in my life; I know it. I cannot give my faith away to anyone, though. People have to find it for themselves. Speaking for myself, I am sure there is a plan. I keep going only by telling myself that there is a reason for everything. Perhaps it's just to be able to help out someone else someday, when the same thing happens to them. But for me, that's a good enough reason. I may never understand it, really. That I believe there is a purpose for everything in God's plan, even when I don't understand it, is the essence of my faith."

I had no response to Joel's speech. I could not deny that something had arranged the stars and had a hand in placing the rocks and trees and rivers. But I had not given it much thought in the past few years, much less discussed it with anybody, and I was uncomfortable with the topic. I had an appreciation for the wilderness; I was glad it was there, and I wanted more of it. And that was about all I could say.

Mentally, I drifted away from Joel like a wisp of wind. Soon, I got up and went to bed. He stayed out on the river bank for quite a long time after I left him, and by the time he crawled into his sleeping bag, I was already asleep.

Hiking out the six miles to the other end of the trail the next morning, Joel and I again seemed to be residing in separate worlds. I lagged behind him; he stopped and waited for me to catch up to him a couple times. Eventually, he gave up on me and went on by himself. Alone, I walked the trail slowly on the bank above the Yellowstone River's black canyon. Skeletons of small mammals littered the trail, and at one place where I stopped to drink some water, I spied a coyote moving across the plain on the far side of the river a mile or two away. The Indian summer heat and the soothing sound of the flowing river permeated my consciousness. I walked until I had not an argumentative thought in my head. I had to let Joel go; he was on a different path than I was, and eventually I stopped worrying about our differences. That rivers would flow downhill and trees would bend in the afternoon breeze was enough to sustain my faith in the God of my understanding.

When I made my way out to the road, Joel had already hitched a ride back to the trailhead to pick up his truck. I walked another mile into Gardner and found some Mammoth Morons who offered to give me a ride home by way of the hot pots. The warm water of the springs relaxed and revived me.

We left the hot springs after half an hour of soaking and returned to Mammoth. After I ate dinner, and darkness had fallen, I went by myself to climb up to the top of the nameless hill behind the hotel. I needed to be alone. My second summer in Yellowstone was coming to an end.

I thought about the people like Rusty who had brought joy to my life, and those like Joel who had caused me to stop and ponder the mysteries of the spiritual world. And I thought about all the places I had been in the past two summers, places which

were not accessible except by foot and with great effort. A wave
of gratitude for my beloved Yellowstone filled me. In the darkness, sitting on my rock in the wind, I composed a love poem to
Yellowstone and its people.

> *Climb up to my silent mountain*
> *And hold me in your song*
> *Where starry plains chase a bright path*
> *A hundred miles long across the sky.*
>
> *Where the night becomes the music*
> *Of an Indian summer wind.*
> *Embrace me with your eyes.*
> *Let the silence of my mountain*
> *Into your heart*
> *And then keep me there*
> *Forever.*

9

Desert
View

My next year of college was spent at Berkeley. Almost immediately upon arriving at the large campus on the San Francisco Bay, I changed my major from communications to environmental geography and took nothing but earth science and resource management classes. The topics of all my term papers were national parks; I used my studies as an excuse to escape the city for long weekends in the California parks. I wrote about the biogeography of Death Valley in the winter quarter. During my spring quarter I visited Redwood National Park and completed a report about the human influences on the park ecology. For another class I assembled my impressions of Yellowstone, using material from the journals I had kept for two summers. My teachers were pleased with my work, and my dedication to the field of park management increased.

When the school year ended, I went down to Los Angeles and sat around at my parents' house for a week or so, indecisive about my next move. I had not re-applied for a job in Yellowstone. I had decided while I was at Berkeley that I had spent enough time in Mammoth, and I had no desire to work in either of the Old Faithful or Canyon complexes.

I had acquired a small Datsun pickup truck. One day, at the end of June, I loaded it with a summer's worth of play clothes and headed east on Highway 40. I had in mind a vague itinerary: Grand Canyon to Zion to Bryce to the Tetons or Rocky Mountain Park, or something. I was certain that I could find a job somewhere along that route; halfway through the summer, there were always jobs in parks.

Rails keep stray tourists away from the edge of the canyon.

I filled my gas tank in Williams, Arizona and discovered that I had only five dollars left in cash holdings. Undaunted, I started up the spur road out of Williams which led to the South Rim of the Grand Canyon. Besides the five dollar bill, I possessed a hefty portion of optimism. Unconcerned about the shortage of money, I was confident I could find something to do.

It was an hour's drive on a flat road bordered by extinct cinder cones, from Williams to Grand Canyon National Park. Once I passed the park entrance booth, I continued to follow the road for another mile. A turnout marked with the name MATHER POINT beckoned me, so impulsively I made a right turn and stopped in the parking lot.

In front of me, suddenly, the flat ground dropped away, and there was the canyon. I was, at that first viewing, unable to comprehend what I saw. The layers and colors of the canyon's walls looked like an oil painting; my mind was unable to make sense of it. Even with three years of higher education to my credit, I was unable to come up with a more intelligent thought than this: "Something happened here!"

I stared at the canyon until the view at least began to look less foreign. At that time I had no reference point from which to view the canyon. I had no way to understand it. When another bus load of tourists pulled into the parking lot, I decided to leave the viewpoint and tend to the immediate business of hunting for a job.

I found the personnel office tucked in a back room of the El Tovar Hotel, adjacent to the laundry. I took a deep breath, entered, and was granted an interview with a heavy woman who looked overworked.

"What kind of work do you want to do?" she asked me. I had the impression that she had asked that question a few thousand times before.

"Food service is my first choice," I answered, "but I am willing to do anything except housekeeping."

Grand Canyon
National Park

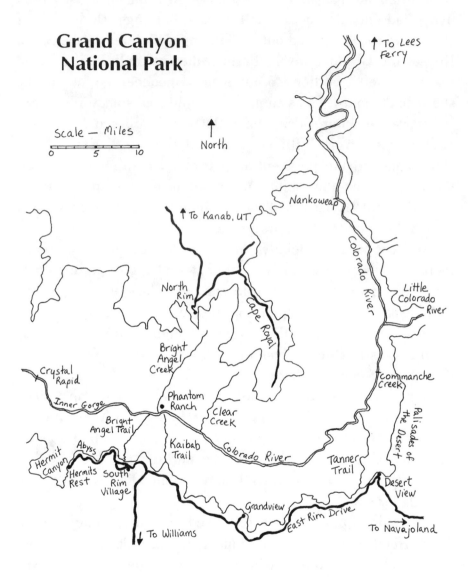

Scale — Miles

0   5   10

North

To Lees
Ferry

To Kanab, UT

Nankoweap

Colorado River

North
Rim

Little
Colorado
River

Cape Royal

Bright
Angel
Creek

Crystal
Rapid

Commanche
Creek

Phantom
Ranch

Clear
Creek

Inner Gorge

Bright
Angel Trail

Kaibab
Trail

Colorado River

Palisades of
the Desert

Abyss

Hermit
Canyon

Hermits
Rest

South
Rim
Village

Tanner
Trail

Desert
View

Grandview

East Rim Drive

To Williams

To Navajoland

"Do you particularly want to be here in the South Rim village?"

"Not necessarily." I had seen some of the South Rim village during the drive in, and had not been overly excited about the four hotels and their attendant restaurants and gift shops, crammed into a couple acres of ground on the lip of the great canyon. I told her about Mammoth.

"I sort of liked being away from the main tourist attraction up there. I feel more comfortable in a smaller area. And I am hoping to have time to do some research for my honors thesis. Are there any places that are off the beaten track here?"

She smiled. "I think I have the perfect job for you. Twenty five miles east of here is an area called Desert View. It has a couple gift shops, a snack bar, a grocery store and a campground. A lot of people come in to the park that way, but most don't stay there very long.

"We have an opening in the snack bar. You would be cooking hamburgers, hot dogs, and eggs to order, and serving ice cream and cold drinks. I'd like to offer you that job. What do you think? Do you want to go out and look at the area first, before making a decision? Do you think you could handle a position like that?"

"I don't think I need to go out there. I'll take it, sight unseen." I did not tell her that I was not exactly in the position to turn down the offer, that my pocket was lined with a lone five dollar bill. I was more than pleased; Desert View sounded like just the sort of place I wanted to spend the summer.

She had me sign some papers. After I finished, she made me an employee identification card.

"O.K.," she said, as she handed me the freshly laminated card. "You start work on Wednesday. When you go out there, look for Cindy. She is your supervisor. She will show you where your housing is, and get you set up."

"Thank you very much," I said with feeling. "I know I will

enjoy this job."

"I hope so," the woman answered, shaking my outstretched hand. "Have a good summer."

Not enough people worked in Desert View to justify the building of an employee dorm. Instead, a scattered collection of trailers and prefab houses provided living quarters for the thirty or so of us who worked there. In addition to the assortment of residences for concession employees, a double row of trailers, set apart from the rest, provided housing for the 15 or 20 National Park Service employees who were also assigned to duty at the outpost on the east end of the South Rim Road.

I shared a prefab house with a native girl who came from Cameron on the Navajo reservation east of Desert View. She went home every weekend and did not spend a lot of time in the house. Nor, for that matter, did I. There was not much to the place: a bathroom, a kitchen and a main room which contained two single beds nailed to the wall.

The job slinging burgers in the Desert View snack bar was in many ways similar to the jobs I had had in Yellowstone. The tourists looked the same, only there were more of them. The people arriving in Desert View had either driven up 30 miles and 3,000 feet in elevation from the Navajo reservation, or they had driven out from the South Rim village in private cars or in an air conditioned tour bus. Either way, they were all hungry. The line for the snack bar often stretched out the doorway and wound around through the aisles of the gift shop. With that volume of people passing through, I usually had no time to make small talk with the tourists. I tipped my Grand Canyon visor down to keep my eyes from meeting theirs. My hands flew, working the deep fryer, grill, milk shake machine, and cash register all at once. No one was concerned with the quality of the food we served at the snack bar; the idea was simply to get them served as quickly as possible.

Few of the tourists lingered in Desert View. There was one small campground available for travelers to use, if they arrived early enough to reserve a site. Otherwise, the nearest lodging was back at the village. The people came out to Desert View primarily to see the spectacular, sweeping vista of colorful flat lands of the Painted Desert from the top of the Watchtower. Once that mission was accomplished, and they had sufficiently filled their stomachs with hot dogs and ice cream, they turned around and went back to the village.

The Watchtower was a structure built in the 1930s by the Fred Harvey Company, for which I worked. Designed by a woman architect named Mary Jane Colter, it was modeled after the kivas, or ceremonial rooms, found in ruins of the ancient tribes who inhabited the desert and canyons of the Colorado Plateau a millennia ago. Many people who visited the Watchtower assumed it was an authentic kiva. It was not. Though there were some Tusayan Indian ruins several miles west of Desert View, there were no ruins right close to the Desert View settlement. Ancient people who used kivas had generally stayed near streams and rivers, nowhere near the quasi-kiva known as the Watchtower.

The view from Desert View was stupendous. From its perch on the south rim, the Watchtower overlooked a great bend where the Colorado River was joined by the turquoise waters of the Little Colorado River. Along the rim just south of the confluence and thousands of feet above it, the Palisades of the Desert formed a sheer cliff which appeared to hang suspended in midair, shimmering in the summer heat. Beyond the Grand Canyon, the view extended eastward. One could see the Navajo reservation, the Painted Desert, and, on clear days, the hump of Navajo Mountain, 200 miles distant.

I was dismayed to notice that, some days, the view to the east was obscured by a yellow haze. When tourists asked about the smog, I answered their questions by alternately blaming the coal-powered Black Canyon Power Plant near Navajo Mountain and the winds that blew smog in from Los Angeles. Fortunately, smoggy days were few, and the majority of the time the spectacular view was unobscured.

On my lunch hour, I took a hot dog from the snack shop and sat out on the rim of the Grand Canyon to eat. I found a place to sit away from the tourists, and it was there that I first began to become acquainted with the canyon. The view became familiar, yet it was never familiar. I learned that the canyon changed moods by the hour, depending on the slant of the sun, the presence of clouds, and the advance of the summer monsoon season. A raven often joined me for lunch, perching on a dead tree near my view point and watching my every move in hopes I would drop some food. I watched the raven fly effortlessly down into the canyon, soaring on updrafts and covering several hundred feet of altitude in seconds. From that raven I began to get a perspective on the size of the canyon. I had, of course, read the statistics: a mile deep, 14 miles wide, 208 miles long. But the numbers meant nothing to me without a reference point such as the bird.

I was jealous of the ease with which the large bird traveled past the sheer walls of jumbled rock below me until it disappeared into a point; and it occurred to me that birds were the only animals really suited for canyon travel. It did not matter to the birds whether the ground beneath them was horizontal or vertical, so they were able to gain access to the whole of it. At that time, I was still merely staring at the canyon. I was afraid of the canyon for most of my first summer there. If I hiked down there, I thought, looking down into its depths from Desert View, I might never be able to make the trip back out.

I was content just to listen as the wind whispered through branches of pinyon and juniper trees and the canyon wrens whistled down the sunset. And I learned that the Grand Canyon possessed a power. I felt the power but did not truly understand it. Over the years I learned that nobody reckoned with it anyway. It just was, and I felt very small and humble as I sat on the rim each day eating a hot dog and watching the canyon's colors change before my eyes.

The small population of employees at Desert View limited my choices for friends. Shortly after my arrival at that outpost, I formed an alliance with three men who shared a prefab house. They were all from Philadelphia. I met Tom first; he and I had a stormy relationship which consisted mostly of drinking rum and playing music. He thought he was a rock guitarist, and my singing became more and more off key the more I drank. It was not a match made in heaven. We did not have much in common besides a drinking problem, but through him I met the other two, John and Charlie, and the four of us became fast friends and running buddies for the remainder of the summer.

John had worked a couple seasons at the Grand Canyon already, and had earned a reputation as a gracious host. There was always beer in his refrigerator, and he was ever willing to invite one more person to pull up a chair around the small table in his living room. He put up a variety of travelers at his place during the course of the summer: two attractive women from Florida, a couple city boys from east Los Angeles, and a huge man named Don who was covered with tattoos and sported a shaved head long before that style became popular. Don bragged that he had outstanding warrants in at least eight states, but nevertheless he was always given a traveler's welcome at John's place when he showed up.

I ate dinner at John's more than I ate at my own home, and I enjoyed making a meal for all of them too. Shooting down the beer chasers, high as a kite, I would put some slop together and call it lasagna. No one ever complained about the food I made, and I was happy to make myself useful in some way and thus earn a return invitation for the following evening.

Each Desert View sunset is spectacular in its own way.

The third of the Philadelphia trio was a kleptomaniac named Charlie. Charlie worked with me in the snack bar, where he put his sticky fingers to good use. I never quite saw how he did it, but he had the ability to ring up a sale and take the money from the tourists. At the end of the shift, the money in the register would balance but he would have 20 or 30 dollars in his pocket. He financed his airplane ticket back to Philadelphia that way. Charlie was always laughing and telling jokes; he was easy to be around.

Typical evenings at John's house began after we all got off work and most of the tourists had emptied out of Desert View.

We convened for beer and storytelling in the kitchen, and John or I would prepare some sort of dinner. Then we took a bottle of rum and went out to watch the sunset from the rim of the canyon.

"Remember the sunsets," Tom would always tell me. "No matter what else slips your mind, remember the sunsets." The line was spoken with the feeling that could only be expressed by one drunk to another.

And I did remember them. I remembered them so well they haunted me even after I left the canyon and returned to my native California at summer's end. Each sunset was different, depending on the cloud cover and the weather. The canyon was absolutely still before the sun sank below the horizon, as if holding its breath while the most dazzling oranges and yellows crept across the expanse of sky. The ancient rock of the canyon turned gray, then blue, then purple. At the moment the sun sank below the edge of the sky, a hot wind blasted up out of the gaping hole below our feet. Color in the sky often lingered for hours after the sun had disappeared.

After the show was over, we went back to John's house to commence singing, partying, telling jokes, and making too much noise for the neighbors' tastes. Night after night, the same pattern repeated itself. Several times during the long, hot summer, the Chosen Few From Desert View, as we called ourselves, took field trips away from home. We invaded the bars in the village, Lake Powell for water skiing and Telluride, Colorado for a jazz festival.

In August, we made the trip down to the bottom of the Grand Canyon. I had grown sufficiently comfortable by that time with the canyon that I swallowed my fear, hefted a pack onto my back, and followed my friends down the sloping trail. When we got to the bottom, I turned and looked up at the rim, a mile above my head and floating like a dream. I wondered if I would ever get back to it.

Worrying about the return trip took some of the fun out of being at the bottom of the Grand Canyon, but my fears were unfounded. I discovered the following day that all the space, after all, could only be covered one step at a time. My friends encouraged and cajoled me into continuing upward, and we rimmed out just before sunset. A great sense of accomplishment filled me when I completed that first hike. The canyon began to take on earthly dimensions. I was starting to know it.

Always, we Chosen Few were together that summer. The camaraderie I felt with the men from Philadelphia left a warm glow long after we had gone our separate ways.

It was the summer of Skylab. We hunted the skies for flaming shards of satellite, swearing we saw them among the millions of stars spread out across the black sky above the canyon. We agreed that the Grand Canyon was the perfect place for Skylab to fall, because there was already a hole there. When we heard that a newspaper was offering a cash reward for the first person to bring back a piece of the satellite, we planned our race into the canyon to get it, and then we planned what we would do with the money we were going to win. We were genuinely disappointed when we learned that Skylab crashed somewhere in the Australian Outback and that some ten year old boy had claimed the prize.

My first summer at the Grand Canyon went by quickly in a blur of sunsets and parties. I left reluctantly in mid-September for Berkeley, but in the span of one short summer at Desert View the Grand Canyon had snared me. I decided to write my honors thesis on the subject of wildlife management at the Grand Canyon, which gave me an excuse to return to the canyon for a couple of long weekends during the school year. In June of 1980, after I graduated with high honors from Berkeley with a degree in geography, I wasted no time in returning to the canyon. And there I stayed for the next four years, getting to know it on its own terms.

10

❖

Hermits Rest

The Hermit was Louis Boucher, a miner who lived down at Dripping Springs from 1898 to 1912.

The building was constructed in 1914 by the Santa Fe Railroad. The Hermit never lived there.

And the bathrooms are located behind the building, next to the parking lot.

I repeated those sentences thousands of times during the year that I worked as assistant manager of Hermits Rest Curio Shop, at the end of the Grand Canyon's West Rim Drive.

I had been recommended for rehire at the end of the previous summer's employment in Desert View—a miracle in itself considering the company I kept. A couple weeks after I graduated from Berkeley, I began working the cash register at Hermits Rest for $4.65 per hour. At first I commuted eight miles from the South Rim Village out to the store every day, but by the middle of the summer the Fred Harvey Company allowed me to move out to a trailer behind Hermits Rest. I lived in that trailer, with two parakeets and two neighbors for company, for a year.

Hermits Rest was another of the Fred Harvey buildings designed by the architect Mary Jane Colter. Originally, the building consisted of just one room, most of which was modeled into a huge, domed fireplace. Sections of Ponderosa pine tree trunks, carved out on one side, provided travelers with a comfortable seat inside the dome from which they could enjoy the roaring fire. A room was added on to one side of the main room and used as a bunkhouse for employees. When park visitation increased, the employees were moved out and the room was converted to shop space, where Papago baskets, Navajo rugs, Zuni jewelry and Mesa Verde pottery were displayed. The building, quarried entirely from Grand Canyon stone, overlooked a wide, yawning side canyon of the Grand.

During the summer months, 15,000 people per day rode free Park Service mini-buses out to Hermits Rest. The West Rim Drive was really more the attraction of the trip than was the gift shop at the end of the road. Spectacular views of the canyon could be seen from Hopi and Pima points; and the Abyss, a vertical cliff dropping off 2,000 feet from the rim before it leveled out at the Hermit Shale level, was also a tourist draw.

The eight-mile-long drive had been closed to private vehicles several years earlier, for the duration of the summer. Lack of parking spaces at view points made driving hazardous on a narrow road with hairpin curves. Park officials decided the visitors would be safer riding in mini-buses with a top speed of 15 or 20 miles per hour than driving their own cars or RVs, where a glance at the Grand Canyon at the wrong time might result in a vehicle disappearing into the Abyss. In the winter months the West Rim Drive was reopened with a posted speed limit of 35. The fastest I ever made the drive was at 60 miles an hour, but I usually kept my speed down to 45 out of respect for that 2,000 foot drop.

The most frequent complaint we heard from the tourists who made the trip out to Hermits by mini-bus was the unavailability of water along the road. At the pace by which the mini-buses traveled, it took nearly an hour for the people to arrive, with parched mouths, at Hermits Rest. A large glass of lemonade cost 65 cents; many were dismayed to find that the water fountain was inoperable and ice water sold for a dime.

The summer tourists bought souvenirs. Our biggest sellers were tee shirts, cheap souvenir spoons, postcards, and leather coin purses. We carried a selection of natural history books for the literate West Rim visitors, as well as authentic Indian crafts for those who remembered to pack their Visa cards.

Other items which sold well were uncut geodes, Shimayo rugs, and wampum. I never understood why people who had traveled hundreds of miles to visit the Grand Canyon would buy those particular items, because they came from central Arizona, northern New Mexico, and Cape Cod, respectively. But nevertheless, they sold well, which I supposed was why the Fred Harvey Company continued to stock them.

Although the Grand Canyon was not a park noted especially for its wildlife, animals indigenous to the Hermits Rest area frequently made appearances to startle shop visitors. The appearance of one creature on a hot August morning made a spectacular scene, simply by moving across the stone floor.

It was an amber-colored millipede, about four inches in length. There were a number of tourists in the store when the millipede showed up. I was at the cash register nearest the door, busily ringing up key chains, when I heard a piercing scream. I looked up and saw four women running in four different directions.

"What's wrong?" I shouted.

One woman had leaped up onto the ponderosa pine log chair. Still screaming, she pointed at the floor. My eyes followed her finger and I saw the creature inching its way steadily toward her.

"No problem, ma'am," I said as I came from behind the counter and picked up a book about Indian jewelry from the display. "They won't hurt you."

"Get it out of here!" she yelled. "It's so big and ugly!"

"Yes, ma'am, we do grow them big here at the Grand Canyon," I answered. I scooped the millipede up onto the book cover and carefully carried it outside. I took it around to the back of the building and gently slid it from the book cover to the ground.

"There you go," I told it softly. "Now you can enjoy the peace and quiet. I wish I could join you, but duty calls."

When I returned to the shop, the woman had climbed down from the chair, and appeared to have mellowed. I knew she would be all right when she grabbed my sleeve as I headed back to the cash register.

"Did the Hermit build this place?" she asked. "And where are the bathrooms?"

On several successive mornings in the winter, I opened the store and discovered that the small closet which contained our stock of candy bars had been broken into. Snickers bars appeared to be the focus of the larceny; each morning I found that several of them had been partially consumed, while other brands of candy were left untouched. The screen doors on the closet, reinforced with wood, were supposed to protect the candy supply, but the doors had been torn off their hinges. Whatever had done the damage was surely larger than a mouse. I set a live trap one night in order to catch the culprit.

Next morning, I entered the store and heard the loudest, shrillest screams I had ever heard in my life. It sounded like a small child was being murdered. I hurried back to the stock room and discovered that a small, angry ringtail cat had been caught in the trap. The animal looked like a cross between a skunk and a raccoon. Its eyes shone with rage and its snarling, sharp teeth bit the air savagely as I approached. Park Service biologists were summoned. By the time they arrived, I had gingerly moved the cage containing the ringtail cat outside, where its foul odor would not ruin shop customers' appetites. One biologist stepped up to the the cage with authority, and told me he was going to release the creature nearby.

"If you do that," I protested, "it will come right back and get into our Snickers again. I've seen how they get in—they've eaten a hole through the rafters, and they climb down through the roof."

"Park Service policy dictates that wildlife should neither be destroyed nor relocated," the biologist said. He sounded like a management plan. I was suddenly reminded of the ranger who had tried to convince my Dad that throwing rocks into the Merced River would upset the balance of nature.

"This ringtail has an established habitat here," the biologist went on. He reached for the cage, and the cat snarled at him. "If we move it elsewhere, it may not be able to adapt to the new environment."

I said, "You mean, it will have to learn to find its food in the woods, instead of in the candy closet."

"It may have a family here, and a nest. We can't interrupt the natural balance of its ecosystem," the biologist continued as if I hadn't spoken.

At that I laughed out loud. "Don't be throwing those big words around with me; believe it or not, I have a college degree too. That cat's ecosystem consists of Snickers bars for food and the roof of the gift shop for a nest. Is that what you're trying to preserve?"

The biologist angrily picked up the cage. The ringtail screamed obscenities at him. "Shouldn't you be getting back to work? I think I hear the tourists calling you." And off he walked with the cat.

After that, the store continued to be vandalized by the

ringtail cat or one of its family members. I got in the habit of leaving an unwrapped Snickers bar within easy reach of the cats' access hole into the stock room, as this seemed to be the action advocated by the biologist. I figured that if I could not fight them I would join them in their wildlife protection techniques. Immediately the destructive vandalism ceased; but every morning when I opened the store, I found that the Snickers bar had disappeared.

Once I moved out to the trailer behind Hermits Rest, I stayed out there most of the time, coming into the village only once every three or four days for supplies and some contact with other people. The couple who managed the store were my only neighbors out at Hermits. While I enjoyed visiting with them occasionally in the evening, I kept to myself for the most part that year.

I had no television in the trailer, which was just as well because reception was lousy. I spent a lot of time reading, writing letters, and listening to the radio in the evening. After dark I could tune in to an Albuquerque station which broadcast a mystery story every night at ten o'clock. The show was done in the old radio broadcasting style where different people spoke the parts for each character and sound effects were added. I greatly enjoyed the quiet serenity of living on the rim of the canyon without anyone bothering me. I became a bit of a hermit myself while I was there.

My two parakeets flew free in the trailer. Since I did not share the living space with anyone else, I gave up trying to keep the birds caged or training them to mind me. Essentially they were wild birds which flew around the trailer at will and made their home on the curtain rods and cupboard tops. Often when I was in the shower, one or the other of them would fly through the bathroom, startling me with their noisy beating wings.

From Dripping Springs, a narrow trail leads down to Hermit Canyon.

One spring day while I was at work, an employee of the housing office entered my trailer ostensibly to see if any furniture needed replacing. The poor man nearly had a coronary when he saw the birds and the mess they had made underneath the curtain rods. He said nothing to me, but the next day I received a scathing letter from the Fred Harvey Company which threatened to terminate my employment if I did not get rid of the birds. I was busted. Muttering apologies to the birds, I chased them around my trailer for half the evening before I finally got them both stuffed back into their cage. Then I gave them to a friend in the village to keep for me, and spent another day cleaning and fumigating the trailer.

On days off I spent a good deal of time exploring the Hermit Basin area near the shop. The basin was a wide, bowl-shaped side canyon off Hermit Canyon, full of fascinating magical places to which I would return again and again.

I was walking one day below the rim, less than a mile from my trailer, when I stopped to sit on a ledge of Coconino Sandstone and enjoy the sun. The rock upon which I sat felt rough on my bare legs. Shifting to find a more comfortable position, I took a closer look at the sandstone. Embedded in the rock, I saw sea shells. They were scallops, bivalves similar to those I used to find in broken pieces on the beaches of California. Not even yet fossilized, the shells embedded in the sandstone indicated that a sea had apparently covered the whole Colorado Plateau before the land rose to its present elevation of 7,000 feet and the Colorado River and erosion combined to sculpt the Grand Canyon.

Not far from the shell cliffs, I came upon a series of natural bridges. The largest of the bridges was four feet wide, twenty five feet long, and spanned a ravine about five feet deep. By walking up and down the ravine, I discovered that natural bridges crossed it at intervals of several hundred feet. Never in all my walking along the South Rim of the canyon had I encountered bridges like that. Fortunately, very few locals at the canyon knew about the existence of those bridges. Except for showing a couple of close friends, I kept my mouth shut about the location of the bridges.

Every few weeks during my year at Hermits Rest, I made the three-mile hike down to Dripping Springs. Tucked back in a corner of the Hermit Basin, Dripping Springs was a special place for me to go to escape the madness of the busy gift shop on the rim.

During the early part of the century, Dripping Springs had been the home of Louis Boucher, an eccentric miner who rode a white mule, cultivated fruit trees and kept corrals full of horses, mules and sheep at his hideaway in the canyon. The name of the place was inspired by a spring which dripped from the ceiling of a domed cave into a pool. At the front of the cave was a grassy area and stands of fruit trees that had been planted by the Hermit. The view of the Grand Canyon proper was blocked by a steep wall to the left of the cave, so that when I sat by the spring in the warm sun, I felt I might as well have been in the Verde Valley or in Canyon de Chelly as in the Grand, isolated as Dripping Springs was from the rest of the canyon.

But from the sojourns into the Hermit Basin I always had to return. The tourists would not wait. They pounded on the door at a quarter to eight and lingered over the tee shirts long after closing time. The summer madness was draining but I stayed around after the crowds abated, and was lucky enough to continue working at Hermits Rest through the winter.

In the winter months, opening Hermits Rest was a pleasure. I hauled a couple loads of firewood into the store in the morning and started a big, friendly blaze in the oversized fireplace. Then I sat in one of the ponderosa chairs, sipping the house specialty —powdered hot chocolate mixed with strong coffee—for an hour or more before the first visitors arrived. Some days, when a quantity of snow had fallen, nobody ventured out until the road was cleared, usually around noon. Winter visitors were never in a hurry. They lingered, asking about the Hermit and taking time to listen to the full story, which I relished telling when my audience was rapt. I especially enjoyed showing them Indian jewelry; with enough time to point out the craftsmanship of each piece and tell them about the jeweler who had created it, I made more sales of handmade jewelry during the winter months than I ever did in the hectic summer.

According to park statistics, the average time a visitor stayed at the Grand Canyon was less than two hours. I could have sworn at times that some of those summer tourists were trying to lower that average. They were the ones who shoved each other out of the way at the cash register line. They were the ones who took pictures of each other out on the porch, "to prove," they said loudly, "that we were here." They were the ones like a large woman in a pink sun hat who shouted everyone down on a hot summer day to inquire of me, "Is that the Grand Canal out there or what?"

Still, I relished answering a question like that infinitely more than the one about the bathrooms.

11

❖❖

The
Tanner Trail

The view had not changed much in 400 years. When Don Pedro de Lopez de Cardenas and his men paused on the precipice, near where I stood, 400 years ago, their overwhelming emotion was dismay. For the next three days they had tried to descend to the river. The farther into the canyon they climbed, the more distant the river seemed; it was a mirage, an impossible task for them to cross the canyon.

In the middle of winter the vast gap below the rim seemed as empty and illusive to me as it must have to the Cardenas party. Nevertheless, I took a deep breath and began my descent into a v-shaped notch spread with several inches of fresh snow. At the bottom of the notch began a route which led down through the layers of canyon and on, in a roundabout way, right down to the bank of the cold sparkling Colorado River.

It was January. My backpack weighed nearly 60 pounds, loaded down with food, water and supplies for a four-day hike. At no time of year was foot traffic heavy on the trail I had chosen to follow, for the more popular routes into the canyon lay west of the Tanner Trail. At that time of year, I shared the steep and narrow descent with no one.

Since I lived at the Grand Canyon, I had the privilege of finding solitude in its vast side canyons and endless plateaus by hiking while the tourists were in Belize or New Zealand. The canyon was a local's playground during the winter months, when tourist traffic was sparse. By late March, flowers began to bloom tentatively in the lower reaches of the canyon. The green of new life crept slowly up the steep canyon walls. And the park visitors returned, led by college students on spring break.

In the winter months, clouds often fill the canyon.

Simmering in the heat of Arizona sun, the canyon filled with hikers by May and the onslaught of humanity continued until the tamarisk down by the river turned gold. Then in November, snow dusted the rims of the chasm, clearing out all but a few adventurous souls. And the spaces of air and columns of rock no longer reverberated with the thud of Vibram soles. The canyon endured all seasons and changed, its rocks eroding and its river widening and its plants growing and its lizards sunning, whether anyone was there to see it or not.

Down the back of Tanner Wash I began my descent. The trail was not much more than a jumble of boulders strewn over steep walls of Coconino Sandstone untouched by the weak rays of winter sun. I did not exactly hike down that portion of trail; a more correct term was "controlled free fall." My pack made me top-heavy and my knees shook with the strain of holding in place each downward step.

I took some solace in the knowledge that ascending the steep wash would be easier on my return trip. Climbing uphill strained my reserves of energy, but that strain, I thought, was nothing compared with the difficulty of keeping my balance and a semblance of control on the trip down. After a couple miles of controlled free fall, I crossed a land bridge of rich red soil and began following a long, circuitous route which was more horizontal than vertical—much to the relief of my knees. I was able to cover that ground more quickly, falling into a rhythm of step and meditation. I followed a contour around Escalante Butte, treading on the fine dust of the Supai formation, just above the sheer Redwall Limestone.

I was comfortable traveling through the familiar landscape of stunted juniper trees, gray and twisted bark growing roughly over their distorted frames. Blue bellied lizards and collared lizards zipped about on the red slabs of Esplanade sandstone. Patches of old snow lingered in the shade, but already most of the snow which had fallen a couple days before had evaporated or been soaked up in the red soil and turned to dust.

Before descending through the Redwall, I made a detour, leaving the heavy pack near the trail and walking around to the front of Cardenas Butte. As I approached the edge of the plateau, a cool, stiff wind rushed up from below to meet me. In spite of an air temperature of 50 degrees, I had worked up a sweat on the swift descent from the rim and the wind quickly chilled me. Wary of hypothermia, I did not stay long, but spent just a few minutes absorbing the view.

Descending into the canyon takes a hiker
from snow into a milder climate quite rapidly.

I was standing on the edge of a cliff. Luminous desert air filled the space 1,000 feet below me before it blended with the solid ground of the distant Tonto plateau. The deep green Colorado River shimmered engagingly, but it seemed to be no closer than it had been when I began the hike several hours earlier. Beyond a wide S-curve described by the river, the purples and reds of the northern wall of the canyon faded out to the horizon. Not a human nor a human artifact was visible. I was completely surrounded by canyon, immersed in it, lost in its depths.

I lifted the heavy pack back on and continued down the trail through the Redwall. I climbed over boulders left in the wake of a landslide which occurred some time in the past few thousand years—yesterday, in the geologic timetable of the canyon. The trail then led me through a section of yellow-green pillars known as Bright Angel Shale.

Although only 12 inches wide, the trail was easy to follow as it plunged from the Bright Angel Shale downward across the moonscape plains of the Nankoweap formation. Only the occasional blackbrush grew on the crushed rock barrens. Beyond were acres of tiny round rocks, like so many marbles rolling underneath my boots. The river had disappeared from sight but I knew I would come upon it over the next rise . . . or the next one.

I had not yet seen another human on the Tanner Trail. Although it was never used as frequently as those highway-trails to the west, historically its use had been steady. Originally, the trail was a part of a Hopi route from the South Rim to the salt mines near the confluence of the big and little Colorado Rivers. River legend stated that the Mormon pioneer and polygamist John Lee, of Lees Ferry, buried several pots of gold near the Tanner Trail—never, of course, to be found again.

In the 1800s, the Tanner Trail was used by horse thieves who made their steal from ranches on the Coconino Plateau.

They herded horses down the Tanner Trail to the river, where in pre-Glen Canyon Dam days the river flowed sluggish and knee deep through the S-curve at certain times of the year. Once across the Colorado with their contraband, the thieves ascended to the North Rim via the Nankoweap Trail. Their horses and they were protected from the law by the Grand Canyon, which sheriffs of the Territory of Arizona were reluctant to cross.

At last I passed through the last of the moonscape and reached terraced gravel deposited by river floods. The last half mile of trail looped easily over small rises composed of dried mud and boulders and ended at a sandy beach dotted with leafless tamarisk. I had descended a vertical mile in nine hours. Depending on who was asked, the length of the Tanner Trail was said to be anywhere from eight to twelve miles. As I threw off the dusty boots and smelly socks and thrust my sore feet into the waters of the icy Colorado River, I cast my vote for the higher figure.

I set up camp on the beach at Tanner and reveled for a couple days in the 65 degree heat, clear light, and impeccably blue sky floating above multicolored canyon walls. Ravens visited my camp daily, checking for bits of food I might have dropped. Red ants and mice scavenged nearby. The canyon wrens whistled descending shrill notes as shadows grew long in the late afternoon. The river water flowed slick and swift, throwing driftwood into the back eddies as it went by.

I had come down the Tanner Trail for two reasons: to revitalize my love and commitment to the canyon, and to prove that I could handle a solo hike to the bottom. I had already hiked the Kaibab and Bright Angel trails to the bottom, as well as covering the day hikes to Grandview and across the Tonto Trail. I was not afraid of the canyon, but I had learned to respect it. Running out of water in July or slipping a foothold in January could mean death for a solo hiker. I could not afford to turn my back on the Grand or forget even for a minute who was stronger.

With this wariness always in my subconscious thoughts, I nevertheless enjoyed exploring the area around the S-curve of the Colorado River.

There was no question whether I might have the Tanner beach to myself in January. But trail usage was limited in all areas of the park by the National Park Service, and I knew it would have been impossible to enjoy the canyon wren's song in solitude if I had come in April.

Overcrowding first became evident in the cross-canyon corridor consisting of the Bright Angel and Kaibab Trails. A backcountry management plan was introduced in 1972 after hundreds of people converged at the Bright Angel campground at Phantom Ranch one Easter weekend. Limits were defined by that plan in terms of numbers of people on each trail. Subsequently, the management plan was revised to a zone system whereby people were allocated to each trail according to where they planned to camp.

Protest to the limiting of backcountry permits ran along the lines of, "the people are being denied access to their own park." To that charge, I would have answered (if anyone had asked me) that one could hardly call a six foot wide trail such as the Bright Angel, flowing like a swollen creek with a steady parade of people, a wilderness area; and that any hike along a maintained trail marked on a map could not technically even be called a wilderness journey at all.

The Grand Canyon to anyone who descended it, as I did, without benefit of human companionship, gave the illusion of wilderness. I knew about the Hopis and the horse thieves who traveled my route many years before I was born; but I preferred to believe, while I was sitting on the beach at Tanner, the exquisite illusion which the canyon was so capable of fostering. It was difficult to listen to the swirl of water in the back eddy and imagine Girl Scout groups hanging clotheslines from the tamarisk branches on the beach. It was difficult to stare at the

The upper Colorado River, looking south toward the Tanner beach

changing colors of the canyon wall opposite the beach and
imagine hundreds of river runners viewing the same scene as
they floated down through the S-curve of the river on a hot
summer day. In the summer, even the Tanner Trail was populated. But in January, I went alone to relish the illusion of
wilderness in the canyon.

One day hike I made from Tanner Beach followed the remnants of the old Hopi Trail to the salt mines. Directly below the
Palisades of the Desert I hiked up a wash to reach an amphitheater tucked in a fold of the canyon. The route up Co-

manche Creek drainage traversed asphalt-like slabs of an ancient lava flow. The flow originated near Cardenas Butte and ribbons of its residue were visible across the entire region near the river's S-curve. It had been postulated by some geologists studying the canyon that the lava flow had temporarily dammed the river in much the same way the one at Toroweap many miles downriver did at Lava Falls. Like so many other geologic theories about the canyon, that one had never been proven. As usual, the canyon remained an enigma; it was not talking.

At the head of Comanche Creek was evidence of a catastrophic event in the distant past. The movement of an earthquake broke loose a huge section of Redwall and Muav, two thirds of the way up the canyon wall, and the chunk came crashing down to rest in the lava amphitheater. The debris from the rock fall was hurtled down the Comanche Creek drainage all the way to the river. As I climbed around in the amphitheater, I imagined that the sight and sound of the chunk of rock smacking the basalt must have been awesome.

I reflected on change in the canyon as I walked back to camp. Again the desire to accept the canyon's illusion of eternal steadfastness was tempting. The only moving thing near me was the river. Yet to look around me proved the opposite; rock slides, earthquakes, volcanic eruptions and the less violent changes of erosion by rain and wind and river had all occurred and left their evidence for me to inspect. It was, I decided, human-centered to assume that all the movement, building up and breaking down, should have come to a halt just because a national park had been created in that spot.

If anything, the Grand Canyon's fame encouraged an acceleration of the processes of change. Did hundreds of feet tramping through the washes and sliding over the marbles in the Nankoweap formation have any less effect on the canyon than the pelt of rain and wind? I thought not. By our presence, people hastened the erosion process.

The fact that humans had no control over catastrophic events such as volcanic eruptions and earthquakes which tore chunks of rock away from cliffs was comforting to me. The canyon did assert itself. People were forced to back off in the face of such powerful events; yet when the front quieted, armies of backpackers moved in again, believing the canyon to be tamed and conquered.

Recalling the Comanche Creek amphitheater, I knew with certainty that the dominance of people over the canyon was only temporary. The truth was that hikers like me, scampering along the dusty river trail back to camp, would perish without a whisper of protest, if the canyon flexed its rocky muscles again when we happened to be standing in the wrong place.

On the fourth morning of my stay at Tanner, I loaded up for the long walk back out of the hole. My pack, emptied of most of my food and water, seemed light as I set off over the conglomerates and moonscape and pink dust toward the rim.

Hiking out of the canyon was a study in concentration, each foot moving out and up, mechanically. I hiked steadily for hours without a stop, for I knew the value of an even pace. After awhile, I ceased to think about any particular thing; my entire consciousness was centered on the steady upward push.

The canyon did not surprise me with any shortcuts or flat stretches. It was nothing if not straightforward. Since I was not a bird, I could not possibly get from here to there without walking every step of the way.

Sunlight was waning as I crossed the land bridge and started up the last steep ravine of the trail in Tanner Wash. With every step my muscles screamed. My reserve of strength was dwindling, and the rim was still quite a distance above me.

I pled with the canyon to compromise. It refused. I was forced to take it as it was offered, on its own terms. I felt myself losing the struggle with the sheer rock walls . . . and then, suddenly, I was out. The uphill climb ended abruptly. Rimmed out,

I found myself looking over a tableland forested with pinon and juniper—no more canyon. I was free of it. A car whizzed by on the nearby East Rim Drive, drawing me back to the reality of the world beyond the canyon.

As the sun began its descent to the horizon, I stood in the snow near my truck and gazed back down into the canyon. I could see most of the route I had followed. I saw the S-curve of the river and the beach on which I had camped. The canyon layers glowed orange and ruby and violet in the setting sun.

Looking down into it, I did not possess the victorious jubilation of a conqueror. The canyon showed me its power and its strength. The benign illusion was shattered. I took my place in the ranks of small, humble humans beside the mighty canyon with joy, for though I could not control it, it allowed me to co-exist—if I dared.

12

❖❖

Phantom Ranch

When the opportunity arose, I jumped at the chance to live and work at the bottom of the Grand Canyon. Along the 250-mile Colorado River corridor, there was only one place where anybody lived permanently. At river mile 90, directly below the South Rim Village and at the lower end of the Bright Angel and Kaibab Trails, was a guest ranch called Phantom Ranch.

The ranch provided lodging and meals for tourists who rode mules from the rim to the river, as well as offering dorm-style accommodations for hikers who preferred not to camp. I was hired as one of 14 ranch hands to provide some of the comforts of home in one of the most remote locations in the entire National Park system.

I took a couple boxes of essentials—clothing, camping gear, and several pairs of shoes—to the mule barns on the South Rim. The wrangler there promised to haul them down next time he took a supply train to Phantom. I then loaded my backpack and set off down the Kaibab Trail to my new home.

Springs emerge from the Redwall layer
throughout the Grand Canyon.

The trail was the shortest and most direct route to the bottom of the canyon. It was also one of the steepest. I thoroughly enjoyed the hike, because for the first time since I had begun to hike the canyon, I was not thinking about the dreaded trip back out. I was going in to the hole to stay.

Though it was only mid-May, the inner canyon was already baking in the heat of summer. It took me two and a half hours to get to the bottom of the canyon. I crossed a suspension bridge and followed the trail for another half mile along the far side of the river, until it intersected with Bright Angel Creek, a cheerful, bubbling stream. I walked along a path next to the creek for another quarter mile, and then I was at the ranch.

It was a large complex which seemed to spring up unexpectedly in the middle of that vast empty canyon. The ranch consisted of a combination dining hall, sundry store, kitchen, laundry room and employees' "family room." There were small cabins and larger dormitories containing eight to ten beds each, scattered in a rough circle around the lodge; an employee dorm, three people to a room; and stables for the mules. The black granite walls of Bright Angel Canyon rose sharply on either side of the complex. And far above, a mile in the air, was the distant outline of the Grand Canyon's South Rim.

A ranch hand, I soon learned, was a jack of all trades. The 14 of us rotated daily through the different tasks, and work days often lasted 12 hours. Because of the heat, which could reach 115 degrees in the summer, we worked split shifts or took frequent breaks during the day, as nobody could tolerate working outdoors for very long when the sun beat down. The work week was ten days on, four days off, so that on "weekends" we could hike out to the rim, or else have time to go hiking in other areas of the canyon.

The tasks I was expected to perform were varied and challenging. As a maid, I stripped and changed 80 beds, cleaned the cabins, and did all the ranch laundry. As a waitress, I served meals to ranch guests and then doubled as cocktail waitress during beer hall, selling cans of beer for $1.50 apiece. As a cook, I did all the meal preparation, and as dishwasher I had to do all the kitchen cleanup and assist the cook. The other job was as retail salesperson; there I stood at the sundry store win-

dow, handing out hot dogs and lemonade bearing a remarkable
similarity to those sold at Hermits Rest and Desert View. I also
peddled moleskin, sunburn lotion, and plenty of information
and advice for hikers.

I learned from the other employees to be an opportunist. A
fifth of whiskey went for 30 dollars on the Phantom Ranch
black market. A ride out of the canyon on mule back for a blis-
tered and discouraged hiker went for a lot more. Once, two of
my fellow employees made 20 dollars each by retrieving the
backpack of a poor fellow who had hiked to Clear Creek, eight
miles upriver from the ranch, and had become too tired and de-
hydrated to carry his own pack back. Supplies were scarce at
the bottom of the canyon; I learned that everything could be had
for a price. There were advantages to living at the ranch.

All our visitors were short-timers. I always liked to watch
them ride off, uncomfortable in the saddle of a mule due to the
residual aches of the previous day's ride down. It was a wonderful feeling to be staying at Phantom, calling it home and
knowing that if I went back out to the civilized world, I would
be returning to the ranch soon. In the evening, after the sun
went down and the black granite schist began to cool, I walked
out by Bright Angel Creek or down to the Colorado River to
listen to the canyon wrens and watch the river flow. And I felt
the canyon wrap itself around me, enclosing me in its embrace
of rock and heat and glowing warm light. My skin became
browner and my appearance less studied. I began to feel as if I
were a part of the folds of the canyon. Living inside of it, I felt
secure.

Phantom Ranch had an illustrious history. Over the years, it
had been visited by presidents, movie stars, famous writers and
painters. A log book in the beer hall/dining room which had
been signed by visitors since the 1930s provided a history of
the ranch. Some of the comments written by visitors were flow-
ery; others bordered on the profound. The one most memorable

to me was written by a soldier who came down during a leave from the Second World War. "I wish I could stay at Phantom Ranch forever," he wrote. "The Army would never find me here."

A woman known as "Big Red" initiated me to the customs of the Phantom Ranch world on my first day of work. She and I were assigned the "maid" position for the day, and I watched in amazement as she stripped beds in five seconds and carried huge piles of clean sheets from one cabin to another in the 110 degree heat. She talked nonstop while she worked, so by listening to her chatter I picked up a lot of information about the finer points of life on the ranch. She threw a fresh sheet onto a bed. "Look," she said. "You put the sheet right in the middle with the fold along this line. Then you open it the length of the bed, then unfold it the other way." Her hands flew as she talked.

"Tuck the ends under like this. Square the corners. We do this part together. Tuck in the long edge and pull it tight. That's all. Making beds is easy."

"I can't seem to do it that fast," I complained. "Slow it down, will you?"

"No, you speed it up. You'll catch on soon enough," she told me, starting on another bed. "Don't worry, honey. If you stay down here long enough, you will be able to do this in your sleep."

She laughed loudly at her own joke, showing big crooked white teeth. Her hair was the color of the dust of the Supai formation, and her face was leathery and bronzed like that of an old cowboy. Some of the harshness undoubtedly came from the constant exposure to the relentless sun down at Phantom, but I supposed that she had a lot of tales to tell as well.

As we worked, I learned that Big Red had been a ranch

hand at Phantom for nearly ten years. She had at one time been married to a cowboy who rode on the rodeo circuit. The man was long gone but the products of their marriage, two grown children, still existed. Her daughter was a blackjack dealer in Las Vegas, a fact of which Big Red was very proud.

"She makes her own way," she told me as we walked empty handed back to the laundry room to fetch another pile of clean sheets. "My daughter doesn't ask me for nothing. She doesn't have a man to lean on, so she takes care of herself. I sometimes wish I had had the choices she has. Women are so much more independent today. When I was her age, I thought that marrying that jerk was my only option short of staying at home, an old maid."

We walked a few steps in silence. "My boy, though, he's another story. Maybe you met him already? He's a wrangler. Comes down here every few days with the mules. Joey? Looks like me?"

"No, I don't think I know him," I said. "Not yet, anyway."

"Well don't get too friendly with him. He looks like me but his habits are like his father's. He will grab you, but he won't hold on to you. I am the only stable influence in his life. Me! Can you imagine?"

As soon as we finished putting the sheets on the beds in all the cabins, Big Red threw down the pile of dirty laundry which still needed to be washed.

"Let's take a break," she suggested. I followed her out of the cabin and staggered a little when the heat struck me full force. She walked around behind the lodge and down a path through the bushes. At the other end of the path was a swimming hole, about 20 feet across and three feet deep. It had been created when someone built a rock dam across Bright Angel Creek.

Without hesitation, Big Red stripped off her clothes. She stepped into the water, then turned to look at me.

"Come on," she encouraged. "We don't worry about formalities like bathing suits here. We are family. Jump in."

I took my clothes off self-consciously and stepped into the cool water. I was immediately glad I had done so. As the air around me sizzled with heat, I sank gratefully up to my neck into the refreshing water of the pool.

When we had been there only a couple minutes, Tom and Jack, two of our fellow ranch hands, showed up.

"Hey guys," Big Red said, standing up. "Have you met Kitty yet?"

"How's it going," Jack said.

"What are you doing today?" Tom asked Red.

"I'm teaching her how to make a bed," Red said. "What about you guys?"

"We got the kitchen today," Tom answered. "We're on break for an hour or so until lunch time."

He and Jack stripped their clothes off casually and stepped into the pool.

"Want a beer?" Tom's question sounded rhetorical. Without waiting for an answer, he produced one and passed it to Red.

Our break lasted half an hour. Finally, Big Red motioned for me to get out of the swimming hole.

"We got work to do," she said.

As the days went by, I found out that most of the jobs were plain hard work, but I was grateful to Big Red and the others for showing me how much easier it was to clean 20 shower stalls or wash 60 sets of white sheets when a frequent break schedule was included in the itinerary. Working inside the lodge was even more pleasant, as the ranch stereo was always blasting good old 1960s rock and roll.

From seven to nine o'clock in the evening, beer hall was open. On the nights I was waitressing, I was on the run during those two hours, serving the tourists and listening to their stories as I had done in Yellowstone. I found that I was no longer attentive to their tales; I had the attitude that their lives beyond the rim of the canyon were outside of the realm of my concern. I was bored by their identical stories of journeys down the trail; after all, I lived in the canyon and they had nothing new to tell me. I listened with half an ear or no ear at all, simply nodding and smiling and serving beer by the six pack to tables full of rowdy young men from Germany and Denmark and New York.

On the evenings I did not have to work, I sat at a table with some of the other employees, telling stories or playing cards. One guy who worked there was quite an accomplished guitar player. He often got up and played old favorites, to which we enthusiastically sang along. With a spirited crowd in the beer hall, the singing sessions lasted long after the bar had closed.

We who worked at the ranch were an odd group. I supposed that anyone content to live down at the bottom of the canyon had to be at least a little bit out of touch with the real world. Phantom smacked of escapism; there was not a television nor a radio to be had down there, and no one possessed nor cared to possess any knowledge of current events. But the really odd thing was the way it all turned around, once I had been there for a few weeks. I began to believe that the real world, the one that mattered, was at Phantom; it was the rest of the world that was out of touch. It was hard to argue with the heat and the oppressive vertical walls of canyon, hard to even concentrate on anything above the line of the canyon lip staring down at me from the sky. So slowly that I almost did not notice the change, the rim and the world beyond it slipped away. The other ranch hands said that their experiences in the outside world justified their presence at Phantom. It began to make sense to me that they, and I, were the only ones who really had an understanding of the world, and that was our reason for rejecting it.

The woman who managed the ranch was about 80 pounds overweight and declared that she hated men the way someone else might state that they hated spinach. She had a three year old daughter by a Navajo man; the daughter lived on the rim with a friend. She told me stories one evening about how the man had chased her and her daughter around the house with a butcher knife. In her version of the story, of course, the attack was unprovoked. I did not blame her for being down on men after that experience; I agreed wholeheartedly with her sentiments, although I did not subscribe to them for myself. When she questioned me about my feelings toward men, I just got us each another beer and asked her again to tell me about the time he gave her a black eye the day before her parents were to arrive for a visit.

That was how I got along with the others at the ranch: I nodded and asked questions and then went about my own affairs. Perhaps they thought I was a bit strange and noncommittal, but no one spent much time analyzing me, any more than I did analyzing them. The point was that it did not matter what had happened to bring us to Phantom. Now that we were there, we all felt safe. With the heat and the foreign tourists and the occasional food shortages we could cope.

I stayed at Phantom for a little more than a month. I thought I would never leave. But finally, inexorably, the real world intervened, in the form of a broken sewer line. The sewage treatment system for the whole ranch went belly up before the broken line was noticed, and by that time it was too late to make repairs. The leach fields ceased to function. The smell of human excrement filled the hot canyon air. Alarmed, the ranch manager put in an emergency request to the maintenance division on the rim and they rode down the same day by helicopter to survey the situation. The result was that they condemned the ranch.

The word spread quickly from one ranch hand to the next. I heard it when I was eating lunch one mid-afternoon, on a break from cooking the meals. Jack and Big Red were sitting quietly at the other end of the table as I sat down.

"Hey," I said to them, noticing their low voices. "What's the deal here? Someone die?"

"Yes," Red said glumly. "We did." She told me about the judgment of the company maintenance men. "They say the ranch has to be shut down for at least six months. We're all out of here, man. We're history. We gotta move."

"How can we?" I said, shocked. "Where are we going to go? They can't make me leave. I like it here."

"We have no choice. We have to leave. You had better make some plans quick," Jack said. "Hey, why don't you come over after dinner tonight? Tom is trying to organize something for us to do so we can stay together. Maybe we can go tour the country or something."

"Maybe we can get married, too," Big Red said sarcastically. For all her cynicism, she looked as if she was about to cry.

I smiled at her. "We'll find something. I'm sure it will work out. They can't keep us away forever."

Big Red just stared at me with the eyes that would not tolerate lies, even in the name of kindness. "Right. What else is there? After Phantom, what else can there be?"

I ate my lunch in silence. I had not considered the possibility that I could not stay at Phantom indefinitely. Mentally, I turned over the prospects for other employment: Yellowstone, no; Hermits or Desert View, no for the same reason; maybe the North Rim, or maybe Alaska? Perhaps. I was not sure what I ought to do next. Thinking of the alternatives, I realized that I was glad, in a little corner of my mind, to have a reason to leave the ranch. I had taken to it so quickly that it frightened me. But I did not think that I had changed too much to go back into the real world. If I had been at Phantom for two years, or ten, I might have been panicked or depressed as Big Red was. She had been there so long that she knew no other way of life. I still did; the opportunity to extricate myself was still available. When I went to Jack's room that evening, I found my co-workers chatting excitedly about buying a van and making a trip across the United States. They were going to stick together. I sat back and chose not to participate in the discussion. When Jack asked for commitment, I said I could not promise him one. Their discussion turned into an argument about whether to drive to Mexico or Canada; I quietly slipped out of the room.

I followed the path next to Bright Angel Creek until I reached the Colorado River. Moving noiselessly over the trail, I walked past some ruins of Anasazi Indian dwellings and up to the suspension bridge. Underneath the bridge I sat for a long time, soaking up the heat which still clung to the rocks at the water's edge. Swiftly the river slipped by; moonlight reflecting from the choppy surface of a back eddy before me shattered into a million shards of light.

My eyes caught the movement of a chunk of wood bobbing along in the river's current. It floated down toward me; then the greedy fingers of the eddy caught and held it. Round and round it whirled. Its edges were being pulled under by the strength of the invisible river current. I watched it for a long time as it spun around in one spot. Eventually, the wood broke free of the whirlpool's grip. Immediately, it shot downstream.

The journey of the chunk of wood continued, and sitting in the moonlight at Phantom, I knew suddenly that I was capable of doing the same thing. I did not have to leave the canyon just because I had to leave Phantom. I would simply have to find another place as compelling as Phantom, and keep going. I was not ready to become part owner of an old van, part leader of a gang of misfits. Once a member of the Phantom Ranch family, I knew I never would be excommunicated. But like Red's daughter, I had other options.

Two days later I climbed out of Phantom without the security of knowing when I would next return. I did not travel far.

Almost before I had time to get acclimatized to the 7,000 foot
elevation of the South Rim again, I found myself a whole new
niche. Because the sewage backed up at Phantom, I got out of
there and became a parkie—a real one, an employee of the National Park Service.

13

❖

The
Park Service

I never got a job with the
National Park Service by beating out hundreds of other aspiring
rangers on seasonal employment registers. Years later, when I
was asked by some college students how best to distinguish
themselves among a sea of eager applicants vying for a handful
of ranger jobs, I advised them to do two things: volunteer for the
Park Service and make contacts. That combination worked for
me and for many others I knew who had managed to stand out
on a long list of qualified applicants.

I volunteered for the Division of Resource Management on
the South Rim after the job at Phantom Ranch fell through. One
day I was asked to shuttle a vehicle up to Lees Ferry, at the
head of the Grand Canyon, for a river patrol trip; it was during
that overnight trip to the ferry that I made a contact which led
to my first Park Service job.

The Canyon District supervisor was in need of a clerk. The
young woman who held the clerk job was a bored 19 year old,
home from college for the summer. She had been hired by virtue

140

of the fact that she was the daughter of one of the park's division managers. When I met the ranger in charge of the district, he was about to lose his clerk, as she was returning to college; I was an unemployed, overqualified and overeager prospect with a college degree and a willingness to do anything to get my foot in the door. It was a windfall for both of us that we met. I had one other thing going for me that helped me get the job. The clerk position was one which did not provide housing for its appointee. A loophole in the hiring laws allowed the park to put someone on an 11 month seasonal appointment if that person was not in need of housing.

I had been involved in a relationship with a man who was a permanent Park Service employee in the maintenance division. I had moved in with him on a temporary basis the day I climbed out of Phantom for the last time. The job offer with the Canyon District, I told him, was a wonderful career opportunity for me, but I had to provide my own housing to get the job, so he agreed to let me stay with him. We moved a couple blocks down the street, into a stone duplex which had been built originally as housing for railroad employees in the 1910s. I began the job as district clerk in August of 1981.

The typing, filing, telephone answering and correspondence routing tasks were simple. Doing the budget, calculating travel vouchers, and compiling payroll were somewhat more challenging aspects of the job. I was clerk for the entire Canyon District, comprised of three subdistricts: the River Subdistrict, the Backcountry Subdistrict and the Cross-Canyon Corridor Subdistrict. In essence, the 33 employees in the Canyon District were responsible for patrolling and managing everything below the rim of the Grand Canyon, and I was in charge of all their paperwork. At first, I was eager to do whatever was asked of me in that job. But as the months wore on, I became frustrated with the fact that I was really just a glorified secretary. I did a good job, but that very fact kept me at the desk. I desired to get out of the office, participate in river trips, go on back-country patrols, respond with the other Canyon District rangers to search and rescue missions. Unfortunately, I got the reputation early on for being good with the phones and paperwork, so my opportunities to work in the field were limited.

My supervisor encouraged me to learn some ranger skills first hand, on my own time. I took his advice and put a lot of energy into that task during my first year of Park Service employment. I took courses on search and rescue, fire fighting, and technical climbing. I also completed a four month long course on emergency medical service and was certified by the State of Arizona as an Emergency Medical Technician.

Still, my chances to get out of the office were few. My name was on all the callout lists but I never got called. When the real incidents occurred, they passed me over for people who had more experience than I did. They were always shouting over their shoulders for me to please answer all the phones as they ran out the door to rescue some poor tourist who had fallen into the canyon.

Ultimately, I got my experience in those field activities in the same way I had snagged the Park Service job in the first place, by volunteering and by grabbing onto a contact with both hands. I learned to be resourceful about getting myself involved. Since none of my co-workers thought to draft me for the field activities, I volunteered myself.

Just getting to the site of the emergency was half the battle. Once there, standing around, I could easily wiggle my way into some form of participation. The first time that formula worked successfully for me was when a search began one November morning for a hiker who had been reported overdue. Most of the Canyon District rangers were immediately dispatched into the canyon to do a "hasty search," a quick once-over of the area to look for the missing man before the operation escalated into a full-blown search. Alone, I sat in the office becoming more and more impatient, wanting the experience of being on the big search I knew would occur if the man was not found quickly.

Finally, somebody called and asked if I knew of anyone who was available to go pick up an overhead projector at park headquarters. Without hesitation, I volunteered to do it myself. I forwarded my phones to the clerk downstairs, got in my truck and drove over to get the projector at breakneck speed. My heart was pounding. I wanted to be on the search.

I fetched the projector and drove back to the search headquarters, in the maintenance shop. Into the shop parking lot I drove too fast, eager to join the team. I backed into a parking space and heard the crash of glass. Stunned, I stopped and got out of my truck to find that, in my haste, I had backed into a forklift. The forks had taken out the entire back window of my truck's camper shell.

Undaunted, I brushed the broken glass off the projector and carried it into the building. I did not tell anyone about my broken window, afraid that they would banish me back to the office again, disgusted at my carelessness.

I placed the projector on a table. Ten or twelve people were bustling around the large room, setting up charts, taking notes, and talking urgently in low voices. I spotted Paul, the one who had requested the projector, and approached him boldly.

"I just brought in the projector. It's on the table," I said. The ranger to whom I was speaking, dressed in a bright yellow fire shirt tucked into green ranger jeans, barely looked up. "What did you want me to do with it?"

Paul considered me for a moment. Absently, he ran his fingers through a neatly trimmed beard. He seemed to be thinking about many things at once.

"Can you draw a map?" he asked me.

"Sure!" I answered too quickly and too loudly. "I took a Cartography class in college, and—"

"Great," he interrupted, handing me some colored felt

markers. "Project a map of the search area onto that big sheet of butcher paper. Hang it on the wall. We need an enlarged map of the area so we can keep track of which areas we are searching. Look here."

He showed me a topographical map of the Grand Canyon. "Here—" he marked a spot on the map "—is the point this guy was last seen. And here is where we found his pack. Here is the area we will be searching. Do you know Phantom?"

"I do. I used to work down there."

Paul looked right into my eyes for a second. "Great," he said again. "So get drawing."

I set up the projector and commenced working on the map. Drawing carefully, I concentrated on what I knew of the area in which the search was centered. The missing hiker had disappeared somewhere between Phantom Ranch, where he was camped, and Clear Creek, eight miles by faint trail up the canyon from Phantom. As I worked, several people involved in the search paused on their way to or from an errand to admire the emerging drawing I was creating.

I worked slowly, in part to lengthen my contact with the principals of the search effort. They still had not officially offered to sign me up for the event, but I hoped that if I drew a good enough map they would find something else for me to do. Paul, I had gathered from conversations I overheard around the room, was designated as search boss. He came back over to where I was working carrying a roll of Mylar under his arm. I helped him overlay the map with Mylar, and we began drawing in the areas which were being searched by my Canyon District co-workers.

"You did a good job with this," he said. I glowed in his praise. He was a permanent ranger with years of search experience, so when he noticed my work, I knew it was something special. Before that day, he had only spoken to me to ask me to type something or look up a figure in the budget.

"Now, the search teams are meeting in a few minutes here for a briefing. I want you to sit in on it too. Can you do that, or do you have to get back to the office?"

"I can sit in," I offered quickly. No one had told me it was all right to leave the office; however, since I had forwarded the phones downstairs, I was not about to go back and un-forward them. Not after smashing my truck window with a fork lift. Not after spending months attending training sessions on my own time. I intended to be at that meeting if it meant calling in sick at the office.

"Do you want me to be on a search team?" I tried to ask Paul the question casually.

"No." My heart sank. "No," he said, "I want you to be in charge of supply."

"What's that?"

"Support for the search teams," the search boss explained. "You get everything we need. If we need vehicles, you find them. If we need food for the field troops, you get it. If we need more searchers, you call them up and get them here. Can you do that?"

"Certainly," I answered without hesitation. That I was not getting my chance to go out in the field did not surprise me, considering my history in the Park Service so far. I was used to being stuck in the office. However, it was a chance to be part of the team, to observe from the command post the inner workings of the search. I made a decision right then that I would obtain whatever supplies they needed for that search. If that was where they wanted me, that was where I would shine. No job was too small for this budding ranger. I put my name on the search pay-roll roster.

People began to drift in to the maintenance shop and gather around my map. When about 40 people, most of them Park Service employees, plus a few volunteers, had assembled, Paul quieted everybody down and began to speak.

"We are looking for a solo hiker. Now, the man was camping at Phantom Ranch. He was last seen there two days ago. He left his backpack hanging on the pole in the campground and left, presumably for a day hike up to Clear Creek.

"Some people coming back from Clear Creek said they were certain they saw a man matching his description about a mile up the trail from Phantom. They said he had a small red day pack and was wearing a lightweight blue jacket and tennis shoes. He never returned to Phantom. No one saw him after that time.

"The missing man is in his late 20s. He's a citizen of South Yemen currently attending a junior college in California. He doesn't appear to have had a lot of backcountry experience, and he has never before visited the Grand Canyon. He's been in the United States for a couple years and does speak good English.

"The hasty teams we sent down this morning have completed a search of the trail from Phantom to Clear Creek. No clues have been discovered yet. You have been assigned to teams of four people. If you'll all look at the map here, I will show you which areas each team will cover in their search."

Paul drew out areas for each team on the Mylar overlaying the map. That section of the Grand Canyon, though visible from the South Rim Village, was rugged and seldom traveled by hikers. Searching in that area would be slow; the areas assigned to each team looked relatively small, but I knew that it would take most of a day for the teams to complete a thorough ground search of each area.

"To complicate matters," Paul went on, "we just got a weather report from the National Weather Service. They are saying more rain and increasing clouds. Maybe some snow on the rims. Wind. Not the greatest time of year to be out for a stroll in the canyon with a thin jacket and tennis shoes on. So, folks, it is urgent that you waste no time in getting down to the search areas. Your speed might well have a bearing on the survival of the missing man. This is hypothermia weather, and don't any of you forget it. Dress accordingly. The last thing we want to do is start a search for one of you people."

The searchers broke into small groups to discuss gear they would be packing and meeting times for the hike in to Clear Creek. I stood apart from them, unsure what to do next. I did not have to wonder for very long, however. Paul approached me immediately.

"Here is where you come in," he said. "You've got to get some gear together for the search teams. Let's see . . . got a pencil?"

I fumbled for one. "Go ahead," I said finally.

"Everyone will need fire shirts, like this one," Paul said, indicating his own yellow shirt. "Head lamps. Raingear. C-rations. Climbing rope. Whatever other gear we can come up with. Go out to the rescue cache and bring in everything you can find. Make sure there are batteries for the head lamps. You may have to send someone over to the store to get those. Then we need to arrange transportation out to the Kaibab trailhead for anyone who needs it. That will give you a starting point. You'll come up with more equipment needs as you go along."

"Where do I set up?"

"Over there in the corner. Push a couple tables together and stake out enough space for boxes full of gear. You'll need a sign-out sheet to make sure all the gear is returned when this search is over. Payroll has the list of names. Any questions?"

"Only one," I said, grinning at him. "Can I wear one of those yellow shirts too?"

"You bet," he answered. "You are on the team."

I spent the remainder of the day and evening gathering gear. I wasn't finished making preparations until about 11:00 that night, and when I finally got home from the search headquarters I was too excited and full of nervous energy to fall asleep quickly. The atmosphere of urgency surrounding the search had affected me. As I finally began to fall asleep, I had to force my mind away from lists of equipment and supplies I knew I would need to procure if the search continued past the next day.

I arrived at the maintenance shop at 5:30 the next morning. Already half a dozen bleary eyed rangers, heading the plans, payroll, investigations, communications, public information, and air operations departments of the search effort, were there, commiserating over coffee about the coming day's activities. They greeted me with a warmth I had never before felt from any of them in the office. Our shared concern for the safety of the missing hiker and the ground search teams looking for him had, for the moment, erased the lines of hierarchy between clerk and ranger. I had a feeling of belonging in the inner circle. I wore my yellow shirt with pride.

The searchers began to arrive at six. After signing up at the payroll table, they filed past me one at a time. I issued equipment and wrote their names down as fast as I could. By the time they all had gone through the line they looked to me like a blur of yellow. Once that task was completed and they were out the door, I began to gather more equipment. If the hiker was not found by noon, Paul told me, more searchers would be recruited. I was to be prepared for a doubling of the number of ground forces.

At the end of my first full day on the search, no one had found the man from South Yemen. I stayed at the shop, working, until the evening briefing session; this I attended without even being asked. I listened to rangers with many years of search experience put forth theories about the location of the missing hiker and formulate ideas for the search effort to pursue on the morrow. When they said that they would be trying to get another 20 to 30 searchers on the ground, I knew I had to get busy and come up with some more equipment. Again that evening, I did not arrive home until after 11:00 P.M.

By the next day, tempers were beginning to wear thin. Everyone down in the canyon and at the command post had been running on pure nervous search energy; the collective lack of sleep was beginning to take its toll. Still, the hiker had not been located, so everyone attempted to put personal feelings aside and concentrate on the task at hand.

For me, the rosy glow of being a part of the effort wore off as I too became weary beyond salvation from the long hours and the constant intensity. I lost track of time and completely forgot what it was like to be anywhere but behind my tables at the supply area or in a park service van running errands to the store or to park headquarters. My yellow shirt was getting grimy. Still I did not resign my position. I knew I was involved in something spectacular in the history of the park; people were saying that this was the largest and most thorough search they had ever seen staged at the Grand Canyon.

The operation continued to escalate. We called in volunteers from Coconino County Search and Rescue. We acquired two fixed wing planes and six helicopters to fly the area. Dogs trained to sniff out missing people were flown in from Tucson. The dogs and handlers were in the search headquarters just long enough to check out some gear from me, then were whisked down to the search area by helicopter. At the height of the search effort, there were more than 100 people walking the Clear Creek area. Still, no hiker was found.

One team followed Clear Creek drainage down to the Colorado River. On the sand where the creek emptied into the river, the team discovered a couple of footprints which matched the size and type of the missing man's footgear. That was all. No other clues were found by any of the teams.

While the fresh recruits poured in, I sat at my table and checked out equipment. I gave them C-rations and raingear and tents and sleeping bags. I had a couple people working underneath me by then, and I kept them busy shuttling vehicles and buying batteries and rain ponchos by the dozen. On the third day of the search, the teams who had been down in the canyon since the beginning of the search radioed up that they were running out of food. Ever the resourceful supply manager, I ordered 110 hot lunches from a local lodge. I then arranged with the heliport manager to have the lunches flown down to the ground troops as soon as there was a break in the clouds. I was later told by some of the people who received the lunches that although they did not arrive warm, the food was nevertheless delicious and it boosted everybody's morale to receive it.

Like everybody else involved in the search effort, I worked feverishly. And as I worked, I turned over the problem of the missing hiker in my mind. All my co-workers were also discussing the mystery; the theories were disparate and fascinating. Each theory that had even half a chance of being plausible made its way to the ears of the search boss. His job was to incorporate every possible scenario into his plans.

On day four, the effort began to take on an air of desperation. The ground searchers had followed every lead, checked out every potential clue, literally left no stone unturned in their efforts to discover what had happened to the man from South Yemen.

The weather got worse. Some snow did fall on the rim, and rain poured down on the search teams who were combing the canyon. Clouds hung on the canyon walls and prevented helicopters from flying.

At the end of the fourth day, the search was finally called off. Teams were given permission to come out of the canyon. As each group arrived at the maintenance shop, they checked their gear in with me. None of us spoke much as I collected dirty tents, mud-caked fire shirts and head lamps with dead batteries. To have looked so thoroughly for a man and been unable to find even a shoelace which belonged to him was heartbreaking to all of them. After I got them all checked in, I abandoned the table piled high with search equipment and followed them into a room adjoining the maintenance shop where chairs had been set up for a debriefing. There, Paul, who looked more frazzled than anyone else, spoke in a hoarse voice which could barely be heard. To all those who participated, he said, he owed an explanation. It was obvious to him and everyone else at the command post that every place the man could possibly have been had been searched. That left two possible answers to the puzzle.

One was that the man could have gone to Clear Creek and followed the drainage down to the river. There he either accidentally fell into the river or had attempted to swim back to Phantom. Either way, he had drowned in the river.

The other was that he set up the whole situation to make it appear that he had vanished. Then he walked out to the North Rim at night and disappeared into Utah. Investigation had uncovered the fact that he was about to be deported back to South Yemen, and he had been unwilling to return to his native land. Perhaps he tried to disappear so that he could be declared dead, and thus would be able to acquire a new identity and stay forever in the United States.

No trace of the man from South Yemen was ever found. He was not the first person to vanish in the Grand Canyon. However, what distinguished his disappearance, besides the suspicious circumstances surrounding it, was the exhaustive effort made by the searchers. It was, according to one ranger who was quoted in a Phoenix newspaper, the most thoroughly conducted search he had ever seen in 15 years of search and rescue work at the Grand Canyon.

Only one conclusion was ever reached: that the missing man was not in the Grand Canyon between Phantom Ranch and Clear Creek.

14

❖❖

The
Colorado River

During the hike down to Phantom Ranch on a cool, clear morning in late October, my thoughts were not on the scenery or the steep Kaibab trail. The often quoted words of explorer John Wesley Powell, written as he was on the brink of a plunge into then uncharted territory of the Colorado River through Grand Canyon, pounded out a rhythm in my head. He wrote:

> We are three quarters of a mile into the depths of the earth, and the great river shrinks into insignificance, as it dashes its angry waves against the walls and cliffs.... We have an unknown distance yet to run, an unknown river yet to explore. What falls there are, we know not; what rocks beset the channel, we know not; what walls rise over the river, we know not.

Like Powell, I was going to run the Colorado River, challenge the rapids and see the sights along the way. When Powell traversed the river in 1872, he was not on a pleasure trip; his purpose was geological research on a canyon which was at that time only a blank spot on the map. I felt akin to Powell as I hiked to Phantom to meet the trip, for I too was to be a part of a research expedition on the river.

The purpose of my trip was to gather information quantifying the environmental health of the river corridor. The dozen people with whom I was traveling on the trip, all sent by the National Park Service, represented a wide variety of backgrounds. They were boatmen from the River Subdistrict, botanists from the Museum of Northern Arizona, backcountry trail patrol rangers, an archaeologist, and several resource management specialists. I was along officially to become oriented to the river, so that I might better answer questions asked of me by hopeful river runners at my job as Canyon District clerk. Unofficially, I was the chief research assistant and bottle washer.

Since we all were in some capacity working for or with the Park Service, we were all there for a similar reason: to preserve and protect the Grand Canyon for the enjoyment of future generations. This particular goal was extremely difficult in the case of the Colorado River, due to the high visitor use of the river during the summer months. Every year some 15,000 people made the trip through the Grand. Commercial trips were booked months before their launch dates, and private groups endured up to five years' wait before being offered a permit to make the trip.

The impacts of all those visitors on river beaches and attraction sites were increasing at an alarming rate; trash, vegetation trampling, accelerated erosion, multiple trailing, accidental fires, and congestion were some of the assaults to which the river environment was being subjected. Preservation and protection were the mandates of the Park Service, but public pressure to allow even more people to run the river each year was also rising.

The completion in 1977 of several years of research yielded a conclusion that the river corridor had been impacted from

National Park Service rafts carry all the gear for the trip.

heavy usage. Some corrective action needed to be taken. When the Colorado River Management Plan was released in 1981, it called for the initiation of a resource monitoring program whereby the Park Service could document the impact of river runners and be alerted to any potential environmental problems before they got out of hand. The 1981 plan set user-days at 169,950 per year, the highest figure ever in the history of river

management; but at the same time, it called for a strict monitoring program to assure that visitors who made the trip year
after year would continue to be awed by the primitive beauty of
the river.

It was late fall. The tamarisk trees along the river were
bright gold and the temperature hovered near 70 degrees at
midday. The last of the commercial river trips had come and
gone. I joined the research expedition at Phantom Ranch to accompany the group downriver to Diamond Creek. Alone on the
river save one or two isolated private groups, we pushed off the
sandy beach at Phantom in search of marks that the summer
season of river runners had left on the Grand Canyon.

Our boats, loaded down with equipment and supplies for
ten days on the river, plowed through more than a dozen rapids
for the entire day below Phantom. In 18-foot-long oar-powered
rafts our expedition was almost noiseless. At times the only
sound was the wooden oars slicing tersely through the glassy
river surface. Then, half a mile below, a rapid crashing around
house-sized boulders would break the silence to make its presence known. In the novice whitewater rafters like me,
adrenaline flowed. But the experienced boatmen ran to the left
on the slick tongue of the rapid, and seconds later the boats
were once again sliding across smooth water.

Once through the inner gorge, we pulled in to camp at Bass
Beach. The next morning, the boats were unloaded, equipment
was removed from the bilge bags, and the resource monitoring
program was initiated on the beach. I watched with interest
while one of the botanists from the museum demonstrated a
method of measuring impacts of human use on the beach vegetation. He laid a 100 meter tape measure along a line which had
been chosen from an aerial photograph of the beach. Along every five meters of the line, he put down a one-meter wooden
square, inventoried the plants inside of it, then estimated the
percentage of perennial vegetation cover, as opposed to bare

ground.

As he worked, I followed him, carrying his notebooks and plant samples, and asking him questions about his project.

"The idea," he explained patiently, "is to check the same areas again next year. We will make comparisons and look for a trend over a period of time."

"That sounds fine in theory," I answered. "But in practice it seems inconclusive. Wouldn't it be more accurate if you had started this fifteen years earlier, when less than 1,000 people in the world had run the river?"

The botanist stood up from the quadrant he had been stooping over. He looked at me with an irritation usually reserved for tourists. "The monitoring program did not begin until 1981. You know that. We've got to start with the base line data we gather now."

I got the distinct impression that the botanist did not want to be bothered by my questions. As soon as I had the opportunity, I escaped from the task of assisting the botanist in his painstaking exercise of counting plants inside a square of wood. Instead, I volunteered to accompany Trinkle, the park archaeologist, over to Shinumo Canyon. We hiked up to a terrace overlooking Bass Beach. Without breaking stride, Trinkle pointed out the ruins of some ancient Indian dwellings along the ledge.

"Are we going to stop and look at them?" I asked.

"Not this time. I mapped them last time I was down here. The main thing I have to do today is to survey the old Bass Camp in the next canyon," Trinkle replied.

"So, your projects on this trip are not necessarily along the same lines as those of the botanists and resource management people?"

"Not exactly." Trinkle was a swift hiker; even though she was shorter than I was by several inches, I had to increase my pace to keep up with her. "I am part of the division of resource management too, but my area of interest is the cultural resources. You know—human history in the canyon."

"You mean like the ancient Anasazis? Or something more recent?"

"I am interested in all of it. The Anasazi and the later tribes to settle here, and the early pioneers as well. Do you know anything about Bass?"

I smiled, proud that I had done my homework before the river trip. "He ran the Bass hunting camp on the South Rim, and guided people across the canyon to the North Rim on trails he built himself. This is one of them, isn't it?"

Some of the historical items at Bass Camp on the Colorado River.

"Yes," Trinkle replied. "This trail leads down to one of Bass's camps, where he had a tent dwelling, a garden, and a large orchard. Did you know his wife was the first white woman to raise a family on the South Rim?"

"No, I didn't know that. How many kids did she have?"

"Four. Watch out now, this part of the trail is difficult. We're going down there." Trinkle pointed down a steep incline to the floor of a side canyon. We were perhaps a mile downriver from Bass Beach.

Carefully we descended into the cool shadows of Shinumo Canyon. A short distance from the path we had followed, I saw ancient tin cans strewn about, caught underneath the edges of canyon rocks and squashed flat beneath trees. As we moved up the canyon, Trinkle pointed out broken pieces of dishes, a length of tent cloth, and even an old rusty Yukon stove.

While Trinkle spent most of an hour mapping the locations of Bass's belongings, I walked around the old camp poking at the piles of garbage and guessing at the purpose the old Grand Canyon pioneer had had for each item. Finally Trinkle said she was finished with her survey.

"Not much change here since last year," she commented as she replaced her notebook carefully into her day pack. "It doesn't look like many people have been up here."

"I hope you don't mind me asking a stupid question," I said, remembering the botanist I had tried to question that morning.

"Go ahead."

"Well, to the naked eye, this Bass camp appears to be nothing more than a garbage dump. Why don't we just clean it up and forget about it?"

"That's not a dumb question," Trinkle said. "Cultural resources are difficult to define. There is no question about whether we need to preserve a dwelling site of ancient native inhabitants of the canyon; everyone can appreciate the exotic and mysterious nature of those stone dwellings and granaries. But sites like this one have value too in the modern history of the canyon. Bass wasn't a tourist who left his lunch sack on the trail. He was a pioneer in the era when the Grand Canyon was first being settled by white people. In deference to his contributions to the canyon's exploration, this site is left untouched.

"It is ambiguous, I know. But I don't write the management plans." Trinkle laughed. "I have to agree with you that it looks more like a city dump than a historical site. My real love is studying the archaeological areas. When we get downriver farther, I'll take you along to help me map some of those, O.K.?"

"I'd like that," I said. I found Trinkle's candor and cheerfulness refreshing. I resolved to spend more time with her during the next few days.

After we left Bass Camp, our expedition continued on down the river. We ran rapids with descriptive names like Fishtail and Upset, stopping along the way to complete monitoring surveys. The beaches chosen for resource monitoring were supposed to represent a cross section of high and low use areas along the river corridor. Some, no more than isolated, windswept stretches of sand, were seldom used, and the research turned up very little evidence of human impact. Others, more scenic and comfortable, showed the scars of heavy visitation.

We passed through Granite Narrows at river mile 133, where the powerful thrust of the Colorado River was funneled through a narrow black granite passageway less than 100 feet wide. Within the Narrows, the sun had not yet risen, and a chill pervaded the atmosphere. After a mile long stretch of river, we emerged from the Narrows to gaze on Deer Creek Falls.

Deer Creek Falls, one of the most well known of Grand Canyon attraction sites, rendered innumerable rave reviews from writers, artists and river runners since John Wesley Powell first set eyes on it. Even when compared to the many other wa-

terfalls along the river, Deer Creek stood out in travelers'
minds. On his 1872 expedition, Powell paused in his scientific
analysis of Grand Canyon geology to note the falls: "Just after
dinner, we pass a stream on the right, which leaps into the Colorado by a direct fall of more than 100 feet, forming a beautiful
cascade. On the rocks in the cavelike chamber are ferns, with
delicate fronds and enameled stalks."

Some more logistical pluses, as well, accounted for Deer
Creek's popularity. While most other river attraction sites, such
as Beaver Falls on Havasu Creek, were several miles' hike from
the river, Deer Creek's cascade was less than 200 yards from
the edge of the river. Thus, the site was especially popular with
the people on those commercial trips which covered the length
of the canyon in a week or less, leaving little time for extensive
side canyon exploration.

Another point in favor of Deer Creek was its geographical
location on the river. At the foot of the Granite Narrows, the
black schist disappeared beneath the surface of the river. The
Colorado's banks opened out into several large sandy beaches
lined above with Tapeats sandstone, creating ideal campsites
within a mile of Deer Creek Falls. In addition, swimming below
the falls, hiking up the creek, and exploring nearby Indian ruins were popular layover day activities for both commercial and
private river runners.

During our expedition's stay at Deer Creek, we executed
another method of resource monitoring involving the taking of
sand samples. We collected samples from the beaches near
Deer Creek, which would later be analyzed for charcoal content.
When measured against a graded gray scale, the percentage of
charcoal in the sand indicated comparative levels of campfire
use on the beaches.

Having a campfire during a river trip was itself no crime.
Regulations concerning the type of wood a river runner could
burn, and the manner in which it was burned, however, were

strict. Open fires on the sand were prohibited; all boating parties were required to use a fire pan, or shallow metal box, in order to catch all charred wood and ashes and pack them out.

Low impact camping techniques were stressed by river managers. The actual requirements of low impact use, such as burning a fire in a metal pan, packing out all human waste, and laying a ground cloth below the kitchen area to catch every fallen particle of food, appeared to me to be picayune. But I was educated by the river rangers on the trip, who emphasized that all those steps were essential to hold the impact of 15,000 visitors each year to an absolute minimum.

After we finished collecting sand, I accompanied several of the rangers on a hike above the falls to a campground along upper Deer Creek. There, I was surprised to see that some of the cottonwood trees were scorched black and the ground was covered with a solid layer of charcoal. I asked one of the rangers what had happened.

"Several years ago," he answered, "some people were camped up here. While burning toilet paper in the morning before breaking camp, they accidentally ignited the surrounding desert brush. The fire spread quickly. What you see is the result of their carelessness."

"Fire scarring is not permanent, though," I observed. "It looks bad now, but the effects will eventually disappear. In a lot of places fire managers just let a fire burn. So what's the big deal?"

"It's really not a big deal in that sense," he agreed. "But in an aesthetic sense, the scars of a fire are ugly. Especially one like this, that was caused by carelessness. It reminds me of the presence of people in this area which is supposed to be wilderness."

"That's true. Even though the Colorado River is not exactly a wilderness area, I guess it is important to try to maintain that illusion. People expect it to appear untouched by human impacts."

"That is what people come down here for," the ranger agreed. "Aesthetics are as important a reason for preserving an area as the presence of any unusual natural feature. In the case of Deer Creek Falls, the reputation of the place depends to a large extent on aesthetics. We've got to keep trying to educate the people who use this area about the importance of walking lightly."

After we completed a hike to the far end of the side canyon, picking up garbage all the way, we descended back down to the river and crossed to our campsite on the opposite side of the river from the falls. It was Halloween on the Colorado River. I had been on the river for four days already, or maybe five; I had completely lost track of the time. I had sand in my sleeping bag, and the coffee was never hot enough. I needed a shower in the worst way. The pure physical discomforts of field work were becoming evident. Exhausted and sunburned after a long day at the falls, I ate a hearty dinner of *chile relleno* casserole baked in a Dutch oven and then left the group after dinner.

Moving to a private vista of the Colorado on an overhanging rock down the river from our camp, I watched the river slide by. Darkness crept into the Grand Canyon's inner gorge slowly. The full moon rose above the cliffs of black Vishnu schist, throwing reflections off the surface of the swiftly flowing river. The sounds of tamarisk branches rustling in the breeze and a rapid roaring in the distance downriver pleased my ears like music.

My thoughts flowed from one subject to another as the river ran by below my dangling legs. One thing that struck me as really odd about the Colorado River was the way the water level rose and fell. Each evening during the river trip, we tied our rubber rafts to the tamarisk trees at water's edge and set up camp for the night. By morning, the water had receded so sharply that our boats were left high and dry on the sand. For no apparent reason, the river level changed constantly.

The explanation lay in the workings of Glen Canyon Dam. Water releases controlled by a computer correlated to power demands in Phoenix, Las Vegas, and other great cities of the southwest. Fluctuations in the water level were a great concern to river runners on the Colorado because of the effect on the safety and aesthetic beauty of the river below the dam in the Grand Canyon. Further increasing of the power output from the dam was vigorously opposed by a group of strange bedfellows: the commercial boating companies, environmental groups, and the National Park Service. Bureau of Reclamation officials, in charge of the dam's operation, insisted just as vigorously upon the necessity of producing more power at Glen Canyon Dam.

The studies made on the Grand Canyon's riparian environment in the 1970s pointed to Glen Canyon Dam as the major contributing factor to the drastic alterations in both number and type of flora and fauna along the river. The most obvious addition to exotic vegetation species along the post-dam river banks was tamarisk. A native of the Middle East, tamarisk grew to a height of over eight feet and was nearly impossible to eradicate once it gained a root hold. The bush grew thick along the river's former high water line, crowding out historically native plant species.

Another change was wrought on the river's physiography with the completion of Glen Canyon Dam in 1963. The Colorado was referred to by Mormon pioneers in the 1800s as "too thin to plow, too thick to drink" because of its enormous silt content. The opaque, reddish nature of the river was lent by the rust colored soil of the Utah deserts, carried by the waters of the Colorado River.

Lake Powell, the reservoir created by Glen Canyon Dam, retained all that silt, and the silt was piling up behind the dam at a rate many people considered alarming. As a result of the blockade, the river in the canyon began to run clear enough to see through.

The temperature of the river, too, changed dramatically as a result of the presence of Glen Canyon Dam. Before the dam, the river's temperature hovered around 40 degrees during the winter months and rose to 80 degrees or more toward the end of the summer. After the dam, water released into the Colorado came from the bottom of Lake Powell, where Arizona sunlight never penetrated. The resulting river temperature varied annually less than ten degrees, with an average temperature of about 45 degrees. Native fish such as the Humpback Chub, Razorback Sucker, and Colorado Squawfish, accustomed over the millennia to spawn in seasonably warmer waters, either concentrated their populations in small areas such as the mouth of the Little Colorado River, or became extinct in the Grand Canyon area completely since the dam stabilized the river temperature.

The construction of Glen Canyon Dam was an ecological disaster for the Grand Canyon; but it was, so to speak, water under the bridge by the time I and my river running companions got onto the scene. All we could do by 1981 was attempt to prevent further alterations to the river environment caused by drastic increases or decreases in output from the dam. Although the Park Service's mandate was to preserve and protect, we were working in direct opposition to the mandate of the Bureau of Reclamation, which had a sanction to exploit renewable resources to produce water and power for an energy-hungry nation.

Advocates of the dam believed that their purpose was noble. Those terminal environmentalists and members of the Colorado River Fan Club who chastised the dam and its creators knew that, at a time when the search for domestic sources of energy was at its most intense, they represented a minority view. In the short run, anyway.

But in the long run—that is, in the very long run where time was counted as the Canyon counts it, in increments of a million years—havoc caused by the dam was at best an annoyance, and at worst, very temporary.

In the not too distant geologic past, volcanic lava spewing across the river at Prospect Canyon created a dam 2,300 feet above the present river level. Geologists surmised that the dam may have inundated the river corridor all the way upriver to Lees Ferry.

Eventually, of course, the surging waters of the Colorado broke through that dam and thundered onward, and the river migrated back down to its former bed. Modern dams, built of technology and cement, were ultimately subject to the identical fate. When that happened—and I hoped not to be standing on the delta at Phantom Ranch when it did—the tamarisk would all be cleaned out with one swipe. The beaches would be given a master spring cleaning. The Humpback Chubs, if any still existed, would once again roam at will in the warm, silt laden waters of the Colorado.

On down the river our expedition rowed, passing Matkatamiba, Havasu, and Whitmore Canyons at a rate of 15 miles per day with a stiff wind in our faces. One afternoon, the boat I was riding in stopped at a nondescript side canyon a few miles below Lava Falls. While the boatman lounged on the sand, taking a well deserved break after making a perfect run through the falls, Trinkle and I hiked up the side canyon half a mile to an archaeological site. Trinkle knew exactly where she was going; I, never having been there before, followed her silently around the twists and turns of the narrowing canyon.

Finally Trinkle stopped walking. At first I did not see anything extraordinary about the place. To my untrained eyes, the only unusual feature was an artificial-looking mound of dirt pushed up against the sheer rock of the canyon wall. A profound silence crept into the canyon. No wind stirred the blackbrush; no clouds swept the sky high above the canyon walls.

"What is it?" My voice came out as a whisper.

"It's called a midden," Trinkle answered in a hushed voice. "Midden is another word for trash heap." She chuckled. "Seems like I spend half my life sorting through other people's garbage. But it's a site of great archaeological value. The midden summarizes generations of native American occupation of the river corridor."

Trinkle opened her day pack, removing her notebook, pencils, and a tape measure. "From 700 A.D. to 1300 A.D., at least four distinct tribes resided in rock dwellings along the Colorado River for some or all of the year. The garbage they left—pot shards, lithics, and fibers of clothing—are the treasures we look for in their middens. We use those items to piece together clues about the history of the ancient inhabitants."

"Four tribes? I thought there were only Anasazi here. What are the others?"

"Starting with the most ancient, the tribes are known by arcaheologists as the Cohonina, the Virgin Anasazi, the Kayenta Anasazi, and the Cerbat."

"How can you tell that they were separate tribes, if they all used the same trash heap?" I asked.

"In between periods of occupation, natural materials—dirt, rocks and native plant pieces—settled on top of the midden. Then, when the next group came in, they used the same midden. We don't know why the Cerbats chose to dump in the same place as the Anasazi, but that's just what they did. At least, it makes it easier for us archaeologists to make comparisons."

I laughed. "That's convenient. Nice of the natives to leave such a good record for us. I'm sure they weren't thinking about us, though."

"No." Trinkle's face turned serious. "In fact, to tell you the truth, I don't think the ancients really like us to be poking around in their garbage. I don't mean to scare you or anything,

Kitty, but I ought to tell you that some really freaky things have happened to me when I was at some of these archaeological sites. It's almost as if—don't laugh—the spirits of the ancient ones are still hovering around here, watching me."

"I am not laughing, Trinkle, really. One time when I was up at Lake Powell I discovered a dwelling site stuck up on a cliff near the edge of the lake. I wanted to go up and look at it. I don't know what happened, but I tripped on something and fell on my face, right below the ruins. All the time I was there I had a feeling that I was not welcome . . . almost like the feeling I have right now. I never mentioned that experience to anyone, because I thought they would say I was crazy."

Indian ruins present a target for souvenir hunters on river trips.

"You know what I'm talking about, then," Trinkle said. "I was up near Deer Creek a couple years ago, collecting some pot shards for our museum display. I had found four beautiful shards from the Virgin Anasazi era, and had placed them on a flat rock. I turned my back for a few seconds, and when I looked back there, the shards had disappeared! I looked for them for an hour. I don't know to this day what happened to them, but I concluded that someone didn't want me to have them.

"Most scientific people will not bring up the subject of spirits in the ancient sites. But if you talk to them privately, almost everyone in this field has had his or her share of weird experiences. It doesn't stop me from doing this work. But I do move with caution. I would advise you to do the same."

"I will," I promised. "Now, what kind of work do you need to do at this site?"

"We need to measure it. You hold this end of the tape measure and jump up on top of the midden. I'll call out the measurements in each direction, and you write them down."

Trinkle used a compass to get bearings for the measurements. With caution, I climbed atop the midden, which was about four feet high. Squatting down to place the end of the tape measure at just the right spot, I noticed bits of pottery sticking out of the mound. Unable to resist taking a closer look, I reached for one of the shards of pottery and pulled it out of the midden. It was brick red with a black zigzag design. For one long moment, I was tempted to slip the shard into my pocket. Trinkle was not looking. I stood up, and began to move my hand toward the pocket of my shorts.

The wall of the side canyon rose vertically behind me. I had not noticed any prominent extrusions of rock on the wall, but as I stood, somehow my shoulder bumped the canyon wall. Like a shove from an unseen foe, the canyon wall pushed me off balance. Before I could comprehend what had happened, I was tumbling head over heels. I fell off the midden, did a somersault in midair, and landed hard on my rear end on the ground. The pot shard I had been trying to steal flew out of my hand during my fall and disappeared.

"Are you all right?" Trinkle called to me with concern. I was too embarrassed to tell her that I had been attempting to take a souvenir from the midden. I looked down and mumbled something about losing my balance. I stood up, dusted off my pants, and looked around the side canyon. I saw nothing; no one was there except for me and Trinkle. Yet I felt their presence. Under my breath I whispered something to the effect of an apology; then I took the end of the tape measure and climbed back up on the midden.

A shout from Trinkle made me turn quickly. "What is it?" I yelled.

"My glasses," she said. "I bent over, and they slid right off my nose and fell to the ground. And, I don't know, I guess I stepped on them. They're broken."

I carefully climbed back down from the midden. "Trinkle, are we just about done here? I mean, I think we've been here long enough. I am getting the creeps. Let's get back to the river and the rest of our people. It is just a little too weird up here. Sorry to be chickening out on you, but . . . ."

"No, I think so too. Sometimes they don't seem to mind us poking through their belongings, but today they definitely are not tolerant of us. I got the measurements I needed. I was supposed to collect some samples here too, but I think I'll tell my supervisor that we ran out of time. I'd just as soon not take anything with us."

As soon as we had walked down around the corner, out of sight of the midden, I felt an immediate relief. The atmosphere did not seem so heavy, and it was just a benign, sunny autumn day again. Lighthearted, without a pot shard in my pocket to haunt me, I moved quickly back down the canyon at Trinkle's side.

"What is the purpose of taking measurements of that midden?" I asked her. Idly, I noticed that I was no longer speaking in a whisper.

"Problems, both human caused and natural, threaten the archaeological sites in the canyon," Trinkle said. "Erosion, the process through which the canyon was formed, continues; and as the canyon walls crumble and collapse, the middens and dwelling sites of the native occupants are washing away. The more immediate threat to sites such as this one, though, is the people it attracts. Souvenir hunters searching through the archaeological sites for pieces of pottery and baskets form trails crisscrossing through the area. The result is acceleration of erosion and destruction of the sites."

"I would think you would want to go ahead and excavate the sites then. That would seem to be the only way you could retrieve the information you need before the sites are destroyed."

"Some do want to excavate, yes," Trinkle said. "But others in the Park Service see excavation as diametrically opposed to the mandate to preserve and protect the canyon's cultural resources. It is a controversy which has not yet been resolved. So, for now, sites like this one here sit waiting—for flash floods, for greedy river runners seeking souvenirs, or for excavation—whichever fate comes first."

Trinkle and I arrived back at the beach, where our boatman was sound asleep on the sand. We woke him up and continued our journey down the river. He let me take a turn at the oars. I was surprised at the strength required just to pull the heavy wooden oars out of the water and move them forward for the next stroke. After a while, I learned how to move the boat with the river's current, guiding it with my strokes and looking ahead to read the water for an upcoming rapid.

At dusk, we pulled in to a wide, sandy beach where we would be making our last camp of the trip. As I opened my river bags and shook out my hopelessly sandy sleeping bag, I began to think up a theme song for the trip: " 'Twas the night before takeout, and all through the camp, our T-shirts are filthy, our boat shorts are damp . . ."

As daylight waned, I abandoned my effort to be witty. Walking along the beach below our camp, I thought about the trip I had just made. Tomorrow, I thought, we would be arriving at Diamond Creek, the point of termination for our trip. There a rough, rutted dirt road led back to Highway 40 and civilization. Already, the canyon's walls had begun to widen out in anticipation of Lake Mead. Side canyons were no longer steep and narrow, but broad and rolling. The rapids were becoming more tame, and the nights were getting warmer; the end of the trip was in sight. After 12 days on the river, I felt rejuvenated.

It was a world of contrasts down on the river: the profound beauty of delicate waterfalls in side canyons and the shocking violence of untamed rapids. For a short time, I had become a part of the dynamic, living, changing forces of the Colorado River.

On that final evening, the stars in the sky seemed endless in number. The frequency of meteors was astounding. I wondered if a major meteor shower was occurring. I did not know, but my wishes were coming fast on every shooting star I saw. All were variations on the same theme: that we humans find it in our hearts to preserve and protect the canyon for eternity.

The river flowed peacefully a few yards below my campsite; I realized that its sounds had been permanently etched in my mind. The call of a lone canyon wren floated down from a cliff high above. The moon, in its last quarter, rose over the black edge of the gorge, casting shadows on the awesome landscape.

And later, lying in my warm, sandy, sleeping bag for the last time on the final night of my first river trip, I heard the strains of music from a river song. As the words became louder in my head, I hoped that the whole world of river runners would also hear them some night while they were blasting through the

canyon next season. "Peace, I ask of thee, oh River, Peace,
Peace, Peace. When I learn to live serenely, cares will
cease . . ." The sound of slick water moving over canyon rock
was the last thing I heard before I fell into a deep, dreamless
sleep.

15

❖

High Water

After I finished the appointment as Canyon District Clerk in the fall of 1982, I acquired another eleven-month seasonal appointment with the Park Service. Though still technically a clerk, I filled a position infinitely more complex and interesting than the secretarial job I had held previously in the Canyon District. My job title was River Permits Clerk, and I worked in the highly visible River Permits Office of the River Subdistrict.

My job duties in a nutshell were to complete all the paperwork connected with river trips on the Colorado River. That meant dealing with both the commercial outfitters and the private, do-it-yourself groups running trips on the Grand. The commercial and the private sectors of river runners were often at odds with each other. A great degree of diplomacy was demanded of me so that I did not alienate either group, nor show any favoritism in awarding trips to them.

The Colorado River Management Plan, ten years in the writing, was implemented when I began my employment in the

River Subdistrict. For the first time, the river managers had a document which backed their authority for mandating use levels, trip sizes, required equipment and experience on trips, and methods for allocating trips. But the document was written by faceless resource managers in the Western Regional Office of the National Park Service, far removed from the Colorado River. It was my task to translate the words of the management plan into workable systems which applied to the entire river running community without violating any mandates nor stepping on any toes.

Much of my work day was spent on the telephone. I answered the questions of people wanting to buy a slot on a commercial trip or plan a private one. I talked technically about river trips to those people who were scheduled to run each year, advising them on every aspect of their planned journey from equipment to campsites.

I fielded a number of calls from the media who wanted river running information. Everyone was curious about the permit allocation system and the mechanics of putting together a trip. During the 18 months I worked in the River Permits Office, I was quoted in the *New York Times*, *River Runner* and *Canoe* magazines, and the *Los Angeles Times*. My information about the river was boundless, and I enjoyed my role as chief disseminator of information and champion of the Colorado River Management Plan.

I was not an expert river runner, but I did not pretend to be one, either. I went on a total of four river trips in those years, acting as cook or swamper, but I did not know the technicalities of running the Colorado. I had the ability, however, to describe the river to callers; I could talk all day about "the hole below the rock on the left side at the top of Hance Rapid," or the "standing waves and eddy lines near the landing at Phantom." I learned the language and landmarks of the river and used them effectively.

My real strength was my comprehension of the intricacies of the permit system and the complicated user day allocation guidelines. During the time I worked in the Permits Office, I understood the mechanics of who got which trips better than anyone else.

The commercial company owners met annually in December; that was the only time of the year when I saw them all together. The river company owners were minor celebrities. Martin Litton, unofficial spokesman for the environmental activists within the river running community and owner of a small company which used wooden dories to carry passengers down the river, was always there with a pitch for the preservation of the canyon, even at the expense of a profit for himself. Georgie, Woman of The River, sat with the men, face tough as leather and permanently tanned from the years of piloting pontoon boats under the relentless sun of summer in the canyon. Fred Burke, Richard Bangs, Rob Elliot, and the rest were household names in the world of river running. They were the elite; they held Grand Canyon permits. There were 21 commercial river running companies, and though nobody dared to put a monetary value on their contracts with the National Park Service, the right to run trips on the most famous and tightly controlled stretch of whitewater in the United States was obviously both an extremely valuable and jealously guarded commodity to all of them.

During the meetings each December, which lasted several days, I had a part in the agenda. I talked about the brass tacks of their operations; armed with pages of statistics, I showed them how their user-day allocations, mandated by the management plan, had been utilized. Because I prepared weeks ahead of time for the annual meeting, running and re-running the numbers through the computer, the outfitters grew to respect my calculations. Seldom did they question the totals I produced of their user day counts. Naturally, the smaller companies demanded more user days while the companies who ran huge swarms of people down the river held on tightly to their quotas. When I introduced a workable system of pooling unused allocations, which could then be put up for grabs by any of the companies during the course of the high use season, they greeted that proposition with unanimous approval.

I also mediated the circus of bidding for the next year's launch dates during those outfitter meetings. A maximum of 150 passengers could leave Lees Ferry each day during the summer. I stood at the podium, calculator in hand, as the representatives for each company shouted out their preferred launch dates. It usually took several hours to hammer out a schedule that was acceptable to all the outfitters. Though everyone yelled and the atmosphere of the meeting became quite hectic, I was required to remain impartial, showing no favoritism toward any one company. Through the personal contact at the meetings, I got to be friendly with the company owners, and was able to enjoy a good working relationship with all of them. They called me often during the river running season, to shift dates around and add or subtract trips. They came to trust me, often asking for me by name when they called.

Working with the private trips was an entirely different but no less challenging experience. The waiting list for non-commercial trips was 2,700 names long; if each person waited placidly until his or her name rose to the top of the list, they were looking at a seven- or eight-year wait to run the river. Many of the non-commercial river runners raged at the unfairness of the user day allocation in the management plan; non-commercial trips had less than half the number of user days as the commercial trips.

The irony was that, small as it was, the user day allocation for private river users was never fully utilized, due to a high number of trip cancellations at the last minute. Private trips had to be planned a year in advance. When a trip leader broke his leg or could not get time off work or encountered some other unforeseen roadblock to his trip, there was no way to reissue the trip to someone else on the waiting list, so the launch date went unused.

When I began working in the River Permits Office, the disparity between private user days available and those actually used was a grave problem. We worked out a system to modify the waiting list method of obtaining a trip. The way it worked was that, when anyone scheduled for a private trip launch date cancelled, their launch date automatically became available to anyone on the waiting list on a first come, first served basis. The modifications to the river permit system were watched closely by the river running community, and consensus was that the first come, first served method was reasonably fair and reasonably successful. On the cutting edge of river permit systems throughout the United States, I knew that the actions of my office were being watched closely. My reward was the grudging admissions by die-hard non-commercial trip advocates that the system, though complicated, was effective in allocating trips to private users in a just manner.

Those who were assigned a private trip launch date were regularly in touch with me to plan their trips and complete all the necessary paperwork. For many of the private groups, I was the only contact they had with the River Subdistrict prior to their launch date at Lees Ferry. I received several letters of appreciation from the privates. One even went so far as to write that "Kitty was the most helpful and the most agreeable person I have ever found in that office."

I loved to receive those letters of thanks. I enjoyed being interviewed as an authority on the most elaborately structured river permits system in the United States. But eventually, discontent crept into my attitude toward that job, as it had into all the other park positions I had held for any length of time. For all the challenge of setting up a permit system, and for all the ego boosting contacts with the media and the famous people who ran commercial trips, I was still stuck in the office. I was the one who was answering phones while everyone else in the River Subdistrict was on the river.

When I had worked in Yellowstone, and the first couple years at the Grand Canyon, it had been enough just to be present in the parks. I used to tell new employees, when they complained about low pay for hard work, that the scenery was worth at least five dollars an hour. For a long time I believed that myself; but by the time I reached the position of River Permits Clerk, just being at the canyon, near the excitement, ceased to be satisfactory as an end in itself. During my time in the River Permits Office, I strove to make a difference in the management of the canyon. I wanted to hold an active and important role in the preservation and protection of the resource. And though I believed I did make a difference in a small way, I grew discontented with the job. I grew tired of clerical work.

Something did happen in the summer of 1983 which lifted me for a time from the drudgery of the office routine. What happened was that the river flooded.

Before Glen Canyon Dam was built in 1959, the Colorado River flooded routinely every year, but it was no big deal because almost nobody was floating it recreationally. After the dam was completed, the flow of the Colorado was regulated by power demands at the dam, and the river level was strictly controlled. Flows were as dependable as the sunset and the presence of canyon wrens. River runners could simply look at the average temperatures in Phoenix and Las Vegas and calculate what the river flow was going to be on any given day.

The snow pack in the Rocky Mountains was unusually heavy and lingered until the end of May in 1983. During Memorial Day weekend, temperatures in the mountains high

A boatman skirts the hole at Crystal Rapid during the flood of 1983.

above the Colorado River soared into the 90s. The snow melted almost instantaneously. All the water from the rapidly melting snow ended up in Lake Powell, causing the lake level to rise at an alarming rate. Dam managers waited as long as they possibly could before making the decision to increase flows. But when the lake level became high enough to threaten the multi-million dollar marina at Wahweap, the Bureau of Reclamation decided to increase the output of water from the dam.

Glen Canyon Dam had been designed to handle occasional water overflows, but nothing of the magnitude of the waters which crowded it in 1983. On June 2, the dam's flow was increased to 40,000 cubic feet per second (cfs). It was quickly discovered that the increase was inadequate to compensate for the inflow of melting snow from the lake's tributaries. Lake Powell continued to rise; water was threatening to spill over the top of the dam. During the next three weeks, the flows released from the dam were steadily increased until, at the peak of the flood, the dam was releasing 92,000 cfs of water into the Colorado River.

As the water level rose along the river, we in the River Subdistrict became concerned for the safety of the people who were running the river. At its normal flow of 30,000 cfs, the river was rated ten on a scale from one to ten for difficulty. But the boatmen who were piloting the boats down the river were familiar with every hole and rock at the normal water level, and thus could run it with a minimum of trouble. When flows were increased, however, the river changed. Rapids became unrecognizable stretches of radical whitewater. Rocks were submerged; beaches and landmarks were wiped out. Suddenly it was an unfamiliar river. The Park Service was responsible for the welfare of those who had happened to be down there when the flows were increased without warning.

A critical point was reached at 70,000 cfs. At that particular water level, most of the major Grand Canyon rapids were washed out. Crystal Rapid, however, was transformed into a nightmarish section of roaring water and standing waves 30 feet high. A monstrous hole engulfed boats large and small, flipped them over and flung them out like driftwood.

In a one week period, when the flow of the river was at 70,000 cfs, four commercial tour boats flipped in Crystal Rapid, throwing a total of 132 people into the 45 degree water of the Grand Canyon's inner gorge.

When word arrived at the South Rim that boats were flipping, most of the river rangers were sent down to aid in the res-

cue. As usual, I was not selected to go into the canyon on the
emergency; my job was to answer the phones and monitor radio
communications between Crystal and the South Rim. As news of
the spectacular result of high water spread to the outside world,
I was inundated by telephone calls. The Associated Press was
calling; Dan Rather discussed the situation on the six o'clock
news. Commercial outfitters wanted to know whether their boats
had been among those that flipped, and private trip leaders
called to ask my advice about whether they ought to cancel or
postpone their planned trips. Alone in the office, I juggled
phone calls in an attempt to keep the world informed of the situation at Crystal Rapid.

Without consulting anybody, because nobody was in the office to consult, I drafted a cancellation policy for private permit
holders who were unwilling to run the river at an unfamiliar
flow level. I assembled a list of the names of people who had
been in the Crystal calamity so I could answer the frantic questions of family members who called to find out if their kin had
been involved. With all my fellow Subdistrict employees down
in the canyon, I became for a few days the entire River
Subdistrict.

Meanwhile, the word came from Crystal that some of the
passengers on the overturned boats had been fished out of the
river by kayakers. Others who had been thrown into the river
had pulled themselves out along the sheer walls of the granite
gorge, where rescue by boat was impossible. Rangers in wet-
suits were dropped by helicopter into the river to attempt to
coax these people back into the water, so that boats could pick
them up.

One man perished in the confusion surrounding the res-
cues. He had been held under water by the pontoon boat on
which he had been riding when it flipped over. He drowned
before anyone could get to him. The rest of the people were
evacuated safely. Fifteen had minor injuries; the rest had a

story of high adventure to tell.

The Bureau of Reclamation continued to raise the flow level on the river as Lake Powell was still in imminent danger of overflowing. Increases in the dam's output came without warning; the biggest problem the River Subdistrict faced was that there was no reliable means of communicating to parties still on the river about the impending increases. With most of the other rangers on the river rescuing passengers on flipping boats, my supervisor, Curt, turned to me to come up with a method of notifying river runners of flow increases.

I typed up messages which stated what the water level was likely to be. "Colorado River flow will increase to 80,000 cfs on Monday," the notes read. "Camp high—be cautious." Each note was placed in a zip-lock bag along with a couple handfuls of sand. To the top of each bag I tied several yards of bright red or yellow flagging tape.

About 100 of the message packets were prepared. I took them to the heliport, where a helicopter whose doors had been removed was waiting for me. I strapped myself into the passenger seat and we flew directly from the South Rim to Lees Ferry.

From the ferry, the helicopter pilot flew his craft down the river corridor at an altitude of 100 feet above the water. Each time we spotted a boating party, whether on the water or camped on a beach, the pilot hovered over them, trying to keep the helicopter still.

Held in by the seat belt only, I leaned out of the craft and dropped a message bag to each party. At first, my aim was not very accurate; the notes ended up in the bushes or on the wrong side of the river. With practice, though, I got better at the art of dive-bombing people with baggies. I hit one group's outhouse tent with a note; at another spot, I accurately threw a message into the lap of a boatman as he was rowing his raft through a rapid.

I was astounded at what I saw from the helicopter. The river level was many feet higher than it had ever been in my lifetime. Sandy beaches were completely obliterated by the churning water of the flood; tamarisk trees were drowned by the deluge. I saw caves, normally used by river parties as lunch stops, filled to their ceilings with water. The river current flowed over the top of a rock on the upper stretch of the river, a rock which normally stuck up like a monument twenty feet above river level. Whole trees uprooted by the force of the flood moved with the current and smashed into the shore in back eddies.

I could hardly believe that this was the same river I had run only a couple months earlier. Then, it had been fairly placid, a deep green color, predictably flowing; now, it was wild, straining to become again what it had been before the dam attempted to leash its power. A thrill of victory stole over me as I examined the destruction of the river corridor beneath the hovering helicopter. Once again, the Grand Canyon had asserted itself. I dropped the warning messages to attempt to protect the lives and property of those who were running the river; but I could not stop the water from rising. Nor did I want to stop it. There was joy in my heart as I completed the mission and returned to the South Rim. The river, the force of water which had helped to create the mighty chasm in the desert, had broken the chains with which modern society had tried to control it. The river's spirit had not been contained.

Altogether, I went on three helicopter missions. Two were to warn boaters about impending high water; the third was to inform them that the water level would be dropping, when the Bureau of Reclamation abruptly stopped running water through the dam's spillways. Leaning out of the helicopter, suspended above the flooding Colorado was the most exciting work of my Park Service career.

That experience also led me to receive an award. Curt nominated me for a special achievement award for my actions above and beyond my job description. What that meant, basically, was that a clerk whose job it was to stay in the office answering telephone calls and scheduling launch dates had no business flying in helicopters, giving interviews with the Associated Press, and implementing management plan revisions. I was proud of my involvement in the emergency operations of the River Subdistrict and pleased that the Park Service recognized that I possessed abilities beyond the scope of my job description.

The high water receded. By mid July, the river was back to normal level, and the lake level again was manageable. The flood had not been of a long enough duration to permanently alter the canyon vegetation; though it had killed a few of the tamarisk bushes and did give the beaches a thorough cleaning, the high water ultimately had little impact on either the river environment or the river running community. I settled back into the mundane tasks of scheduling trips and responding to commercial outfitters' demands for more user days. The excitement passed. The summer of high water moved into autumn, and, bored with my paperwork and my own endless chatter about river running on the telephone, I began to take some action to effect changes in my situation. I could not wait for the next flood of the Colorado River; I was ready to advance in my parkie career.

The eleven-month seasonal position I held in the River Permits Office allowed me to take off a month of my choice. I chose the month of September for my furlough. Alone, I took a three-week vacation in my truck, traveling to the Pacific Northwest. Camping and driving, I saw Oregon, Washington and Idaho. I relished the alone time and spent days listening to music on the stereo and taking long solitary walks in the rain forest.

By the time I returned to the Grand Canyon, I had made the decision to attempt a change in my life. During my travels I had been unable to let go of the conviction that it was time for me to take some steps in a different direction. Without mentioning to anyone what I was doing, I wrote to every place I had ever heard of in the distant land of Alaska. During the winter, when snow blanketed the South Rim of the Grand Canyon and clouds filled the gorge on frosty mornings, I filled out applications for jobs in Alaska. To the Park Service in Denali and Katmai, to the national forests of Chugach and Tongass, to the concession-aires in Glacier Bay and Denali and Lake Clark, I carefully mailed out my resume. Between the lines listing my experience, I attempted to convince someone in the cold northern lands that I was more than just a secretary who had been in the desert too long.

I had been on four Colorado River trips. I had hiked every major trail in the Grand Canyon. I had worked on the rim and on the river. I had, in five years at the Grand Canyon, experi-enced the best it had to offer. I was uncertain whether my pot-pourri of job skills would be of any value to the people who ran the parks in the far north. But I sent the resumes because my soul was stirring with the desire for change.

In March, I traveled to Phoenix to interview for a job with the Denali Park concessionaire. The man who interviewed me told me that I had an excellent chance of being hired. When I returned to the South Rim, a letter from the concessionaire at Glacier Bay waited in my mail box. Glacier Bay also offered me a job as a steward on one of their tour boats. A day later, the Chief Ranger at Denali called to offer me a job as a Park Ser-vice dispatcher at that park.

I mulled it over and asked the opinion of several people who had been to Alaska. Eventually, I decided to take the Park Service job. For one thing, I thought my career would be en-hanced more by a ranger job than by a waitress-type job. And secondly, I believed I would be able to see more of Alaska at Denali, which was on a road system, than I would from Glacier

Bay, which could only be reached by boat or plane.

I resigned from my River Permits Office job in April. I was afraid that Curt would try to talk me out of leaving, but he surprised me with his enthusiasm and encouragement for my desire to go north. He insisted that the River Subdistrict give me a going away party on the South Rim before I left.

At the party, Curt told me that he had been born in the Yukon. He understood the restlessness that was driving me to leave the security of the Grand Canyon. In front of my assembled co-workers, he announced that he had a poem to read to me. It was "The Call of the Wild," by Robert Service. In those words I heard expressed all the reasons I was taking the chance to go explore the world of the Arctic:

THE CALL OF THE WILD

Have you gazed on naked grandeur where there's nothing
*   else to gaze on,*
Set pieces and drop-curtain scenes galore,
Big mountains heaved to heaven, which the blinding sunsets
*   blazon,*
Black canyons where the rapids rip and roar?
Have you swept the visioned valley with the green stream
*   streaking through it,*
Searched the Vastness for a something you have lost?
Have you strung your soul to silence? Then for God's sake go
*   and do it;*
Hear the challenge, learn the lesson, pay the cost.

Have you wandered in the wilderness, the sage-brush
*   desolation,*
The bunch-grass levels where the cattle graze?
Have you whistled bits of rag-time at the end of all creation,
And learned to know the desert's little ways?

Have you camped upon the foothills, have you galloped o'er
the ranges,
Have you roamed the arid sun-lands through and through?
Have you chummed up with the mesa? Do you know its
moods and changes?
Then listen to the Wild—it's calling you.

I drove away from the stone house on Apache Street without announcing my departure. On the way out of the park, I stopped at Mather Point for a few minutes to gaze into the canyon one more time.

Staring down into the depths of rock and color, I picked out areas of the canyon that I knew intimately. There, zigzagging down through the Redwall, were the Christmas tree switchbacks of the Kaibab Trail. Directly across from me on the far side of the river was the Clear Creek drainage in which the man from South Yemen disappeared. Off in the distance to the east, the Palisades of the Desert hung in the air like a rainbow above Comanche Creek.

After five years of living with the canyon, it no longer appeared like a painting to me. I could see the depth and the perspective; it was like a friend whose face I had memorized in all its moods, always changing, yet always familiar.

To the Grand Canyon I conceded that I was going to Alaska without a return ticket. To its silence I whispered goodbye.

16

❖❖

Spring

My plane landed in Anchorage the same day the ice went out of the Nenana River. Somebody in Alaska won several thousand dollars in the Nenana Ice Classic lottery for correctly guessing the minute of spring's official arrival in the arctic. Nobody had made a bet on my arrival; nobody, not even I, knew on the evening of May 7, 1984 that I had come to the Land of the Midnight Sun to stay.

As a Cheechacko, or green newcomer to Alaska, I was unaware that my arrival coincided with the departure of the river ice. During my first few minutes in Alaska at the under-construction Anchorage airport, I concentrated my energy on gathering together my seven pieces of baggage. I tried to call the telephone number someone had given me for a friend of a friend in Anchorage. Receiving no answer, I ditched the pipeliner in a cowboy hat who had followed me off the plane and hailed a taxi.

I stayed my first night in Alaska at the youth hostel on Minnesota Drive. After the long flight north, I suffered from both jet lag and culture shock and was unable to sleep immediately. Throwing a coat over my shoulders, I went outside to sit for a while on a bench in front of the hostel and attempted to absorb the foreign flavor of the far north's biggest city.

Although the clock told me it was after ten in the evening, the sky still glowed with post-sunset brightness. The air was cold and still, in direct contrast to the 95 degree heat I had left that morning in Phoenix. What surprised me the most, as I sat in front of the hostel on that spring evening, however, was the number of cars I saw on the streets of Anchorage. Somehow, the idea had become fixed in my mind that cars were a rarity in the far north. The first of many myths about Alaska was shattered as I watched herds of them move past the hostel.

It was not that I was of the igloos-and-Eskimos school of Alaska perception. I had stared at plenty of coffee table books featuring Alaska as I prepared to leave the Grand Canyon. My mental picture had included log cabins in the woods, perhaps with a view of some unnamed mountains, and a bear strolling past the wood shed. But I had not expected anything quite so urban as Anchorage. Alaska—at least the part of it I saw first— was more civilized than I had imagined it would be.

The next morning, a bus showed up at the hostel to transport me and twelve other seasonal rangers to Denali Park. I had not noticed any of the others the night before in the hostel, but when we assembled at the front door at 8:00 that morning, I saw with some relief that each of them was as heavily laden with luggage as I was. While we loaded our boxes and backpacks into the lower compartment of the bus, we began the familiar parkie ritual of introduction by location, circling verbally like dogs to discover who had been around parks the longest.

Among my Cheechacko traveling companions, several had more years of park experience, but I scored points for having worked in the River Subdistrict. One woman, who was later to become my roommate at Denali, expressed all the parkies' general attitude toward my claim to fame.

"I was an interpreter on the South Rim," she said. "I did programs about the river, but I never got to go on a trip. You did four of them? Wow, you were lucky."

"I worked hard for those trips," I said in defense.

"Why did you ever leave there?" queried a boyish looking man with wire rim glasses and a neatly trimmed red beard. "I think I would have stayed there running the river forever, if I were you."

They were all looking at me. "Time to move on," I explained. "Five years at the Grand Canyon was enough. I've always wanted to come to Alaska and work in the park here. I needed a change from the desert."

For that simple explanation I received nods of approval all around. They understood the concept of parkie wanderlust.

Another woman with a long blonde braid spoke up. "This is my second season at Denali. You'll like it, I'm sure. We are the cream of the crop, as far as seasonals are concerned. You don't get a job in Denali by being an average employee. There are more opportunities for us up here. Six million acres of wilderness. The Grand Canyon doesn't have anything on Denali."

The first stop the bus made, after we and all our belongings were loaded aboard, was at a mall on the edge of town. There, we were instructed to spend two hours shopping for groceries and any other supplies we needed. The girl with the braid, who had assumed the role of tour guide for those of us new to Alaska, advised us that the grocery store at Denali was tiny and its merchandise expensive. She suggested we all stock up on most of the staples we would be needing for the entire summer.

I was again shocked when I walked into the mall. There was a Safeway and a Dunkin' Donuts, a bookstore and several dress shops. Of course, I was aware that Anchorage might be the only place in Alaska which had such a mall, but nevertheless I was taken by surprise to discover its existence in a state which called itself The Last Frontier.

I spent about $200 on food in the Safeway. When I emerged with an overloaded shopping cart, I saw that the others had purchased just as much, if not more, than I had. We wrote our names on each of our grocery bags and piled them into the bus, three bags to a seat. Once the supplies were all loaded, there was scarcely room for the 13 of us to crowd into the first few rows of bus seats.

We left the mall and began the journey north. Within minutes we had left the city limits, moving out through an unpopulated river valley. I settled in to enjoy the scenery on the five hour trip up to Denali Park.

The bare ground and budding tree branches of Anchorage were quickly left behind. It seemed that the closer we got to Denali, the deeper looked the snow on either side of the road. In the interior, it was still winter, though the calendar said it was the first week of May.

Finally the bus turned off the highway and entered the park. A few minutes later, it came to a stop in the seasonal employees' housing area, known locally as C-camp, and I was home. A lot of people were on hand to meet the bus. My supervisor, a fortyish man with a receding hairline and a quick, crooked smile, stuck out his hand and introduced himself to the dispatcher he had hired, sight unseen, a month earlier. I could not help but notice a knot of scruffy looking, mostly bearded men dressed in dirty Levis or Carhartts who stood apart from the bus, watching us disembark. These men, I later learned, were some of the maintenance division seasonals. Most were local residents; they had made a special trek up to C-camp to check out the fresh arrivals to the park. I tried to ignore them as I organized my gear and groceries in a pile, but I felt them looking at me and heard the low rumble of their voices making comments from the sidelines.

C-camp was a cluster of cabins arranged roughly in a circle about a central bathroom and community building. I shared my cabin with another woman, Debbie, who had a job as an interpretive ranger; she was the one who had worked a couple seasons on the South Rim, and it was her first year at Denali also. The cabin we shared was tiny; but it had a refrigerator and a stove and cold running water, and I had a room to myself. I was pleased with the accommodations. For the first time in nearly forever, I had my own space.

The boreal forest surrounding C-camp was still a tangle of black spruce, bare branches, and melting snow. Before my eyes, spring unfolded during the first few days of my sojourn in Alaska.

After spending a couple days getting settled into the cabin and becoming accustomed to the layout of C-camp and Park Headquarters, I decided to walk down to the post office. It could be reached by following the paved road for a couple miles, but I chose the more scenic route of the Rock Creek Trail. Shortly after I set out on the two and a half mile trip, clouds blew in and hovered menacingly over the mountains which ringed the lowlands where the park's civilization was located. Some snow still lay on the trail, and little rivers of melt-off ran down the hillsides. My feet, clad in tennis shoes due to my ignorance of the spring break-up, got soaked.

The wind tore through bare aspen branches. I spotted a large track in the trail which to my inexperienced eyes looked like it belonged to a bear. Frightened, cold and unsure of myself in the wild backwoods of Alaska, I was relieved to finally emerge from the trail at the back of the hotel. Just as I began to breathe easier, movement at the edge of the woods 40 feet away from me caught my eye.

I stared at the massive animal casually devouring whole branches of forest shrubbery. Since the creature appeared to be unaware of my presence, I walked several more steps toward it. I must have stepped on a twig, though, because it suddenly jerked up its head and turned to look right at me. Its brown eyes were the size of ping pong balls.

"Hello, moose," I said.

The moose turned away and trotted off into the woods. I shook my head in amazement as I continued on down to the post office. I had never seen anything quite like that seven foot tall moose. Suddenly feeling lightheaded, I wondered what I had gotten myself into by coming to Alaska. Even after seven years of park residence, I had to acknowledge—if only to myself— that I did not know a lot about living in really wild places.

As I became more assimilated to Denali, I learned that when I went anywhere farther than down to the bathroom at C-camp, I had to be aware of the possible presence of wildlife. In May, especially, both bears and moose were often seen close to the park headquarters and housing areas. The reason was that the moose were preparing to calve, and they chose to do that in our area because of its relatively low elevation and resulting slightly warmer weather and thicker brush cover. Bears, newly awake from hibernation and hungry for a protein-rich meal, followed the moose and attempted to relieve them of their new-born calves.

Debbie came home from a day of training about a week after we had arrived at Denali to tell me that she and the other 20 interpreter trainees had seen a bear down at Riley Creek, near the visitor center.

"Was it close?" I asked her.

"It was about 50 feet away," Debbie said. "We were all walking along the Morino Trail when we heard some splashing noises in the creek. When I looked down, I saw this huge, dark brown bear galloping across the creek toward us."

"Were you scared? What did you do?"

"We all started yelling and waving our arms." Debbie demonstrated as she talked. " 'Hey, bear, hey bear!' we shouted. The bear stopped, right in the middle of the creek. And then it turned and took off the other way."

She laughed. "Poor thing, it probably was a lot more scared than we were, with 20 people all shouting at it."

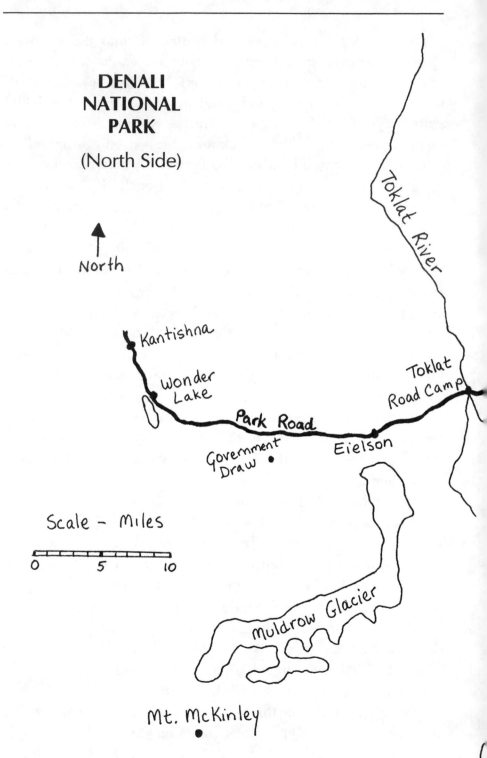

**DENALI
NATIONAL
PARK**

(North Side)

North

Toklat River

Kantishna

Wonder
Lake

Park Road

Toklat
Road Camp

Government
Draw

Eielson

Scale — Miles

0   5   10

Muldrow Glacier

Mt. McKinley

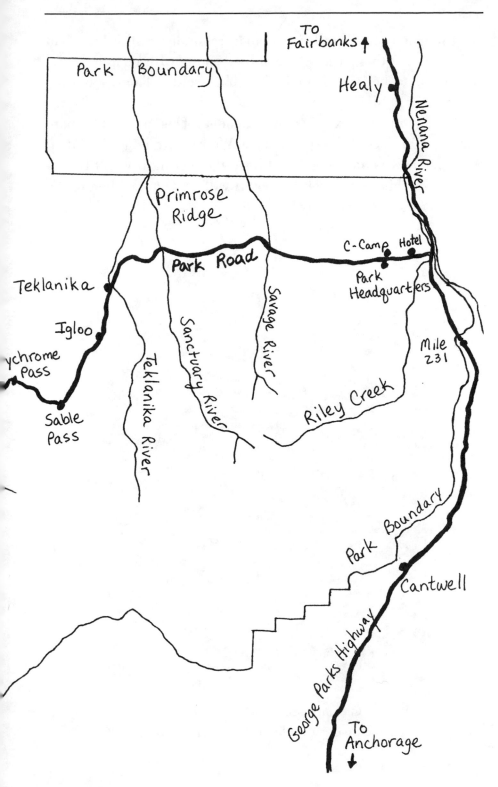

I laughed too. "Well, it's a good reminder, if the bear had forgotten, that this park will soon be teeming with people."

"Hard to believe, isn't it?" Debbie said. "There's no one around now at all."

"Yeah, but you know it will change. This park gets more than 300,000 people every summer. We really ought to enjoy it, as empty as it is now, because I have the feeling it won't be deserted like this very much longer. It will be October before it's again as quiet as it is today."

Glacial streams heavy with silt
cut canyons of relief through the tundra.

As much as I tried to appreciate the open empty spaces, though, I had to admit that I would not really mind the throngs of people; after my experience on the Rock Creek trail, I was leery of the vast wilderness, so full of strange creatures, and I was looking forward to having more of my own species around.

On my twenty-sixth birthday, I boarded an old school bus with the other seasonal Park Service employees, now numbering about 40 including those who had driven up to Denali on the Alcan Highway, to take a tour of the park. The tour was part of a week-long orientation program that we were required to sit through before beginning our jobs. That the park tour fell on my birthday was a really special gift. A bit more savvy to the ways of the wild after a week in Alaska, I was well outfitted for the trip with waterproof boots, gloves, a raincoat and a pair of binoculars for the 50-mile trip into the park.

Under clear and sunny skies, we left park headquarters at 7:00 A.M. The first 12 miles of the Denali Park road were paved, as far as the Savage River. Beyond Savage, the road turned to gravel and snaked over several low passes and across river valleys.

In the morning all the rivers were quite low, though they swelled with spring snow melt by afternoon. The bus followed the road through spruce forests for about 35 miles, then began to climb the steep grade to the top of Sable Pass. By that time, we had collectively spotted ptarmigans, a short eared owl, a jaeger, some moose, Dall sheep, caribou, a harlequin duck, a green winged teal, a marsh hawk and a golden eagle.

At the top of Sable Pass, the vegetation pattern changed. Above the boreal forest, we moved into the realm of tundra. Between Sable and Polychrome Passes, rolling along on a thin strip of gravel surrounded on all sides for as far as I could see with the classic Alaskan postcard scenery of glacial rivers, steep cliffs and mountain upon snow-covered mountain, we saw some tundra-dwelling wildlife: red fox, parky squirrels, hoary marmots, and more sheep.

At the beginning of our ascent of Polychrome Pass, just after crossing the East Fork River, I saw my first grizzly bear. When someone first spotted it below the road on a cliffside, the driver stopped the bus so we could watch it. In an ambling, nonchalant way the bear moved up the cliff and crossed the road ten feet away from the bus. The bear was light colored—almost blonde—and despite its bulk, which I guessed to be 500 pounds, it moved with surprising grace and comfort. The bear embodied power and strength. I could see that it could, if angered, easily have torn me apart. But strangely, the sight of a "griz" so close up had the effect of soothing my fears of the animal. It did not appear to be in the slightest bit interested in the bus or all of us parkies hanging out of the windows clicking our cameras. It simply ambled across the road and off up the hill, digging for roots and eating plants. At one point, the bear pounced on, and caught, a parky squirrel. Calmly, it consumed its midday snack in full view of us on the bus, acting as if we did not exist.

All reported bear attacks in the park, I learned, were a matter of people doing the wrong thing: approaching too closely to take a photo, leaving food out on a tailgate or picnic table, not making noise to alert the bear to their presence. Basically, the bears of Denali wanted nothing to do with the humans, and many of them had never even encountered a human in their lives. Denali was their home; we were only visitors there.

The rule of thumb in wilderness situations involving bears at Denali was this: Never turn your back on a bear. It was I who had to remain aware of the presence of bears in the park. They were not required to remember anything about me.

After lunching at Toklat, the group of us parkies got back on the bus for the three hour return ride to park headquarters. Some were dozing off in the bus seats; everyone had quieted down, lulled by the long ride and the excitement of spotting so much wildlife on the trip out. I leaned my forehead against the window and watched the muddy brush-covered miles of tundra go past until I felt hypnotized by the park's scenery.

I was struck by the fact that although the six million acre park had originally been created because it contained Mt. McKinley, the highest mountain in North America, its true function was as a wildlife sanctuary. Obviously, Mt. McKinley could take care of itself. The frozen slopes of the mountain were in little danger of impact by human beings. But the wildlife needed protection from the encroachment of curious humans who, through their desire to look at the animals, contained the potential to destroy the very thing they came to see.

In Denali, the animals still lived in their own untouched environment; we people, encased in rickety yellow school buses, were the intruders. As an observer, unconnected with the ecosystem outside the window of the bus, I saw that the north was teeming with wildlife, shattering the myth of empty waste-lands in the arctic.

The "food chain" theory I had studied in biology classes was evident in Denali to the point of being elementary. There was one difference from the model I had learned about in school, though. In Denali, humans were not at the top of the food chain. We did not have any power over the wildlife; the best we could do was to leave it alone. Our task, as park rangers, was to attempt to educate park visitors that the park management policy was basically to keep the touch of the human hand from altering the ecosystem. One of the rangers on the bus trip, a returning employee who had conducted an informal tour guide presentation for the rest of us during the journey out to Toklat, said that the park management philosophy could be best summed up in five words.

"Lady, this ain't no zoo!"

As the days of May went by, I watched spring flow over Alaska like lava, bringing the land to life. The crucial factor for the approach of spring was temperature. As soon as the thin, luminous arctic light ceased to be frozen and the entire night slipped by without ice glazing the surface of puddles, spring began. Immediately, plants began making up for lost time. Their development reminded me of time-lapse photography; the exchange of dead sticks for tender green leaves could almost be seen by the naked eye. In the 18 hours of daylight each day of May, vegetation put in two or three days' worth of growth.

Rain showers fell tentatively, but without real seriousness. The moisture in the ground came almost entirely from the melting of the snow and frozen topsoil. The ground underfoot became spongy, mucky, green. Mats of moss thickened and spread. Berry bushes developed bright green leaves and shot toward the sun. Spruce cones dropped to the ground, but did not remain there long; red squirrels snatched them up and chewed them, perching on low spruce branches. The squirrels devoured cones until they were near bursting, and then they tore off to a different tree, screeching "Sick! Sick! Sick!" to me and to the boreal woods.

The sun was deceiving. Though it shined bravely and endlessly, its rays did not bring warmth like that of the desert. But again, the critical point for the growth of plants in the forest was freezing. If the cells of plants did not turn to ice, they grew.

Out the window of my cabin, I saw the line of jagged, snow covered mountains of the Alaska Range. At 11:00 in the evening, weak orange rays of sun created a warm alpenglow of gold on those peaks. The quietness I perceived through the window, looking at that sedate scene, was illusive, for the boreal forest was filled with life and sounds: squirrels chattering, jays and chickadees singing, and the rustle of voles moving about beneath fallen aspen leaves. The black and white spruce forest came to life before my eyes.

Often in those first few weeks in Alaska, I asked myself what I was doing there. I felt like I was in a foreign land.

Hadn't I had everything I needed in Arizona? What had pushed me to leave the clear desert light of the Grand Canyon which I loved so dearly? As the long days of spring passed, I abandoned those questions, becoming completely caught up in the renaissance of new life. Slowly at first, and then more quickly, I began to revel in the midnight sun.

Not because of the Alaskan spring, but along with it, I left the past behind and moved enthusiastically into a completely new phase of my life.

17

❖

Dispatching

Other than my stint at the radios during the high water emergency at the Grand Canyon, I had no experience as a dispatcher prior to the Denali Park job. I had, however, accumulated by that time seven years' worth of experience in answering questions and giving information to national park tourists. It did not take me long to learn the skills of operating the radios, speaking in ten code, and putting together a resource list of phone numbers and people to call in an emergency. Once I became comfortable with the setup of the park communications system, I greatly enjoyed my job as a dispatcher.

I had heard the profession of dispatcher described as "long hours of boredom, punctuated by moments of sheer terror." Although I found little time to be bored because of all my corollary duties, I did find that my adrenaline flowed profusely at those times when I was notified of an emergency somewhere in the park. We had a good number of the usual emergencies which happen anywhere a large number of people are congregated; motor vehicle accidents, heart attacks, broken bones, lost children, and the occasional fire alarm were all incidents I dispatched with calmness and efficiency.

The unusual situations took more imagination and resourcefulness to handle. These events took many hours to resolve and caused me to feel both stressful and intimately involved with Denali Park. They were never explainable in letters to my family in California in one sentence. Occasionally, they were big enough happenings to make the Anchorage newspaper.

The mudslide which occurred while I was dispatching was momentous enough to appear on the front page. It began as rain. In 24 hours, 1.56 inches of rain fell along the Denali Park road. Since it was late July, at the height of the summer tourist season, no one paid the rain much attention. The shuttle buses which carried visitors into the park left as scheduled, every half hour, filled to capacity with people.

At about 5:00 P.M., I was called on the radio by one of the field rangers who was patrolling the road in the Sable Pass area.

"There has been a mudslide," he radioed to me.

"Location?" I asked.

"Mile 44, just past Igloo Creek."

"Is it blocking the road?"

"Affirmative," the ranger shouted. "The slide is 40 feet long and four feet deep. The hillside just collapsed onto the road."

"Any injuries?"

"Negative. I have a bus stopped here. They stopped just a few feet short of the slide. I'm sure more buses will be coming along soon, and it's in a bad spot, on a curve."

"Copy," I acknowledged. "Put out some flares if you can. Send someone up the road to flag down buses. I'll get some equipment out there as soon as I can find some."

I contacted the other rangers on duty in the area and sent them to assist. Those rangers on the park headquarters side of the slide also started out to Igloo Creek to help. Next I called the visitor center, told them of the situation, and advised them to hold all departing buses and stop issuing campground permits for that part of the park.

I notified the Chief of Maintenance at his home a couple blocks from park headquarters. He in turn called out several heavy equipment operators to go out and clear the mud. They were only too happy to assist, as it meant overtime earnings for them.

The rain continued. When the Maintenance Chief arrived at the slide site, he called back in on the radio to inform me that there was no way to get the road cleared for at least several hours.

"How many buses do we have on the other side of the slide?" he asked.

I had been checking with the bus company. "There should be 15 buses," I said. "Approximately 600 people."

"Roger. Eight of them are backed up on the far side of the slide right now. Get some empty buses heading this way from your end, and we'll try to get these folks across the slide."

As the main clearing house for all information on the emergency, I was kept abreast of the situation by those who were on the scene. Some of the hardier occupants of the shuttle buses, those who were wearing appropriate foot gear, walked around below the slide, forded the creek, and got safely to the other side. Others who tried to climb over the hillside above the road ended up covered with mud from head to toe. I sent someone at park headquarters to fetch plastic rain ponchos and blankets to bring to the scene.

The majority of the 600 people stuck behind the mudslide were not dressed to cross it. In high-heeled sandals, polyester pants and baseball caps, the people who had boarded the buses as if on a tour of Europe were not prepared to deal with the mudslide disaster. They were neither willing nor able to cross the roadblock under their own power.

What ensued was a wonderful example of strangers helping strangers. Those who possessed the foot gear and the stamina to cross the swollen creek paired off and made chairs of their clasped hands. They then carried all those people unable to walk across the slide to the safety of the waiting buses on the other side. The evacuation took several hours to complete, but by dusk everybody was safely across the mudslide and headed toward their campgrounds or motels.

Nobody was injured in the ordeal, which made the rescue a success as far as I was concerned. Before the rain stopped, the road had washed out in six places and had to be closed for several days for repairs. It was the first time in almost 20 years that the park road had to be closed during the tourist season. It was that fact which caught the attention of the news media statewide. Reporters called and asked me for information, and one even traveled to Denali to interview some of the people who had been stuck on the other side of the mudslide.

In the next few days, I got many questions from tourists about the road closure. Some were hostile, until I explained—perhaps a bit more graphically than necessary—how the mud had buried the road. Before long I had them all shaking their heads fervently, expressing gratitude that they were not going to be venturing out on that narrow, dangerous road.

The routine emergencies—medical, law enforcement, and traffic related—had routine solutions. I had a flip card file with explicit instructions for all of the commonplace situations. While the intensity of those emergencies was stressful, I at least had a protocol to follow. I learned that imagining the situation in advance, and planning, step by step, what actions I would take, greatly eased my tension when they happened. Aside from once accidentally tripping the park-wide fire siren and setting it to howling in the middle of the night, I made no major mistakes.

I was grateful for the medical experience and training I had acquired at the Grand Canyon, for I was given several opportu-

nities to explain to a frantic caller over the phone how to immo-
bilize a broken bone or stop the bleeding of a wound.

But I had no training in mental illness, and an incident occurred one night which made me yearn for some knowledge of
that problem. A woman who worked at one of the hotels just
outside the park had a history of schizophrenia. I received a
call one evening from a friend of hers who was concerned about
her.

"She didn't show up to work this morning," her friend told
me, "and no one can find her."

"Where are you?" I asked.

"I'm down at the McKinley Park Hotel." The hotel was the
only one located inside park boundaries. "Someone said they
thought they saw her hitchhiking down here this morning."

I obtained a description of the missing woman, and told her
friend to call me back if anything else happened. It was still
early in the evening, with several hours' light yet remaining. I
figured she would show up soon enough; and she did.

The missing girl's friend called me again an hour later.
"Well, I found her," she said. "She walked into the hotel here."

"Is she O.K.?"

"I don't know. She was acting really strange, saying she
heard voices and not making any sense. She said they were
telling her to run. And her eyes were . . ." The friend paused,
searching for the correct words, finding none. "Just wild, I
guess. Panicked. And then, she pulled an eight inch butcher
knife out of her coat. I tried to take it away from her, but she
took off and ran out of the lobby. I don't know where she went.
There's five of us here who know her. We have been trying to
befriend her all summer. We looked for her for awhile, but I
thought I should come back and call you. Maybe you can send
some rangers down to help us look. I don't know what she might
do."

"Did she threaten suicide?"

"She has before, yes."

"Is she on medication?"

"That's the problem, I think. She's fine if she takes her medicine, but she did not take it today. And she told me this morning that she would kill herself before she'd let them take her back to the mental hospital."

"O.K., you stay there for a minute. I'm going to send some rangers down to help you look for her."

I dispatched six rangers, all those I could locate in the area, to search for the sick woman. They went out in groups of two, pairing up with the woman's friends. For several hours they combed the woods around the hotel. They talked among themselves and checked in with me on portable radios, to ensure that they were covering all the areas where she might be.

An hour into the search, one of the rangers called me directly on the radio.

"Did you find her?" I asked quickly.

"Negative," he said, "but I just saw a bear."

Great, I thought. Now we have a woman running around with a knife out there, search parties looking for her, and a bear looking for a meal.

I relayed the message about the bear to all the other search teams, warning them to make a lot of noise as they bush-whacked, so that they would startle neither the woman nor the bear. By three o'clock in the morning, not a trace of the missing woman had been found. The search teams, exhausted, reconvened in the hotel to make a plan for the morning. As they talked, one noticed a shadowy figure slinking through the front door of the hotel.

A ranger said in a low voice over the radio, "I think I see her." Then, there was silence. A couple minutes later, she came back on the radio again.

"The woman ran back out the door, and I am following her. I am going down toward the train depot."

The ranger kept her hand on the radio key, so I could hear all that was said.

She approached the woman. "Hi, my name is Ranger Clare. I'm here to help you. Are you all right?"

There was no answer.

"Here, let me see that knife. Oh, what a nice knife. Can I see it? Here, give it to me . . . that's it. That's a good girl. Can I hold it for a few minutes? Thank you. Where were you tonight? Can you tell me what happened?"

"I don't know," said the voice of the mentally ill woman. "I went for a walk. I don't know what happened, I don't remember. I am just so tired."

"Do you have your pills with you?" Clare asked.

"In my pocket."

"Do you want to take any of them?"

"No, I just want to sleep, just sleep."

"I could use some help now," Clare said into the radio. The other rangers, who by that time had all run down to the train depot, came out of the bushes and helped to lift the sleeping woman and carry her back to the hotel.

By the time I went out of service that evening, it was after 4:00 A.M. and the sky was beginning to brighten. It had been a long, long evening, but I felt satisfied that I had been able to help my co-workers find the woman before the knife or the bear found her and tore her apart.

Besides the radio work, I had the added duties of answering the telephone, responding to written inquiries for park information, calculating park visitor statistics once a month, and filing the law enforcement paperwork. Also, people came into the park headquarters, where the dispatch office was, to obtain special permits to drive on the Denali Park road.

Normally, everyone was expected to take the shuttle bus into the park, but there were some exceptions. Park employees who lived at maintenance camps out along the park road were allowed to drive their private vehicles. Professional photographers who qualified under a complicated application system received permission to drive out. And the small community of gold miners who worked the streams in Kantishna, at the end of the park road beyond Wonder Lake, also were entitled to permits to drive on the road.

The miners were an interesting group of people. Most of them had been mining their claims in Kantishna for many years and resented the stifling regulations the Park Service put on road use. Independent and outspoken, they were often brusque with me and made unreasonable demands for permits. Secretly, I could identify with them, having myself been resentful of the tourists and the ensuing necessity for restrictive rules which I had seen grow to unreasonable proportions during the years I spent in Yosemite. But because I wore the ranger suit, on duty I had to be polite and sympathetic, yet not allow them to bulldoze me into making exceptions to the exceptions in the park road travel policy. The miners and their families tried every trick they could think of to wangle more road travel permits. One was memorable in his approach and his attitude.

The man swaggered into the building one morning while I was on the phone to someone in California. The caller was asking a lot of questions about Denali, so the man had to wait ten minutes or so before he could get my attention. By that time, he was visibly agitated, even though I tried my best to appease him by rolling my eyes as the long distance caller asked me to explain, for the hundredth time that day, why the campground sites could not be reserved a month in advance.

I looked the man over as I walked out of the dispatch office and approached him. He wore big, heavy gold rings on every finger and a chain around his neck which would choke a turkey. I asked which mining claim he was destined for, and he mentioned one which did in fact exist in Kantishna.

"Do you work there?" I asked.

"Hell no," he retorted. "I'm thinking about buying it. But I have to go out and see it first."

"All right," I said, getting out a form. "What type of a vehicle are you driving?"

"It's a bus. A 44 foot bus."

"Oh, no," I said, putting down the pen. "There are over-sized vehicle restrictions. You can't drive that bus on the road except at night."

"Why not?" he roared. "I drive it every place else!"

I sighed. "It's the buses, sir. The shuttle buses. That road is so narrow, two buses can barely squeeze by each other. We don't allow oversize vehicles out there until the shuttle buses are off the road. It is just too dangerous."

"That's ridiculous!" the man shouted. "Don't you know who I am? I'm Bobby Unser, the race car driver!"

"Great. Glad you told me that." I could hardly keep from laughing out loud. A mental image flew through my mind of the Denali Park Road as Indy 500. The man began to pace the room, lambasting the government and the rules and everything, in short, which got in the way of his doing things his own way.

"Sir," I finally said. "Calm down, sir. Now there is nothing you or I can do about the regulations. They can't be changed for you, no matter who you are."

Eventually, he agreed to wait until that evening to drive the road. I was relieved when he finally left, still grumbling about the fact that his famous name did not change his status, as far as the Park Service was concerned. I could not resist shouting after him, as he walked out the door, that the speed limit on the road was 35 miles per hour. I did not think it would do much good. I had seen the way he drove on television.

What he did not realize was that to those of us who lived in national parks, park visitors were like cattle. All of them, presidents and senators and movie stars and sports heroes, melted together in my mind with the fat old ladies and college students from Michigan. My fascination with tourists had long since faded, and jaded by years of living in the parks, I thought of them as bodies only. Another tally on the statistics sheet. Another person who could potentially cause an incident which required ranger response.

In fact, I felt sorry for most of them. They had but a few days to visit the places I knew intimately. I found it becoming more and more difficult to explain to people from the real world what it was like to live in a national park. The scenery and the wildlife and the midnight sun were as foreign to them as these things had been to me during my first week at Denali. Though I knew that a lot of them were genuinely curious about what they saw at the park, somewhere along the line I gradually began to lose my ability to remember how it felt to be new in a park. Living there had become as comfortable to me as Detroit was to them. My explanations and my helpful hints became briefer.

As an insider, I was privy to a great deal of knowledge about what really went on within the park. I heard about the deals made behind closed doors, the favors exchanged through the "good old boy" network of veteran parkies, the occurrences which were carefully swept under the rug.

One of those hush-hush incidents which occurred on my dispatching shift was really too good to keep to myself. It happened in October, after the park area had received several inches of snow and the roads were slippery. A section of the highway between Anchorage and Fairbanks cut through the park's eastern boundary, and it was on a hill on that portion of the highway that Clare, my ranger friend, first discovered that a truck had gone off the road and overturned.

She called it in to me casually, stating that she was going to go look in it to see if there were any people still inside the truck.

When she called back over the radio a few seconds later, I could hardly believe my ears.

"There's no one around," Clare said. "You want to know why? The truck is on its side. I went around the back and looked in the doors, which had been broken open. There were boxes tossed every which way in the back of the truck. They all have that triangle symbol on them. You know—radioactive!"

She gave me the license plate number, and I set about the task of discovering who owned the truck and their whereabouts. I traced it to the University of Alaska, and was finally able to contact a woman in the marine biology department who confirmed that yes, the boxes were radioactive. She assured me that there was nothing to worry about.

"Yeah, that's what they all say," I snapped. "Well, you need to get someone down here to get rid of that truck and its contents."

I was interrupted by a radio call from Clare.

"Got a car coming down the hill," she shouted. "They're sliding sideways. . . . Oh no, they've hit the radioactive truck!"

Fortunately, no injuries resulted from the collision. A few minutes later, another car slid out of control on the icy road and hit the truck a second time. I called the woman at the university again, and told her to please find someone to come get the truck.

My supervisor, the chief ranger, was advised of the situation. He told me to call and report it to whoever was interested in radioactivity.

I thumbed through the Anchorage telephone book and found the number for the Department of Environmental Conservation. A woman answered the phone.

"D.E.C., may I help you?

"I hope so," I said in the most casual voice I could muster. "Could you tell me where to report a nuclear accident?"

A common question from tourists: "Is the mountain out?"

She dropped the phone. After sputtering and stammering, she gave up trying to talk to me and handed me to her supervisor. Calmly, I explained what had happened. He checked with the University and told me the same thing the woman in Fairbanks had said: there was no problem with the broken radioactive boxes.

I remained unconvinced, but with no further instructions from the D.E.C., I was left to just advise Clare to keep the people away from the boxes and set some flares at the top of the hill to avoid any further collisions.

The next morning, the truck was gone. Just like in movies about accidents involving radioactive materials, the owners of the truck had neatly removed the evidence. However, I remained leery for quite a long time after the incident, making it a practice to roll up my window when I drove past that stretch of highway.

Always, always in my park jobs there were the Questions. Denali was no exception. At the Grand Canyon, it had been, "How high are the walls? How deep is the canyon? And what do you do in the winter?" In Denali, "Is the mountain visible?" ranked among the top ten questions. When I was asked that, I radioed out to the Eielson Visitor Center to get the answer. At park headquarters, 85 miles away from the mountain, I had no idea whether or not it was visible when people asked me.

Other questions I found more challenging, because it was difficult to come up with satisfactory answers. Some questions had no answers. For example, many people wanted to know where they could see a moose. There were hundreds of moose living within the boundaries of Denali Park, but I could not at any given moment state the exact location of any of them. Questions such as that were akin to asking somebody, "When will it stop raining?" But the people asked anyway.

Part of the problem was that the majority of the park visitors were from the Lower 48, where things ran on schedules at a split second pace. Even at the other national parks they had visited, events were scheduled: the information booth at Old Faithful predicted the geyser's next eruption to the nearest minute. Compounding the problem was the fact that many of the visitors were on guided tours; the average age of the park visitor to Denali was 53. The "if it's Tuesday, it must be Belgium" mentality that went along with those package tours resulted in questions like the one about the rain.

I did not ever resent the people for being there. What I sincerely wanted to accomplish was the smashing of their fixed ideas about parks and predictability. Denali was like no other place. It was especially dissimilar to the parks Outside. Living in, traveling through, and observing six million acres of sub-arctic wilderness had a profound impact on me. I was dazzled by the lack of human interference with the system. It was this quality I wanted to share.

It was therefore difficult for me to keep my patience when, one day, a man came into the park headquarters to ask about the 90 mile, five hour long bus trip to Wonder Lake.

"Is it worth it?" he asked seriously.

"Is it worth *what*?" I wanted to shout back at him. I wanted to detonate a dynamite blast beneath him so that I might wake him up. I wanted to make him realize that the trip to Wonder Lake was what he traveled 5,000 miles to experience.

But I remained polite. Eight years of national park experience had taught me to think before I spoke.

"Yes, sir," I told him with a smile. "Go out there. It is worth it, believe me."

18

❖

Solstice

The days in Alaska were endless; the sky never darkened. Winter was completely compensated in the northland by the arctic summer light. The atmosphere at latitudes above 60 degrees north was thin, transparent, clear as an unnamed lake. Denali was not quite far enough north to be above the Arctic Circle; yet during the three hours each night when the sun dipped behind the mountains in June, the sky glowed the color of lapis and no stars shone.

On June 21, Alaska was in full summer dress. Vegetation was lush, luxurious, and overwhelmingly green. Tiny tundra wild flowers of every color added splashes of brightness to the endless rolling hills. Mosquitoes, loathsome creatures, thrived, as did the bears, caribou, and sheep.

The Alaska summer screamed at me to shut up and pay attention. And paying attention took all my time; I was unable to close my eyes. I never tired of walking in the boreal forest or the rolling tundra meadows, peering through binoculars at the wildlife and through my close up camera lenses at flowers and lichen until my head throbbed.

The sun never really went away. Light bulbs were redun-

dant at the peak of summer; there was no point in them. The
changing pastels of the sky and the sparkling arctic light provided sufficient illumination.

The energy of the arctic summer infused me with joy.
Bursting with the exuberance siphoned from the hugeness of
the landscape, I walked with a lightness akin to dancing. The
park exceeded my wildest dreams.

Several days before the solstice during my first summer at
Denali, Rob, my sister's high school sweetheart, arrived by
train. Much had changed for both of us since I had seen him
last. After Rob and Christie broke up he had completed college
in San Luis Obispo, then moved back to Los Angeles to work in
the computer field. When he met Jean, the sister of a co-worker,
they fell in love and were married in May of 1984. Rob and
Jean chose to visit Alaska for their honeymoon, and I was
pleased they planned to visit me and Denali during the summer
solstice.

The Park Service in Denali owned and maintained several
rustic log cabins throughout the park. Most were remote and
difficult to reach in the summer; they were used during dog sled
patrol trips in the winter months. Park employees were allowed
to use the cabins in the summer, the only stipulation being that
all supplies were replaced and some firewood was chopped
during the employee's stay.

One of the collateral duties of my dispatch job was to sign
people up for cabin usage. It was no problem, therefore, to put
my own name on the calendar for use of the cabin at Government Draw for the day of the solstice.

Rob and Jean and I boarded the shuttle bus early on the
morning of the 21st of June. They sat together in one seat, and I
sat in the seat in front of them, twisting around to give them a
running commentary. As the bus bounced along the rough
gravel road, I told them stories about the wildlife, park management, and tourists. Rob and Jean asked interested questions

and were genuinely fascinated with the park and Alaska.

Meanwhile, we had a bus driver who thought he was an expert on the park as well. From the minute he opened his mouth, I could tell he was one of those drivers who harbored fantasies of one day becoming a tour guide, because he was repeating with authority every tired rumor ever told about the park. I half expected him to tell the one about the Montana bull shipper. Rob and Jean were not listening to him, but every so often during the first 30 miles of our trip out into the park I caught phrases of the driver's pitch above the groan of the school bus engine, and had to snicker at his rendering of the facts.

We stopped for a ten minute break at Teklanika, derisively known to park employees as "Take-a-leak-a" because it was the first bathroom stop on the trip. As I got back on to the bus, I heard the driver tell several unsuspecting tourists about how a boar had eaten three other bears, bones and all, right here on this road, a few weeks back.

When we had settled back into our seats, Rob asked me if that tale was true.

"Actually," I answered, "he's got it all wrong. I do know the story because I read the case report. What happened was that this mother bear, with two cubs, was out near Toklat when a bear approached them. Boars normally do not have anything to do with other bears, but in May, when they are hungry and just out of hibernation, they have been known to attack their own species.

"So this boar approached the sow. She fought him off. The boar got one of the cubs away from her and swatted it on the back, snapping its spine. The sow fought back. The boar did kill the sow, but the second cub somehow escaped. The boar then partially buried the sow, and just laid on top of her carcass. The cub with the broken back somehow dragged itself up to the road, where it lay for several days. Finally, the Park Service biologists went out there and "dispatched" it—that's their word for shooting it. The reasoning they gave was that it was a traffic hazard. Indeed, that was before the road was closed to private vehicles, and a lot of people drove out there to see the cub and the boar out on the Toklat River bar."

"Did the boar ever eat the sow?" asked Jean.

"No. The boar left the area after a couple days. The biologists figured that the kill was not motivated by hunger so much as it was by jealousy. Boars seem to know that a sow is not interested in them sexually while it has cubs. 'Not tonight, dear, I have a headache' didn't get it, I guess."

We all laughed loudly. Suddenly, I noticed that some other people around us in the back part of the bus were leaning forward, trying to hear what I was saying. With a start, I realized that I had broken a cardinal rule among park employees, one that I learned my first year in Mammoth. Never let on that you work here! It was too late; they began poking me, asking questions and grilling me for inside information.

I knew what was coming. When one man blurted out, "How do you get a job like this?" I had to admit defeat. Rob and Jean thought the questions from the tourists were entertaining. I was a captive of the people in the back few rows of the bus, who were thrilled to have discovered me. Having inadvertently gone public, I surrendered and resigned myself to giving my testimony about the parkie lifestyle until my voice began to go hoarse.

Fortunately, we took a break for half an hour at the Eielson Visitor Center, 65 miles into the park. All the buses stopped there. About half turned around and made the return trip back to headquarters; the rest continued out another 25 miles to Wonder Lake. We went into the visitor center, which was perched on a low tundra hill overlooking the Thoroughfare River and, in the distance, Mount McKinley.

In the summer months, "It," as we park residents fondly referred to McKinley, was visible an average of only one day out of four. Usually, people who made the trip to Eielson Visitor Center gazed out the plate glass window at the front of the visitor center and were told that the mountain would be right there, if it were visible.

When we arrived, only a small part of the north peak of McKinley was visible through the clouds. Rob and Jean and I stood at the window for several minutes, watching the clouds move around in front of the massif. At one moment, we all thought we saw the outline of the snow covered white peak; a moment later, it was again obscured behind the ever-present clouds.

Jean bought a book about the wildlife of Alaska. Rob took some pictures. Before we left the small building, we looked at a chart the Eielson staff kept on the wall near the entrance. It showed, for each day in June, the maximum and minimum temperatures and whether "It" had been visible in the morning, at midday and in the evening. I noticed that the mountain was most often visible in the morning, and that for the past four days, it had not been seen by the Eielson staff at all.

We reboarded the same bus and rode for another couple of miles. The road made several sharp turns and continued out through the uninhabited tundra to the west. Finally, I saw the landmarks I had been looking for: a gravel pit right after a sharp turn to the left, and a small beaver pond on the right. I yelled to the bus driver that we wanted to get off. The bus groaned to a halt in the middle of the narrow dirt road, and we gathered our packs from the back of the bus and leaped out the emergency exit. Away it roared, kicking up dust, leaving the three of us alone in the suddenly quiet high plains of Denali.

We followed the draw for a quarter of a mile, sifting through waist high willow thickets and attempting to avoid the swampy depressions in the hillside. Rob and I spoke loudly to each other, laughing about past experiences we had shared. Jean was silent and walked quite a distance behind us. I had a suspicion that she felt left out; but I had known Rob since I was 13 years old, and I was greatly enjoying his company. I had not realized how much I had desired to see a familiar face until Rob showed up at Denali. He was almost like family to me, and I was, after all, an awfully long way from home.

All of us were acutely aware that we were traveling in bear country. I had heard, and repeated to Rob and Jean, many stories from fellow park employees about bears on the porch of this cabin in past summers. It was for that reason that Rob and I spoke so loudly to each other. The only wildlife we encountered during the hike down the draw, however, was an abundance of mosquitoes.

The draw curved gently to the left. We followed the contour and suddenly came upon the cabin. It was nearly invisible, tucked back against the side of the hill, veiled by out-of-control growth of willow bushes.

The Government Draw cabin was only a couple years old, perfectly constructed and perfectly located. A broad porch in the front afforded a view of the draw and of Gorge Creek down below. We soon discovered that the price of gazing at the view for more than two seconds was that we were eaten alive by the hordes of mosquitoes; our dreamy gazing was thus abruptly cut short. Inside the one room cabin were bunk beds lining one wall and a big wood stove on the opposite side. It was well stocked with food, utensils, cookware, and even a Coleman stove for cooking.

We spent the afternoon and evening exploring the area around the cabin. Down to Gorge Creek we hiked, and over several hills to some large tundra ponds inhabited by beavers. We saw several species of birds and a couple of the resident beavers. An old pile of bear scat was located; but since it was not steaming, we did not become alarmed by its presence. Returning to the cabin, we cooked a dinner of macaroni and cheese and drank some champagne. With vigor, we swatted the mosquitoes which had snuck in when we had had to open the cabin door, and entertained ourselves playing a card game.

Shortly before midnight we put on our hiking boots, smeared a thick layer of bug juice on all visible skin and went outside. Single file, with me in the lead, we crossed the draw and climbed up the steep hillside opposite the cabin to reach the top of a plateau which rose above the surrounding land.

The sun was low in the sky. Spread out before us was the heart of the Alaska Range bathed in the soft orange light of alpenglow. The sky was a rich shade of indigo behind the snow-clad peaks; behind us, the color blended gradually to a brilliant pink the color of fireweed. We stood transfixed by the moment of the solstice.

Rob, Jean Russell and I slap mosquitoes at Government Draw.

"Land of the midnight sun," Jean whispered. "This is incredible."

"Wilderness," Rob added. "Such open space. Such beauty. I never would have believed it if I hadn't seen it myself. This is the best moment of our trip up here. Thank you for bringing us out here, into your world."

"Thank you," I said. "It's special to be able to share this with close friends—both old and new." I smiled at Jean. "I hike alone so often. I spend a lot of time by myself out here, cut off from the rest of the world south of the Alaska Range. I'm glad you can see why I like it here. This is real to me."

"I will always remember the solstice. The way the light strikes those white mountain peaks. . . ." Rob's voice trailed off. Words seemed inadequate to express what we saw, and we three stood in silent wonder for several more minutes.

Eventually, we turned to walk back to the cabin. On top of the plateau, we walked abreast. Awed by the sights and the great silence of the wild tundra, we forgot to make noise. Suddenly, ten feet away from where we walked, there was a flurry of movement. Inadvertently, Jean screamed. I jumped back and yelled, "Hello, bear!" Years of training, beginning with the skit I watched in Mammoth Hot Springs, rendered this greeting automatic.

The caribou had been lying in the willows, resting in the cool evening air. Startled by our noise, he leapt to his feet. For a second he stood his ground and stared right into our eyes. His great antler rack was held proudly high against the deep blue sky. His carriage was dignified; he was at home, and I was acutely aware of being an intruder in his domain. But for that second when our eyes met, I felt, if not his equal, then at least privileged to be a fleeting contemporary in his rugged world.

Without effort, the caribou turned and ran away from us. He moved like water over a smooth stone, hardly expending any effort. He ran with speed and grace, muscles rippling in the midnight sun. In a few seconds, the caribou had disappeared, and we three stood watching where he had run. We were all touched by the magic moment of our rendezvous with the magnificent animal.

The next afternoon, Jean, Rob, and I flagged down a bus as it rattled along the road and caught a ride back to park headquarters. They had to be on their way, so after sleeping one more night on the floor of my cabin in C-camp, they departed for Anchorage on the train.

It was interesting for me, after so many years of living in parks, to once again see the tourist perspective of a "foreign" place. Granted, Rob and Jean did not exactly have a typical tourist experience while they were visiting Denali. It was sunny and warm the entire time they were there, for one thing. Also, they stayed in the cabin down on the draw, rather than camping out in tents and being unable to sleep because every sound and every silence fed the fear that a bear was close by.

But as we had ridden the interminable four hours back over the park road on the bus, their conversation had turned to their eagerness to get back home. Home to them was a world I had long ago rejected without qualms. To them, and to millions like them, a new house with central heating and a king sized waterbed and a brick fireplace and a hot tub in the back yard was the standard. That was what they knew. The wilderness of Alaska was a stupendous diversion, but they never felt that it welcomed them. It was essentially hostile to their way of life.

For the longest time I could not understand why everyone did not choose to live the way I did. The ultimate to me was to have wildness right out the back door, to see fox and moose stroll through my yard, to watch the wildflowers grow up between the cracks on the front porch steps. I loved this in the pinon-juniper forests of northern Arizona as much as I loved it in Denali. To tell the weather by the advance of the clouds, to know without looking at a calendar which phase the moon was in, to smell the moisture in the air and the delicate scent of mountain bluebells: this to me was what life was about. In civilization, for me, that quality was lost. Rob, for all his love of the outdoors, had traded it in when he moved back to Los Angeles. In exchange, he had the familiarity of a neatly trimmed lawn, the security of knowing that a Big Mac was available within 15 minutes of any place, and the safety of creatures like gophers and pigeons and houseflies gracing the terrain.

It was not that I did not like to be clean and warm and comfortable myself. But something always drove me back outside, into the rain and the wind and the wilderness. I was drawn to it; I was unable to turn my back.

The visit from Rob and Jean brought to me the realization that my lifestyle was real to me only. I was unable—and, honestly, I was unwilling—to convince the world that mine was the only way to live. The most I could hope for was that at least some of those city people might some day have the opportunity to glimpse it, as Rob and Jean did, and then to have the sense to appreciate its value.

I was offered a chance to go to the big city just after the solstice. It was the first time I had left the park since I had arrived a month and a half earlier. Deb, a ranger who worked the entrance station and campground desk, invited me to accompany her and "Sheila," her ancient but dependable Volkswagen bug, on the 120 mile trip to Fairbanks. On the way, we must have passed a million aspen trees, tall and white, bushy with green foliage like hippie hair clumped at the apex of their 50 foot trunks. The road roughly paralleled the course of the Nenana River for the first 60 miles; then after it crossed the river at its confluence with the great Tanana River, the route led up over a rolling ridge, from which a view of miles and miles of unpopulated hills and the wide Tanana River valley were visible.

We descended the ridge, and abruptly Fairbanks was upon us. The traffic lights, shopping malls, billboards and radio stations were shocking to me, after having been so long in a place without those hallmarks of civilization. We ate Chinese food for lunch and feasted on 31 Flavors ice cream. After half a day of shopping and driving in circles around the town, Deb and I loaded Sheila's back seat up with groceries from the Safeway and agreed that we had had enough of the city.

Deb grew up in national parks, the daughter of a career Park Service ranger. She had never known any different way of life.

"Didn't you ever wonder what it would be like to live in a city?" I asked her as Sheila coasted loudly down the big grades toward the park.

"The longest time I ever spent in a city was six days," Deb told me. "I went to Los Angeles to visit some relatives. We went to Disneyland and to the beach, but I could not deal with all those people. Everywhere we went there were crowds. My eyes stung from the smog in the air. How did you stand living there?"

"I guess I was used to it," I said. "Once a person is used to having all those people around, it doesn't seem very strange. But also, my family went up to Yosemite every year, so I learned about the wild places. When I found out there were alternatives to city life, I could no longer sit still in Los Angeles. I discovered I could make a living in the places of power. Once in the parks, there was no looking back for me."

"I can imagine!" Deb laughed. "I never even considered another option. I began working in Glacier Park when I was 16, and I have not stopped living in the parks yet."

I had to ask The Question. It was all right for me to ask The Question, though, from one parkie to another. "What do you do in the winter?"

"I work at a ski resort. For several years now I have been teaching cross country skiing at a ranch near Bozeman." Deb chuckled. "You know all those people who come to Denali with

$200 hiking boots, dressed from head to toe in Goretex? Well, they come to the ski resort in the winter. We get doctors, attorneys, C.P.A.s, all kinds of professionals. You should see them in their brand new top-of-the-line ski clothes. They haven't the vaguest idea how to stay warm. After an hour's skiing, they are complaining about the snow and the wind and the cold. Sometimes I wonder why they come at all."

"I think they come for the same reasons we stay. They come to be teased by the wilderness for a couple weeks, perhaps to remind themselves that it is there. Their trip down the river, or into the wilds of Alaska, or whatever, is a once in a lifetime treat. To us, it's a way of life. Sometimes, we even get paid to do it. Isn't it great?"

"It is," Deb sighed. "Frankly, I would not know what else to do."

"It's just as well," I told her. "Cities and television and trying to stay hip in the 1980s are a waste of precious time. It's all pretty phony. This—" I waved my arm at the Alaska Range on the south horizon and the acres of forest surrounding us on all sides, "is real. If they all knew, they'd all be here. I really believe that. The sacrifices we make to live here are small."

"Like driving 120 miles to get an ice cream cone?" Deb laughed. "I don't mind it either. I feel so good when I get back home!"

19

❖

Walking

A national park which had no trails: how could that be? I was thrown off by the prospect of no trails when I first arrived at Denali. A park with no trails was beyond the scope of my experience; in fact, trails had become in my parkie world one of the staples of existence. How was one to get from here to there without those essential arteries? I was baffled at the apparent oversight of park managers in offering an attraction to which there was no obvious access.

I restricted my first explorations of Denali park by foot, therefore, to the few trails which had been constructed around the park headquarters area. The walk from C-camp down to the post office, via the Rock Creek Trail, was, over the months of summer, first a route, then a time trial, and finally a meditative journey for me. I hiked the round trip nearly every day. It took me 40 minutes, give or take a minute or two, to walk it from end to end. Later in the summer, when I had identified and memorized the landmarks, I began to see subtle changes and new arrivals upon the trail. A patch of extraordinarily plump blueberries, a large red squirrel nest in the spruce tree behind the glacier erratic boulder, the track of a fox freshly impressed on the mud: these signs of life stood out against the familiar land-scape of the trail over which I traveled down to fetch news from the outside world in the mornings before my dispatching shift.

I was certain that if I had been an interpreter instead of a dispatcher, I would have been able to give wonderful nature walks along that stretch of Alaskan taiga, for I knew every step of it by rote. I toyed with the idea of offering to give a volunteer program along the Rock Creek Trail during my time off, but soon rejected the inspiration. I hated to see anybody else while I was walking on the trail, and advertising its existence would only encourage the crowds to join me on my solitary morning walks.

The presence of other humans shattered my illusion that I was hiking miles from nowhere. The trail paralleled the high-way and a power line which linked C-camp to the hotel com-plex, so technically it was not even remote. Still, I liked to think of it as 2.4 miles of my own personal ribbon of access to Alaska. I was on speaking terms with the gray jays and squirrels on the Rock Creek Trail, and I knew which trees were sturdy enough to hold my weight while I swung for a moment from their branches.

There were a couple of other maintained trails in the area near park headquarters, most of which were too short to be of much interest to me. The Morino Trail was merely a series of loops which passed from the hotel to the train station, down to the hostel and the backpacker campground, along the river and back up to the hotel. A spur of that trail led across the tracks to the Riley Creek Information Center, and I used that route as a short cut to get to the building. Riley Creek was not called a visitor center, although it functioned as one, because it con-sisted of two double wide trailers, a decor too embarrassing for parkie people to refer to as a visitor center. All the park shuttle buses left from Riley Creek, and campground permits and backcountry use permits were issued from there, so I often had occasion to walk down there. Still I did not consider a stroll on the Morino Trail a real hiking experience; it was merely the shortest distance between two points.

Immediately receiving questions from the tourists about the lack of developed trails in Denali, I began to research the situation. Why the dearth? According to literature printed by the park, the reason no trails had been built was ecological. In a system as delicate as that of the arctic tundra, any trail would encourage hikers to stay on it. The trampling of the tundra by many pairs of boots hastened erosion and ultimate destruction of the vegetation. Therefore, hikers were encouraged to spread out, rather than following each other single file on a hike, so that their impact on the land might be diluted.

When I read that justification, I was filled with joy. After so many years of being told not to step off the marked paths, here was a park management philosophy which encouraged it.

Some controversy had developed among those who advocated various management philosophies in the parks by the 1980s regarding the issue of access. On one side were people who supported difficult access or none at all, placing the challenge for getting into the wilderness squarely on the shoulders of the intrepid and energetic hikers willing to expend great effort in exchange for their breathtaking vistas. In the other corner, spokespeople for the disabled, the elderly and the very young members of society screamed elitism. If national parks were created for the benefit of the many, their argument went, then a way should be found to provide equal access to all groups of visitors.

Before I came to Denali, I had not given much thought to the issue of park access. If anything, I had leaned toward the former position in my viewpoint, fed up by the droves of gawking tourists staring at the Grand Canyon, not understanding its depths. In Denali, however, I became aware of the validity of the demand for access by those unable to walk into the park with two healthy legs.

One of the volunteers who worked in the park both years I was there had no legs. His limbs had been severed below the knees when he was tragically caught beneath the wheels of a freight train. The man, who alternately walked with a prosthesis and rode in a wheelchair, was in Denali for the sole purpose of improving disabled access to the park. He gave interpretive programs and worked at the backcountry desk, but his most important accomplishment was his quiet lobbying to convince park management to bend its rigid rules. Largely through his efforts, at least one bus each day left Riley Creek equipped with a lift for wheelchairs and a specially altered interior which would accommodate the disabled. He also petitioned successfully to ease the method by which people who were physically unable to ride any bus could obtain private vehicle permits to drive the park road.

I used to watch him struggle to get up the steps on the front porch of his cabin in C-camp. I did not offer him any assistance, knowing that he took great pride in his ability to be mobile. I admired his courage and tenacity and was profoundly affected by his one-man effort to create disabled access to Denali where there used to be none.

I became grateful for my own mobility. Young, healthy and able, I only had fear of the unknown and untried standing in the way of my exploration of the park. None of Denali's six million acres was roped off. Except for the occasional bear incident which caused temporary closure of a small section of the park, no restrictions existed on either destination or route for hiking. Backcountry permits were issued according to carrying capacity of each zone. Though the maximum number of people allowed in each backcountry unit was small, the areas were never filled, even on the busiest days of summer. The combination of huge areas and few people brave enough to venture out without a trail into Alaska resulted in near perfect conditions for a hiker craving solitude.

A topographical map was essential equipment for anyone who dared to step off the Denali Park Road. The contour lines on the map indicated the easiest routes over which to travel the land. Though a compass was useless—the magnetic north being many degrees from true north—Mt. McKinley on the horizon served as a wonderfully accurate landmark.

There was another reason that the park shunned the construction of trails, I learned, aside from ecological considerations. Less concrete and more complicated, it was not something that could be explained easily to a tourist on a time schedule, who wanted a pat answer. It was actually a concept that had to be experienced to be understood.

The concept was that we humans had to travel the land of Denali under the same terms as its wildlife traversed it, and for the same reasons.

It was simply the awesome spread of wild lands, mountains and valleys and river beds untouched by human hands that beckoned me. Denali made no concessions to the fears and insecurities of humans. By its staunch presence, trail-less, Denali Park proudly defied civilization. The park's residents, bears and sheep and caribou and moose, moved through it with complete ease, like a breeze moving through spruce branches. I, who also called myself a resident of Denali Park, had to learn to travel it on its own terms.

I stepped out into the park tentatively, willing to try to hike without a planned route but unsure exactly how to go about it. I asked the bus driver to drop me off below the voluptuous curve of Primrose Ridge. After the bus lumbered away from the wide pullout and moved off in a cloud of road dust down the grade to Hogan Creek, I stood looking up at the rise in front of me. The ridge, covered mostly by tundra, sported patches of bare rock. I could see areas where the vegetation did not appear to be very tall, but I was unable to discern anything that resembled a logical route to its summit.

With a shrug I started to climb up the hill. The slope was steeper than it had appeared from the ground. I moved over to my right in an attempt to traverse some less vertical ground, and immediately became mired in a patch of willow which was higher than my head and so tangled that walking proved to be impossible. Forced to retrace my steps, I then tried a route somewhat to the left of my initial attack point. There, the slope steepened to such an extreme that I soon began to feel more like I was executing a technical climb than a stroll on the tundra. Stopping to catch my breath, I looked down at the road. I had achieved almost no altitude, and already I was tiring with the effort of getting up the first hill.

Progress was slow, but as I continued to move upward I began to understand the concept of cross country travel in Alaska. Resistance was least when I followed the natural contours of the land. If I walked on the spine of a hill instead of on its side, the vegetation was sparser. If I opted for a section higher by a foot or two than the land around it, I could avoid stepping in one of the hundreds of hidden water holes. If a stream was large enough to carry boulders, the stream bed provided a highway for me to traverse quickly.

The thought crossed my mind that the animals of the region likely also used those concepts in their wanderings. Without having to consciously think about it, any self-respecting bear would choose the stroll up the river bar over an assault on the tough willow bushes in the steep ravines. I kept a sharp lookout for four-legged fellow travelers on the ridge.

It took me well over an hour to reach the top of Primrose Ridge. Up on the summit, tundra species were dwarfed in size; their leaves were tiny. I had to look closely to see that the variety of lichens, annual greenery and wildflowers was as diverse as that down on the more heavily vegetated lower slopes. I sat on the ridge top and stared for a long time at the scenery laid out below me like a rich tapestry. I saw the section of road I had traveled in the bus that morning, and beyond that I saw the narrow sliver of stream which was the headwaters of the Savage River. Dominating the horizon to the south were the snow covered peaks of the Alaska Range. The distant summit of Mt. McKinley was visible on the edge of the sky.

Although I was on the top of the ridge which carried the name Primrose, I was by no means at the top of the mountains. All around me the land rose to a height much greater than that I had achieved. A quest for the ultimate summit in Alaska suddenly appeared to me to be ridiculous. Unless I was trying to get to the top of McKinley itself, there would always be another mountain higher than the one I was standing on. It would be, I thought, enough to drive me mad.

But only if I was trying to reach that goal. A flash of insight washed over me as I sat on the ridge on that summer afternoon. The reason the dearth of trails in the park had bothered me so much was that it robbed me of a hiking goal. If I were hiking a trail in the woods anywhere else, it would be for the purpose of reaching a lake, or a campsite, or an intersection with another trail. Here, no such goal was available. When I walked into Denali, I was not going anywhere in particular. At some point, halfway through my journey, I would have to turn around and go back to my departure point.

So why hike at all? My standard reason for hiking, to get to someplace, or to be able to say proudly that I hiked a certain number of miles or reached a certain landmark, was invalid in this wilderness with no marked routes. Instead, my reason for hiking had to be merely to experience the joy of the movement itself.

I cultivated the new attitude all summer long, beginning with the hike on Primrose Ridge. I was not, I told myself, there to reach a goal; what I had come to Primrose to accomplish was being done a moment at a time, with every step I took.

Tiny moss campion grows between slabs of Birch Creek Schist.

I suddenly thought of the old folk song about the bear:

The bear went over the mountain, The bear went over the mountain, The bear went over the mountain, To see what he could see. He saw another mountain. . . .

After I ate lunch on the top of Primrose Ridge, I decided to descend the slope on a slightly different course than the one I had followed on the way up. My descent was slow, not so much because of the steep terrain, but because I was fascinated by the tundra life I spotted along the way. Removing my guide to wildflowers from my pack, I tried to identify the flowers at my feet. Some were tiny enough to miss unless I got right down at eye level with them; others were more obvious. Collectively, the tundra wildflowers spanned every color in the rainbow.

Trying to remember all the names of the blooms was like learning a foreign language to me. I said the names out loud; the words felt exotic on my tongue. Pink plume, spring beauty, and monkshood carried descriptive enough names, but the mountain heliotrope, harebell, saxifrage, and moss campion— splashes of bright color hugging the ground, soaking up the arctic sun—had monikers nearly impossible to remember, despite their distinctive appearances. The woolly lousewort, a most beautiful pink flower, had an unfortunately ugly name— memorable, but definitely, in my opinion, not appropriate to its delicate shape and rosy color.

On the curving face of Primrose Ridge, I stopped to rest on a small outcropping of rocks about a third of the way back down. Gradually, I became aware of a slight movement on top of a large rock jutting from the ridge. Stepping slowly and quietly to avoid betraying my presence, I moved closer and peered through my binoculars at the creatures sunning themselves on the rock.

They were hoary marmots. About the size of a football, the marmots looked like a cross between a squirrel and a beaver. Their long silver fur rippled in a slight breeze. The two marmots were not scampering about collecting food and housing materials like squirrels or beavers would have been doing on a warm July day; rather, they appeared to be leisurely taking a siesta, relaxing with no thought about tomorrow on the slope of Primrose Ridge.

Marmots hibernated in the winter, underneath rocks too big and heavy to be moved aside by any of their predators. That explained their apparent lack of enthusiasm for frantic movement so predominant in other species. As I watched the two marmots lazily rolling around on the rock, lethargic and apathetic about my presence, I recalled reading that marmots were one of the few arctic species that mated for life. The minutes flew by uncounted as I continued to spy on the blissful couple languishing in the Alaskan sun.

A hoary marmot sprawls on a ledge near the top of Primrose Ridge.

Many hours after I had left the bus, I finally arrived back down on the road. Standing on its dusty shoulder, I waited only a few minutes for a bus to come by, which I waved down and boarded. I knew I was dirty and smelled of sweat and dank tundra pond water; yet I was not envious of those fresh and clean people on the bus. I had been out on the land, while they had only looked at it through dirty bus windows. I was satisfied with my sojourn to Primrose Ridge. My only goal that day had been to learn something about hiking without trails. Bouncing along toward C-camp in the back of the bus, I was contented that my goal had been reached.

Growing bolder, I took another hike without the benefit of either a trail or a palpable goal to reach the next week. I had mail-ordered some lightweight hiking boots, and when they arrived I decided to give them an immediate field test on the rugged Alaskan wilderness. I left C-camp and walked a short distance to Rock Creek. The stream ran from the Outside Range down past C-camp, crossed under the road, and emptied into Riley Creek, destined for the Nenana, Tanana, and Yukon Rivers. Rock Creek was aptly, if not originally, named, for the broad stream bed was composed entirely of water-rounded boulders and pebbles.

I crossed the creek many times on my journey up the boulder strewn thoroughfare, admiring the fluorescent pink blossoms of river beauty blooming on gravel bars. As I progressed higher up into the headwaters of the creek, I watched the vegetation on the slopes beyond the stream bed change from spruce/aspen taiga to thick stands of willows to, finally, tundra. Hiking with the constraints of neither watch nor timetable, I kept following the creek until I found myself back in a narrow canyon of Birch Creek schist near the creek's source. No vegetation grew in that canyon at all; the shiny, flaky schist, contorted by volcanic action some time in the distant past melted right into the mountain's slopes.

Finally stopping my forward movement, I turned and looked back the way I had come. The bed of the creek twisted snake-like below me, and I could see the tree line where the spruce forest started far below. Suddenly I felt utterly alone. Most of my hiking was done in solitary that summer, not so much because I had no friends to go with as because I chose it that way. I had gone a couple of times on routes with my friend Deb and some of the other rangers, but usually I just left on the spur of the moment with no clear idea of where I was going or when I would return.

Standing at the headwaters of Rock Creek, I looked back down at least three miles' worth of creek bed between me and the civilized world. But the fear of bears and of rain and of those nameless horrors of the wild world had gone out of me, replaced by a joy that knew no bounds. I leapt from rock to rock on my way back down the creek. I was free because there was no trail I had to follow. There was no rule that said I had to turn left here or hike ten more miles before I got to where I was going. And no guide book told me what I would find on my journey. It was there for me to discover in my own way.

Finally, after half a lifetime of searching, I had found what I had been seeking in the power spots of the country. I remembered a line which had been written by the great naturalist John Muir in his book, *Travels In Alaska*, back in 1915: "There can be no happiness in this world or in any other for those who may not be happy here." Joy bubbled from within, nurtured by the stirring of summer wind and bolstered by the free flowing clear water rushing over the stones beneath my feet.

I was no longer dissatisfied with where I was going. In the terms of the wilderness, I was already there, on the journey, en route; and that was the goal. It did not matter whether I changed anything about park management or even if I changed people's perception of the parks. Finally, I knew that I was just there to learn how to travel through it and allow myself to be changed by it. It was that quality, the joy of being alive and un-encumbered, that I so admired in the wildlife of Denali, and it was that quality which I might be able to impart to park visitors —if I could embrace it.

"To see what he could see, to see what he could see," I sang. The aspen leaves quivered in harmony. "The bear went over the mountain to see what he could see." The tumbling wa-ter pounded out a bass line to my melody. "He saw another mountain. . . ." The cloud-shrouded foothills of the Alaska Range glowed on the south horizon. They did not comment on my exuberance, but I did not ask them to sing along. I did not ask them anything. They, and I, possessed the freedom just to be ourselves.

20

❖

Bus Living

It all began with a telephone message. A man called Denali Park one evening wanting to speak to a Brian Kemsley. I looked the name up on the list of employees and told the caller that Brian worked at Toklat, 50 miles from the nearest telephone. I volunteered to copy down a complicated message from the man, who was calling from Oregon, involving something about a job with the Alaska Railroad. I put the message in the box of mail to be taken out to Toklat and thought no more about the incident.

Several days later, a tall, dark haired man with startling blue eyes appeared in the headquarters building and introduced himself to me as Brian.

"Were you the one who took the message for me?" he asked.

"The one about the railroad? Yes, that was me." I wondered what I had done wrong.

"Well, I just wanted to thank you. That was the most clear and complete telephone message I have ever received," he said, smiling.

"Oh," I stammered, "no problem, Brian. I just wrote down

what he said."

"I never get messages like that in Toklat," he told me. "I'm so far out in the boonies that if I ever get a phone message at all, it is always at least two weeks late. Usually, it makes no sense. You know, that kind of a message deserves a hug."

With no warning, Brian embraced me. I liked the way his arms felt, strong and certain, around me. The hug lasted a bit longer than it should have. After he left the building, I sat at my desk staring into space for a while, thinking about the hug I had just received. Could he be interested in more than a thank you? I considered that possibility, but finally decided he was just one of those Thespian types who hugs everybody.

The next week, however, Brian showed up at park head-quarters again. He was with a couple other men, but somehow he managed to send them both on errands so that he could speak to me alone.

Brian looked over at the door through which he had sent his two friends. "I'll get to the point," he said. "Would you like to go out to dinner with me?"

I was caught off guard. Stalling, I asked, "Where?"

"Up in Clear, there is a nice restaurant."

"Where is Clear?"

"About 40 miles north of here. So—do you want to go?" I considered the offer, and could not think of a good reason to refuse Brian's invitation.

"Sure," I told Brian. "How about next Thursday?"

The next Thursday Brian arrived at exactly five minutes past the appointed hour to pick me up at C-camp. He made a nervous joke about being fashionably late; I did not confide to him that I had been ready for an hour. Self consciously I ran a comb through my already combed hair and straightened an imaginary wrinkle in my blouse.

Feeling as inexperienced as a schoolgirl, I wondered if my clothes were right. Briefly I had considered wearing a skirt, but

I decided on pants because, after all, this was the interior of Alaska. Nobody outside of Anchorage on a Saturday night was expected to wear a dress. I noticed immediately that Brian, in new Levis and a button down shirt, had made an effort to dress nicely by adding a wool vest. The vest had ivory buttons and a little metal camel pin on the lapel; the vest looked home made, and it fit Brian's large frame perfectly.

He led me to a white van in the parking lot. As he started out of the lot, I told him that it was a treat for me to get away from C-camp.

"I usually only get out of here on foot or on the shuttle bus," I said.

"You don't have a car?"

"I have a truck, but it's at my sister's house in California. I didn't bring it up here, because I wasn't sure whether I would want to stay in Alaska."

"So this is your first year at Denali?" Brian asked. I knew he was making small talk, but I was glad to have a willing recipient for at least a small portion of my life's story. I had, lately, been spending a lot of time alone.

"My first year, yes. It's my eighth year working in parks, though. I worked in Yellowstone and the Grand Canyon, but I ended up here because I thought Denali would be the ultimate Parkie paradise."

"And is it turning out to be that?"

"In most ways, yes. The ultimate wilderness. The ultimate in open spaces. Some things aren't so great, like the experiment in group living we call C-camp."

Brian's blue eyes twinkled. "I know about that. I lived in C-camp for two summers. I got pretty tired of the parkies discussing brands of hiking boots beneath your window, the earnest conversations about slide show topics in the laundry room—"

"And the way the water scalds you in the shower when

someone flushes a toilet, right?" I joined him in laughter. "How long have you been in Denali?"

"This is my fourth year here. Two seasons in C-camp, two in Toklat. Before that I worked maintenance in Skagway, at Klondike Historical Park."

"What do you do in Toklat?"

"I'm a mechanic, a wrench." Brian held out a large hand so that I could see the grease that was permanently embedded in his fingernails. "But my real love is jewelry. In years past, I made a living as a silversmith selling hippie jewelry. I'd like to get into it again sometime, and try to make a go of it as a real jeweler, setting diamonds and working in gold."

"I took a jewelry class in high school one time," I told him. "It seemed to be a more interesting way to fulfill the art requirement than painting or drawing, which I cannot do. I made a tiger's eye bracelet. But I admit, I wasn't very good at making jewelry."

"You must have some sort of an artistic bent," he observed. "I don't know, I sense that in you."

"Well, it's certainly not any sort of work with my hands. But I consider myself to be a writer. I paint pictures with words. Your speaking of dreams, becoming a jeweler, prompts me to confess my own. And if I could have my dream, I would be a writer living in a cabin in the woods of Alaska."

I suddenly felt foolish, telling my most secret dreams to this man I had just met, about whom I knew almost nothing. I snuck a glance at him, though, and saw no look of alarm on his face. He was nodding; he seemed to understand the yearning I had expressed. Slowly I relaxed, settling back in the van's bucket seat.

"Anyway, for now I am a parkie. I haven't known any other way of life than this for a lot of years. It seems beyond my comprehension to get to the point of living in a house that is my own. Perhaps it will happen some day. Do you own a house?"

"Of sorts," Brian answered. "I live in a bus. My house has wheels, so it goes wherever I go. I am sort of a nomad, moving south in the winter and north to Alaska in the summer."

"Carrying your house with you like a turtle!" I nodded. "How neat! My truck is kind of like that, too. It's too small to live in, but it has a nice camper on the back which I live in when I'm traveling."

"Some of the old hippie ways have stayed with me, I'll admit. The good ideas have stayed. The bad ideas I've let go of over the years."

"How old are you?" I asked suddenly.

"Forty," Brian said without a pause. "And you?"

"Twenty six."

We rode in silence for awhile. There was a fourteen year age gap between us, but no age gap appeared to need bridging. He was in the Navy while I was still in first grade. I had an absurd mental picture of the two of us together twenty years ago, but I did not dwell on it. The subject of our age disparity did not come up again as an issue.

After an hour of driving up the Parks Highway which paralleled the Nenana River, we arrived at the Tamarack Lodge. A large log structure surrounded by black spruce forest, the lodge was decorated on the inside with typical Alaskan props—heads of big game animals and paintings of the northern lights slashing through the sky above a field of snow. Only one or two other couples were dining there; obviously Thursday night was not the busiest of the the week for the Tamarack Lodge.

The steak dinner was delicious. Even more delicious was the comfortable familiarity I felt being near this man, Brian. It was almost as if I had met him somewhere before. I did not mention to him my sense of deja vu, nor did I try to understand it myself. Without effort, we conversed about a wide variety of topics over dinner. No snags developed in the tapestry we began weaving together on that Thursday evening in Clear.

After dinner, we drove in comfortable silence back to the park. It was raining, as usual, as we flew over the highway in the gathering dusk of an Alaskan summer night.

Outside of Healy, the van's windshield wipers suddenly stopped working. Cursing, Brian pulled to the shoulder and got out of the van to fix them. As he lifted the hood to rummage about the engine, I watched a road cut next to the parked van fall, bit of mud by bit, to the ground.

Finally Brian got back into the van and tried the wipers. They worked.

"Sorry," he said as he started the engine. He held out a hand. "No matter what I do, I can't seem to keep from getting greasy."

"Hey," I said, "that's pretty funny. The mechanic's car breaks down on his first date. Did you plan this or what?"

"I wish I had," Brian said, laughing, "but it really was an accident."

I pointed at the road cut. "Look at that. The cliff is falling down. If we sit here much longer, we'll be underneath a mud slide."

"We ought to make it home now—of course, unless I run out of gas." Brian's blue eyes twinkled at our shared joke.

When we got back to C-camp, I invited him into my cabin for a cup of coffee. Fortunately, my roommate was gone for the evening.

I made some coffee and carried the cup over to where he sat at the table. Brian took a sip from the mug, then put it down.

"Come over here," he said. He pulled me down on his lap and kissed me for a long time. Again I had a feeling of warmth and security as he held me in his strong arms. He smelled faintly of grease; it was not an unpleasant scent.

"I really enjoyed the evening," I said, when the kiss was finally over.

"Well, let's do it again. Can I take you out again?"

"Yes," I replied. Once more, I was unable to think of a good reason to say no, nor did I particularly want to say no.

I kept expecting something to go wrong between Brian and me—but nothing did. I traveled on the shuttle bus out to Toklat a couple weeks later to visit him on his own turf. I had no difficulty finding the bus he lived in, a 1959 GMC which he had converted into a very comfortable and compact motor home. I had to laugh at the bumper sticker he had attached to one of the bus's side windows: *Don't laugh, your daughter may be in here.* I wondered what my father would say, but I figured he would probably have approved of the company I was keeping.

I had not intended to make a habit of going to stay at Toklat, but more and more often that summer I found myself climbing off the shuttle bus at the low bridge over the Toklat River. He seldom expected me, because there was no way I could call first to announce my arrival. But he always greeted me with the big smile that warmed my heart, and I felt welcome at the bus every time I came out.

Brian had two sons from a previous marriage who were staying with him at Toklat for the summer. Isaac was 12 and Jed was 9 years old. As I continued to make the trip out to Toklat to see Brian on occasional weekends, I discovered that I had bought myself a package deal: I saw all of them at once. The bus was only 30 feet long; the four of us got to know each other pretty well on the days I spent with the three of them.

After working through their initial jealousy at my taking time away from them and their father, the boys seemed to warm to me and even began to show genuine pleasure whenever I arrived. I took the necessary precautions: each time I rode the bus out for a visit, I packed a plastic bag full of fudge or cookies for the boys. It was either the chocolate or my non-threatening presence which finally won them over; they never told me which.

On sunny days, I talked Brian and the boys into going

hiking with me. The bears were thick in the Toklat area, so we all walked together, shouting and laughing to warn the bears of our presence, as we explored the Toklat River in both directions from the road camp where Brian lived. Along the way, we picked up interesting rocks and identified birds.

In September, after the Toklat road camp was closed down due to snow, Brian came in to park headquarters to work at the mechanic shop there. At that time he moved into my C-camp cabin. My roommate had left the park the day after Labor Day, so we had the little place to ourselves.

With more time to spend together, we made plans and dreamed dreams. As the leaves departed from the trees and the earth began to freeze, we talked of traveling and of finding that cabin in the woods. We even discussed some day leaving the employment of the Park Service and living in our own little world, he as a jeweler and me as a writer, walking in the woods on bright mornings and stacking wood in the stove after supper, to hold the frozen night air at bay. And then, as we lay in bed one October night while a light snow fell outside the cozy cabin, Brian asked me to marry him.

I looked over at Brian's now familiar face, the blue eyes bright with love and the smile that lit up his whole face.

"Hey, Brian?" As soon as I began to speak, I knew I was saying the right thing, because I felt no terror, no sense of making a big mistake.

"Yes?" he locked eyes with mine. I felt he could see behind them, right into my soul.

"My answer is yes," I said. "I would like very much to be your wife."

I kept working at Denali Park until the end of October. By that time, winter had commenced in earnest; the temperature stayed below freezing and a foot of snow had fallen and frozen to the earth. I completed a couple of special projects for the Chief Ranger, then was laid off from my job. The last of the tourists had long before left the park. With the promise of a return to employment in April, I prepared to leave Denali.

Brian, who had been laid off from his job at the beginning of October, converted his van into a mini-motor home, complete with a propane Coleman stove for cooking and an electric heater which glowed orange when plugged in, keeping the inside of the van from freezing. Into wooden boxes he packed food and supplies; on top of the trunks he built a folding bed.

We were ready to travel on the first of November. For the first time in six months, I rode south of the Alaska Range to Anchorage. From there we turned east and then south, following a snow-packed Alcan Highway all the way through western Canada. We arrived in Oregon in time to share Thanksgiving dinner with some of Brian's friends. South we continued to move until we reached Los Angeles, where we spent three weeks with my family.

In the bright sun and smog of that city, I found it difficult to describe Alaska to the family; it almost seemed like a dream. Mostly I just poked photographs in their faces and sat under the orange trees, daydreaming about moose and tundra flowers and the way the wind ruffled a bear's blonde coat like fingers in the land of the midnight sun.

Brian and I returned to Alaska in January. That in itself was insanity, for Alaska in January was not the most desirable place in the world to be. Three months of winter still remained. Employment opportunities were scarce to nonexistent, and the snow-covered land was dark and still. Under the circumstances, however, we saw no other options. For one thing, we had gone through almost all our money. For another thing, the smog and four lane highways and the sheer numbers of people in the Lower 48 were unbearable to us. I had not realized how quickly I had become accustomed to silence and space until I left

Alaska. I yearned to have that back. Brian knew where he wanted to be. After living eight years in Alaska, he already knew what I was just discovering: that once I had been there, my spirit could never really leave it. The state was full of people with stories just like mine. They arrived to work for a summer and stayed for thirty years. Alaska's grip, even locked in the deep freeze of arctic winter, had clamped itself onto my heart.

We rode the ferry on a four-day trip from Seattle to Haines. In Haines we unloaded the van and my truck and drove tandem for 1,000 miles on the white ribbon of highway which led back to the Last Frontier. At Dezadeash Lake in the Yukon, and on the flatlands of Big Delta in interior Alaska, I taught Brian how to cross country ski. We stayed several days in Fairbanks before proceeding down the long straight road to Anchorage. It was too cold in that part of the state for the snow to stick on the road. I was hypnotized by the patterns of millions of tiny white flecks of snow swirling across the pavement in the icy wind. Completely transformed by the season, Alaska was a study of still life in black and white in the dead of winter.

We stayed for several weeks with some friends in Anchorage, waiting for the unemployment checks to begin arriving. Whole days were spent in the city library, or parked at one of the snowbound city parks, playing cards, while we tried to maintain sanity and stay out of the way of our patient hosts. By the first of March, we finally had collected enough unemployment money to live on until my job would start at Denali. Back up the Parks Highway we drove until we reached the place where Brian had left his bus for the winter. It was parked on land belonging to some of his acquaintances from the Park Service maintenance division; they had gone to Australia for the winter. Their long driveway at Mile 231 led back a hundred feet or so, to a clearing surrounded by stunted black spruce trees on the flatlands just south of Denali Park.

We pulled to the shoulder of the highway there, our vehicles hugging snow berms as tall as the van, and attempted to walk up the driveway to the bus. I took a step and immediately sank into snow that reached to my hips.

"This is going to be impossible," I said over my shoulder to Brian. "We have to get a shovel."

"There are a couple of shovels in the bus," Brian said. "You wait here. My legs are longer, I'll go back and get them."

He waded off through the snow while I sat in my car with the engine on to stay warm. A sharp cold wind cut down from the nearby foothills of the Alaska Range. The sky was blue-gray like slate directly overhead, fading into almost pure white to the southwest.

A few minutes later, Brian came back to the cars with two shovels.

"Is everything all right in there?" I asked, indicating the bus, which resembled a hibernating polar bear nestled back among the trees with three feet of snow balanced on its roof.

"It's all just the way I left it. Freezing cold in there. We've got a lot of work to do."

We began to shovel the snow. After an hour of labor which produced a healthy sweat despite the cold wind, we had removed enough snow to pull both our cars into the driveway and to create a narrow trail from there to the bus. At that point, we decided to quit shoveling and hire someone to plow the rest of the driveway out in another day or two. The sun, still hidden behind thick clouds, dove headlong toward the Alaska Range. The sky was just beginning to spit tiny snowflakes as we climbed up the stairwell into the bus.

Behind the driver's seat, one wall of the bus and the back end were lined with windows. The kitchen counter ran almost the length of the passenger side of the bus beneath the windows. There was a wood stove at one end and an icebox at the other. On the driver's side, Brian had built a small jewelry bench, a closet set into the wall, and bunk beds where his kids slept when they stayed with him. In the very back of the bus, the bed was built crosswise, offering a great view of the forest and the Alaska Range.

The space was tiny for two people; we could barely squeeze past each other in the corridor between the bunk beds and the kitchen counter. But it was our own space. After four months of living in the van and then in someone's back bedroom in Anchorage, I was thrilled to have a place I could call my own.

We had few luxuries living in a bus at Mile 231 in the middle of nowhere in interior Alaska. There was, of course, no electricity or running water. For dish water and sponge bath water, we used melted snow; that problem was easy to resolve since a supply awaited our use right outside the door. The abundant supply of snow also served as a cooling agent in the "refrigerator." The pan full of snow had to be changed once a day, but it kept the cooler sufficiently chilly to preserve eggs, cheese, and other perishables. We did not take a chance with items like milk and produce; we drank that sterilized milk which came in a box ("A staple of Bush living," Brian assured me when I expressed doubts about its palatability), and ate a lot of canned vegetables while we were there.

For illumination, we used a kerosene lamp. The bus was set up to run a couple of electric lights off a twelve volt car battery, but we used those lights sparingly. The propane heater also ran on the batteries. Since the heater ran nearly constantly, the batteries petered out every couple days.

We devised a system to keep the batteries in working order. We had four rechargeable car batteries. One would be hooked up for use, while a second, fully charged battery was placed next to the first one to allow for a quick switch when the heater gave out, which invariably happened at three or four o'clock in the morning. The other two batteries we took up to C-camp in the park, 15 miles from where we were camped. Brian had a friend who was living there for the winter, working full time as a heavy equipment operator at Denali. He allowed us to hook our battery charger up on the porch of his cabin.

Every couple days we made a trip to the park, where we rotated the batteries, filled up five gallon water jugs, and occasionally stole a hot shower from the C-camp bathrooms. We also became renegade dumpers, selecting a different garbage bin each time we needed to deposit the frozen contents of our outdoor toilet. The Park Service was unaware that we were using their facilities, but we rationalized that I would be going back to work there soon, and they certainly would not want us to freeze to death waiting for the season to start.

The propane heater was an unreliable source of heat for the bus, and far too wimpy to successfully counteract temperatures which dipped to 20 or 30 below at night. The bus, lacking insulation of any kind, required a greater source of heat to keep it warm. Our main source of heat, therefore, was the wood stove.

The stove was small; when packed full of wood and blazing, it kept the bus toasty warm, but the wood burned off quickly. Maintaining a temperature above freezing in the bus required frequent reloading of the stove. Many nights we went to bed with the fire roaring in the stove and the bus a comfortable, almost too hot, 70 degrees. One of us would awaken at four or five in the morning with a sudden realization that our noses were freezing, and find that the temperature inside the bus had dipped to 10 or 15 degrees. We grudgingly took turns getting out from under the down comforter to rekindle the stove.

There was not a woodpile at the bus. The people who owned the land lived there only during the summer; they had had no need to cut firewood. Even if they had, we would not have felt right about using it. One of the unwritten rules of the Alaska Bush was that one should never use up someone else's woodpile. The first few days we were there, we cut up a couple of downed trees near the bus to fuel the stove. However, that supply quickly dwindled, and we were in a quandary about where to get more wood. Most of the land surrounding our campsite was owned either privately or by native corporations. Cutting wood on park service land was out of the question. We did not own a snow machine which would take us to legal woodcutting areas deep in the woods.

What we did have were bow saws and cross-country skis. Our method of gathering wood utilized those tools. We set out on skis and went half a mile or more back into the woods behind our campsite. We were on native land, but we figured they would not miss a few dead trees carefully culled from their grounds. We were selective in our choices of firewood; green trees were no good, because we did not have the time nor the space to dry them before using. We looked for dead snags, the taller the better. With bow saws, we felled them. I had never before had occasion to cut down a tree; it was satisfying for me to saw and saw through the snags and finally hear that delicious thud when the dead tree went down into three feet of snow. Most of the trees we got were twenty to thirty feet long and six to eight inches in diameter.

After the trees were down, we situated ourselves. I was on the front end and Brian brought up the rear. Under our right arms we tucked the ends of each tree; in our left arms we held both ski poles. And we skied home in this manner. It must have been a comical sight to see us moving silently through the woods carrying our poached trees.

One tree at a time, we hauled the wood back to the bus. It took a full day of sawing and skiing for us to assemble three days' worth of wood. Although it was not an efficient system, we did the best we could with the resources at hand, and we managed to stay supplied with wood the whole time we were living in the bus.

During the portions of days not taken up by chores, I did a lot of skiing. The snowfall had been unusually heavy that year, which made for almost perfect skiing conditions. Right near the bus, I discovered the existence of miles and miles of dog sled trails. Several of the residents in that area just south of McKinley owned dog teams; a couple even ran in the Yukon Quest dog sled race, and many more ran trap lines or simply ran their dogs on pleasure trips. I skied the dog trails often. Packed down by dog feet and sled runners, the trails were as fast as any groomed cross country ski trail in Anchorage and just as much fun. Occasionally I met a dog team on the trail. The teams usually approached silently, so I had to keep a sharp eye out for them. I never had a mishap with them; I managed to get out of their way each time I saw them, and stood quietly by the side of the trail while they passed.

We took our skis along when we made the trips up to Denali for water and battery exchange. The park road was open and kept plowed up to Savage River year round. When we drove up there, we found the rolling tundra slopes nestled in between the Alaska Range and the Outside Range delightful for skiing. Covered by four or more feet of snow, the slopes around Savage were untouched by skis. Many days we set out from the road, and enjoyed hours of exploring cross country and flying down gentle slopes into bowls of powder.

Daylight lasted until seven or eight o'clock in the evening and the weather was often sunny. The daytime temperature soared to 20 or 25 degrees; conditions for skiing were absolutely perfect. Choices of destination were limited only by our stamina and chore schedule in the six million acre wilderness of Denali.

The bears were in hibernation, but most of the other wildlife was out and about. Skiing through the land around Savage River, I saw pure white ptarmigans with feathers on their feet. Tracks in the snow told tales of foxes chasing and sometimes catching the hardy white birds. Moose were very common also. Concerned mostly with finding enough willow branches to eat, the moose never bothered me, scarcely looking up as I skied silently through their territory.

In the evenings, chores completed, Brian and I enjoyed each other's company. Often we played cards or read books, sitting next to the wood stove at the front of the bus. One problem immediately emerged after we moved into the bus: Brian owned only one chair. We dealt with this problem by playing six rounds of Yahtzee each night right after dinner. Whoever had the highest score at the end of six rounds won the right to sit in the chair for the following day. The loser was relegated to an overturned five gallon bucket with a pillow on top of it.

Isolated as we were from other people, Brian and I had plenty of time during the six weeks we spent camping in the bus at Mile 231 for reflection. We had been through a lot of experiences together during our travels earlier that winter; the stress of traveling and camping and talking out our next move had solidified our relationship. In Brian I had found everything I wanted in a companion. He was my best friend, pal, skiing partner, fellow renegade and soul mate.

After our evening game of Yahtzee and relaxing, we stoked up the fire in the wood stove and went to bed early. Snuggled beneath flannel sheets and a thick down comforter in the back of the old bus, I felt more secure and content than I had ever been before in my life.

Out the back windows of the bus, when the moon was full, we could see the spruce trees. Outlined against the white snow, they waited patiently in the cold night air for the coming of summer.

When the moon was not out, on clear nights I could see a million stars spread out across the sky. The northern lights danced silently on the pinpoints of starlight. Most of the time the aurora was comprised of jagged white bands; occasionally, the white was complimented by greenish swatches of swaying light. Once we saw blood red lights set the frozen sky on fire.

The aurora was indescribable, unpaintable, impossible to

put to music. I knew that, yet I, like all others who saw the aurora, was moved to try to explain to a piece of paper the feelings the lights evoked in me on cold spring nights deep in the interior of Alaska.

Supine, frozen
Like a downed log on the permafrost
I stay, eyes unable to turn,
Riveted on the light show
Superimposed on the North Star.
Anticipating symmetry,
I see none.
Following those waves of light
Undulating, creeping, dashing madly free-form.
Anticipating drumrolls of sound,
I hear none.
Straining my ears for melodies
Entwined in cold silence.
Anticipating nothing,
I feel something intangible
In the powerful void of black sky.
The midnight aurora again
Flows without preamble,
Sliding like water across an icebound pond
Coming from nowhere,
Consisting of nothing I can touch.
Glowing elusive particles
Of luminous rainbow dust.

Often when I awoke in the middle of the night, nose tingling with cold which reminded me that the stove needed to be fed, I lay for a moment before arising and watched the mysterious lights of the aurora pass across the wide sky. I did not understand the northern lights any better than I understood the ways of the Alaskan wildlife or the change of seasons. I could not explain my Alaska, but I knew that I loved it. Finally, I had come home.

21

❖❖

Wildlife

When I left park headquarters at midnight after my shift, the sun had retreated behind the Outside Range but enough light remained for me to see where I was going without the use of a flashlight. I walked up the road and turned on a short path which led to the one room cabin serving as the district ranger's office. With a jingle I removed a set of keys from my pocket to open the cabin door.

Suddenly, in the brush to my left I saw movement—lots of it. The noise made by the keys had startled a moose which was browsing five feet from where I stood. She emerged from the thick vegetation and for a moment stood nose to nose with me. I was startled by her massive body; her shoulder towered two feet above my head.

Quickly I turned around and race-walked back down the road, the moose trotting two paces behind me. My heart pounded with fear as she chased me. Several hundred yards down the road, I slowed and glanced back over my shoulder. The moose had abandoned her pursuit of me, but held her ground firmly in the middle of the road, eyeing me with distrust. As I watched, a baby moose calf, no more than two weeks old, emerged from the willow bushes near the cabin and started toward its mother on wobbly legs.

Besides serving as a backdrop for Mt. McKinley, the highest mountain in North America, Denali Park was best known for its abundance of wildlife. The park was home to relatively large populations of "The Big Four": grizzly bears, Dall sheep, moose and caribou—as well as 33 other species of mammals. At the same time, summer visitation in the park topped 400,000 people in the 1985 season. Given the high density of both humans and wildlife in Denali, it was inevitable that man and beast would occasionally cross paths.

Wildlife-related incidents made up the bulk of the calls I dispatched when I worked at Denali for two seasons. The most common complaint I received was that a "moose jam" had developed, usually in the vicinity of the hotel or the train depot. A motorist, noticing a moose near the road, would stop to photograph it. Others driving past would also stop to see what the first person was looking at. They, too, exited their cars to get a closer look at the moose. Before long, cars were double and triple parked on the narrow road. Invariably the moose, nervous around humans, ambled away from the road. The tourists followed it like children following the ice cream truck, leaving their vehicles to block traffic going in both directions on the park road.

At about that time, I received a call from a hotel or railroad employee advising me of the moose jam. I then dispatched a ranger to the scene, where he or she would contact the people and urge them to stop pursuit of the moose and return to their vehicles. Usually the ranger ended up giving an informal talk to the gathered tourists about the wild nature of the animals in the park and the dangers of approaching them—the standard "This ain't no zoo, lady" routine. Despite our efforts to educate people about keeping their distance, the moose jam calls came in regularly, a couple of times a week.

Wildlife thrives in the spectacular scenery near Polychrome Pass.

The park road that snaked over passes and around hairpin turns for 90 miles through the heart of Denali was the site of human/animal encounters far less often than other heavily traveled roads in Alaska. The main reason for the lack of wildlife fatalities on the park road was that most of the summer traffic on the road was shuttle and tour buses which were driven by people experienced in watching for wildlife. Passengers on the buses were also straining to glimpse animals along the road. With forty pairs of eyes scanning the road, it was almost impossible for a bus driver to miss noticing the presence of an animal blocking the bus's passage.

The situation changed, however, after Labor Day. When the shuttle buses ceased running, the entire length of the park road was thrown open to private vehicle travel. If the weather was good and no early snowfall prohibited travel, half the population of Alaska showed up the week after Labor Day to drive the road.

In the fall of 1984, weather and road conditions after the buses stopped running were perfect for travel all the way to Wonder Lake. During a two day period just after the road was opened, a record 1,100 vehicles made the trip out into the park.

Dispatching was hectic that weekend; a carnival atmosphere prevailed in Denali Park. I received reports of moose jams, bear jams and caribou being chased down the road for miles. I sent one ranger to investigate a report of vehicles leapfrogging along Sable Pass, preventing a bear from crossing the road. Another ranger called in to report that he had cited some people in a four wheel drive vehicle for doing doughnuts on the tundra. Campers set up tents in turnouts from Savage to Igloo Canyon, and people in several locations were reported to be feeding potato chips to every bold parky squirrel in sight.

Before the weekend was over, tragedy struck. A magnificent Dall ram with a full curl horn crossed the road at Hogan Creek at the wrong time. A motorist came around the corner too fast and struck and mortally wounded the sheep. The accident was reported by another traveler who happened upon the scene and discovered the wounded ram beside the road; the person who hit it never did confess.

As a result of the ram incident and others that weekend, the park put into effect the following year a week-long delay in the opening of the road. Postponing the opening of the road to private vehicles until the middle of September almost guaranteed that a heavy snowfall would close all but the first 30 miles, dampening the enthusiasm of those who wanted to drive their cars into the park.

After that change was made, the park never again had 1,100 cars on the road at the same time, doubtlessly to the great relief of the wildlife that had survived the "wild weekend" of 1984.

I witnessed the demise of a moose on the park road one night in October, after a recent snowstorm had left the road icy and slick. Usually, I walked the quarter mile from the dispatch office to C-camp, but because the road was so icy that night, Clare stopped in and offered to give me a ride up to my cabin. We pulled out onto the road and started to drive the short distance to C-camp.

Rounding a wide turn, Clare's patrol car headlights illuminated some movement at the side of the road.

"What is that?" she exclaimed.

I strained to make out the dark shapes heaving violently in the ditch. "It's a bear!" I shouted. "A bear that's on a kill. Is it on another bear?"

"I can't see," Clare replied. "I'll turn around."

We pulled into the C-camp driveway and Clare made a quick U-turn. Returning to the area, she aimed the headlights directly at the bear.

We both saw in an instant what was happening. A full grown moose lay in the ditch, apparently dead. Its foreleg was broken and was nearly severed at the joint. The bear, a large and well fed grizzly, was busily tearing the moose apart.

Quickly Clare drove me back up to C-camp. "Tell everyone to stay in their cabins," she instructed me. "I will get Ken and some of the others to go get rid of that bear." Frightened by the idea that a bear with a taste of warm blood on its tongue was so near to the cluster of C-camp cabins, I asked Brian to accompany me to knock on each cabin door and warn my co-workers about the danger. Without saying anything, Brian slipped a handgun into his pocket. I was not about to protest his action.

Meanwhile, Clare and four other rangers went back to the

battle site. Because the kill was so near C-camp and presented a danger to its residents, they decided that the dead moose needed to be removed from the area. They shot their rifles into the air to temporarily scare the bear away from the moose carcass. Quickly, they loaded the moose into the back of a truck and took it several miles up the road, away from the residential area.

I had mixed feelings about that decision. Certainly I did not feel comfortable knowing that a bear was eating a moose a stone's throw away from my cabin; but the idea of an angry bear looking for the dinner it had earned was even less appealing. We did not, however, see the bear in the C-camp area again after that night.

Early the next morning, I went outside to look for tracks. In the fresh snow, the prints left by the animals told the whole story to me clearly.

From the maintenance shop above C-camp, I found two sets of moose tracks, indicating that a full grown moose and a baby moose calf had been running for their lives. The tracks, as well as a large set of bear paw prints, led past my cabin, and down through C-camp. The three sets of tracks approached the icy road. At the road was the kill site. It appeared that the mother moose leapt from the woods onto the road, slid and fell, snapping one of her spindly legs. Unable to get up, she fell prey to the bear.

I found one set of tracks leading away from the site of the moose's demise: those of the calf. It had apparently escaped almost certain death at the jaws of the bear, because of its mother's unfortunate slip.

Fate seemed cruel for many of the Denali animals. But unless a violent episode of killing occurred in close proximity to the people who lived in or visited the park, managers insisted on letting nature run its course. While I felt sorry for the individual animals that fell victim to a natural death, in time I began to understand the overall picture.

Eat or be eaten: that was the rule. The strong survived, and the weak became food for the strong. I learned that fate was not cruel, nor was it unjust. It just was, and none of the animals questioned it. Systematically, I began to weed out anthropomorphic thoughts from my head. I, too, learned to accept the law of the land.

One day in June, I had the opportunity to go out on the park road in a private vehicle. I was invited to accompany Rick, a Park Service interpreter whose avocation was photography. He had been successful enough at selling his wildlife photos to qualify for a road driving permit. The permit was for him and his vehicle; nothing in the rules prevented him from taking along an amateur photographer for company. I eagerly accepted Rick's invitation to spend a day on the park road, searching for wildlife.

I carried four lenses, a tripod, and plenty of film. Rick came by my C-camp cabin at 7:00 in the morning to pick me up. As we drove out of the parking lot and made a right turn on the park road, I asked him about his photography.

"Is it just a hobby for you, or what?" I knew that to obtain a professional photographer's permit to drive the park road, Rick would have had to sell several photographs, to prove that he was serious about the art.

"It's a lot more than a hobby," he replied. "I started out doing it for fun, but it has gotten to the point where I spend every minute of my free time taking pictures and sorting slides."

"Where have you sold your photos?" I was curious about the professional photography business. "Do you just mail them in, or does somebody ask you for them?"

"I had an agent for awhile. I sent hundreds of photos at a time to this place. Perhaps you've heard of it—Third Eye Pho-

tography. That method is a lot easier, because they take care of
the business end, finding markets for your shots. But, it doesn't
pay as well as when I do all that work myself. Anyway, to answer your question, I've had pictures in *Alaska Magazine*, on
calendars, in *Ranger Rick Magazine*, and in several books. I
have been pretty successful at it, if I say so myself."

"Would you like to do that full time at some point in the
future?" I asked.

"Yes, of course. But you know, it's hard to make a living as
a wildlife photographer in Alaska. There are so many of us.
Some day, I'd like to publish a book of photographs. But for
now, I'm still working as a ranger."

I took a deep breath. "Well, Rick, I hope I'm not alienating
you by saying this, but surely you've heard it before. Don't you
think that being a park employee gives you an unfair advantage
over the other people who travel up here to photograph wildlife
for a week or two in the fall? I mean, you're here all the time.
You go out and take pictures every day. Do they resent you at
all?"

"I suppose they do." Rick surprised me by not reacting de-
fensively to my comment. "The thing is, I work for a living. I
give slide shows and nature walks to tourists, and tell them
about the sled dogs three times a day. I am careful never to take
any pictures while I am on duty, in uniform. If I happen to live
here, then what I do on my free time is my own choice. I prefer
not to think that I am making a profit off the park. No, the way I
look at it, I am using my art to further the education of people
about Alaskan wildlife. Does that make sense to you?"

"It does." I was impressed by Rick's sense of purpose.
"So—" I indicated the tundra beyond the truck's windows,
"where do we stop first?"

"Wherever we see animals. We are not on a time schedule
today. We'll just go until we see something worth stopping for."

The first thing we found, along Hogan Creek, about a mile

east of the Sanctuary River, was an injured moose calf. The calf
had two puncture wounds, about an inch apart, on its lower
back. One of the wounds cut clear to the bone. Rick said that
the injuries looked like the work of a bear. The poor calf was
not long for this world; unable to stand up, it lay huddled help-
lessly, shivering and wet next to the road.

As we stood looking into the frightened eyes of the calf, a
ranger pulled up. We told him what we had observed. He radioed back to park headquarters with the information.

On the advice of park biologists, we threw a blanket over
the calf, picked it up and moved it across the road and into
some willows. Up a hill several hundred yards away, a cow
moose—probably the mother—looked down at us with interest.
But she did not go near the injured calf. After watching for an
hour, we acknowledged that the scene was not likely to change.
Finally, Rick and I decided to continue on along the road,
leaving the calf to its fate.

Near Teklanika, we saw three bull moose, sporting velvet
covered antlers already a foot long. Then, near Igloo, Rick
pointed out a fox den.

"How did you know it was there?" I asked him, puzzled. I
would never have been able to pick the fox den out on the
rough, rock-strewn hillside.

"I told you I spend a lot of time out here," Rick replied as
he set up his spotting scope. "People think that wildlife photographers just go out for an afternoon, shoot a couple rolls of film,
and then go home and wait for the money to roll in. But really, I
spend a lot more time just observing the animals than I do taking pictures of them."

I looked through the spotting scope after he positioned it in
the direction of the fox den. There, lying in front of the den, I
saw a red fox asleep.

"Funny, I did not see that fox before. Do they sleep all
day?"

Caribou are constantly harassed by mosquitoes and other insects.

"No, they just nap, like dogs," Rick said. "They might be seen hunting, or taking naps, at any time of the day or night."

We continued on over Sable Pass and down to the East Fork River. Two golden eagles soared overhead. They used their large tails like rudders to control their glides. We climbed a hill above the river, set up the spotting scope again, and glassed for a wolf den. The den was about eight miles away from where we were standing, but Rick's scope was powerful. He peered through it for what seemed like forever. I began to get impatient for my turn, when he exclaimed, "There!" and pulled me to the scope.

I looked, and saw the first wolf I had ever laid eyes on. It was white, with thick fur; its body shape reminded me vaguely of a German shepherd. I was excited about the sighting of the elusive animal.

"Can we get closer to them?" I asked.

"Afraid not," said Rick, ever patient. "It is too easy to disturb a wolf. If they even get the inkling that there are humans nearby, wolves will abandon their dens. They have even been known to leave pups behind in their panic to get away from the human scent. No, my philosophy is to wait for them to come closer to me. They do, sometimes. Not today. We'll let them be."

The mother bear and her cub linger quite close to the park road.

I was disappointed, but had to admit that Rick's ethics were sound. Along the Toklat River bar, many caribou—bulls, cows, and calves—were traveling. Some were bedded down in the tundra, while a few stood guard watching for wolves. Others were spread out in small groups of two or three, foraging for lichen, which Rick told me was their staple food.

"In the next couple of weeks, these caribou will begin to consolidate," he said as we drove slowly past the herds. "They will then move to the south side of the Alaska Range, through the pass."

"They're always moving, aren't they?" I commented. "Seems that they hardly stay still, even when they are lying down."

"Yes, caribou are restless. The mosquitoes torture them, and a blow fly that breeds in their noses drive them crazy. They have to keep moving, or the insects will eat them alive."

We had heard from some people up on Polychrome Pass, returning from Eielson Visitor Center, that there had been a sow with a cub hanging around near Stony Creek. So rather than stopping to watch the caribou, Rick and I decided to continue on up the road a few miles to see if we could find the bears. The two bears appeared in front of us after we rounded a curve at the creek. They were foraging for roots along the side of the road.

At least, the mother was foraging. The cub was just following along, leaping and running under its mother's huge legs. We parked the car and watched the two bears for a couple of hours. The sow moved randomly from one place to the next, digging for peavine. The pair slid down a snow bank, wandered up another ravine and crossed the road.

After an hour, the cub seemed to tire. It flopped down in the dwarf willow and began to squeal. Mother bear ignored her cub for a time. Then finally, she gave in, rolled over onto her back, and allowed the cub to climb on her and nurse. Once the cub was satisfied, the sow rolled back over and went to sleep. Hers was not a deep sleep, though; every few minutes she lifted her head up and looked around, checking for predators.

The cub was dark brown, with a white ring around its neck. Rick explained to me in a whisper that many cubs had a ring like that when they were born, but they lost it by the time they were a year old. The mother bear was very blonde. When the wind blew through her coat, though, I could see the dark colored fur underneath. It gave the appearance of a frosted bear, like a woman who had bleached her hair several months ago.

Wildflowers were abundantly distributed in bright splotches of color. All the colors were vivid: green, green tundra, blue sky spotted with white clouds, red and orange patches of lichen on the rocks, and flowers of white, yellow, purple and pink.

Finally, reluctantly, Rick and I decided it was time to head back to C-camp. I had taken eight rolls of pictures, but I had gained from the trip more than what was contained in my camera. A quiet peace moved over me as I sat in the truck while Rick drove expertly over the narrow dirt road back to park headquarters. The animals of Denali were all in their places, and things were right with the world.

22

Bear Maulings

I was able to ski on the hills around Savage River until mid May because the snowfall during the winter of 1985 had been unusually heavy and winter lingered late. The ice went out on the Nenana River on the 12th of May; I drove to work on six inches of new snow on Mothers Day.

Finally the snow began to melt. Nature's timetable clashed with that of the Park Service and the early summer visitors to the park. One complaint I heard often during the opening weeks of the 1985 tourist season was that the road was not yet open. Usually by Memorial Day, or the first week of June at the latest, road maintenance crews had the park road cleared, graded, and ready for travel to Wonder Lake. That year, it was almost solstice before the road was in driveable condition, much to the frustration of that never-ending stream of tourists who had come all the way to Alaska to see Denali Park.

The late spring had another effect on park visitors that year. What happened was attributed to the elements—Denali Park being the wilderness that it was—no more than that. But no allowance for variations in the seasonal timetable was made by the thousands of people who showed up at the park beginning on Memorial Day weekend. As a result, Denali was on the front page of the Anchorage newspaper after two different bears attacked humans in incidents which occurred less than 24 hours apart. Bear attacks were big news in any part of Alaska because they happened so infrequently. Even bigger was the news that the maulings took place in a park where the number of previous bear attacks could be counted on the fingers of both hands, in a national park where no bear had ever killed a person.

Encounters between bears and people were common in the park. The Division of Resource Management kept statistics on what they termed "bear incidents." Not all sightings were considered incidents. If a group of hikers at Stony Hill walked over a rise and saw a mother and cub a quarter mile away, digging for roots, theirs would not be termed an incident. If, however, the group approached the bears until the mother raised her head, stood on her hind feet, or charged them, they could legitimately report an incident.

The presence of bears in camp was also considered an incident. Park biologists were always interested in the bear's behavior in a camp: specifically, did it attempt to obtain food? Was it successful in its quest? They kept close tabs on the bears that caused minor inconveniences for campers, such as a tent ripped to shreds or a backpack larceny. The biologists tried to deter the bears from getting the idea fixed in their minds that people equaled a free handout. Attempting to prevent the Denali bears from meeting the same fate as the Yellowstone bears, park biologists had developed, and were experimenting with, several strategies to deter the bears from becoming unnaturally interested in humans.

One practice employed routinely for all users of Denali's backcountry was the issuance of "bear-resistant food containers." The cylindrical tubes, constructed of sturdy plastic, could be opened at one end by twisting a coin in a slot; they were, however, nearly impossible to get into using only the hands—even if the hands happened to possess three inch long claws.

When the park began issuing the food containers, everyone called them "bear-proof." Then, a wily bear managed to get one open. After that, a memo went around instructing park employees to refer to the tubes as "bear-resistant." Although there was not a repeat of the dexterous bear's performance after that, I secretly thought calling them resistant was a good idea. The phrase "bear-proof" sounded too certain, too guaranteed. A trip into Denali's backcountry, I knew, was always made on the wilderness's terms. Always there had to be that seed of doubt, the sneaking suspicion that there perhaps might be a chance that anyone who went in there might not come back. I was fond of telling people, when they gave me a nervous look, that there was no assurance of security. Denali's backcountry was not for the faint hearted. If calling the containers bear-resistant helped dispel the myth of guaranteed safety, I was happy to use that phrase, along with an ominous description of the one bear that the container, indeed, could not resist.

It was exactly that kind of human-centered attitude of people who wanted to be promised that they would only see bears when they were safely aboard a bus, that I tried to smash. In my small way, I tried to speak for the bears, who were not doing anything wrong. The bears had the right to go anywhere they wanted to go within the park. I was able to spot the fear a mile away: the quivering lip, the wrinkle of a brow across a smooth, tanned forehead, and always the question: "But what do we do if we see a bear?"

Every piece of literature handed out by the Park Service gave practical advice about proper behavior during a bear encounter. The lines most memorable to me were those which understated the obvious:

IF A BEAR TURNS SIDEWAYS AND SHOWS YOU ITS PROFILE, IT IS TRYING TO SHOW YOU THAT IT IS LARGER THAN YOU ARE.

A grizzly bear forages for roots along the Denali Park road.

WHEN A BEAR SNAPS ITS JAWS AND MAKES WOOFING SOUNDS, THIS IS YOUR INVITATION TO LEAVE.

An argument made frequently—and often, by Alaskans— was that it was insane for the Park Service to prohibit firearms in Denali's backcountry. The party line on firearms was this: Denali was preserved for the protection of its wildlife, including the griz. Shooting the wildlife was not a part of the Denali experience. Therefore, hikers in the backcountry were to enter at their own risk, weaponless, to face the possibility of encountering bears without killing on their minds.

The inevitable response to the party line was: "But what if it is charging me? What if I have to defend myself?" I gave a lot of thought to that dilemma, but in the end I had to philosophically align myself with the party line of the Park Service. Taking of bears in defense of life or property (DLP) was legal everywhere else in Alaska. And the number of DLP bears taken every year was quite high. I felt that the bears ought to have a refuge.

Besides, there was the inarguable statistic that a bear had never killed a human in Denali. Almost every charge made by a bear was a bluff. In the cases where a human, charged by a bear, ended up injured, the person was found to have made one of two errors. Either she had come much too close to the bear, or else she had turned tail and run.

"When you run from a bear, you become prey!" How often I repeated those words. Other common sense rules I repeated to potential hikers in the park were to make noise while they walked, to look ahead of where they were going, and to never, ever, get between a sow and her cubs.

Usually the only park visitors who had occasion to find themselves near a bear were the backcountry users. This group was almost always contacted by a backcountry ranger before commencing their trip and given the information about what to do in a bear encounter. Those who did not ask, or to whom it did not occur that they might find themselves eyeball to eyeball with an irate sow grizzly, were the ones who stayed near the hotel and on the bus and inside the visitor center. Therefore, bear/human encounters were fairly uncommon at Denali, and when they happened, they were mostly without adverse results for either the person or the bear.

The monkey wrench in June 1985 was the late snowfall. Routinely in May, before the snow melted at higher elevations, and again in October, when the tundra froze up, moose came down into the Riley Creek Valley and other low lying areas. In the fall they came for the remnants of a willow branch meal, long after the leaves had shed from the willows above 2,000 feet. Their spring migration to the valleys was for the purpose of bearing their calves in an area slightly warmer, with denser underbrush, covered with less snow—in short, a safer area.

Every spring the bears came down to the valleys to feed on moose calves and to await the thaw of the tundra. Ravenous after six months of hibernation, the bears in the spring were fierce and aggressive. What usually happened was that park employees, forewarned of the semiannual bear migration, took extra precautions to avoid running into bears during the couple of weeks they were around, chasing moose through C-camp and across the front porch of the hotel. By the time the summer tourists began to arrive at Denali en masse, the tundra was free from the iron grip of winter; moose calves had learned to run away, and the bears had returned to the more remote areas of the park.

But because of the delayed spring in 1985, the moose dropped their calves later than usual. Bears stayed around in the low lying areas, waiting for their moose calf meals, and when the throngs began to arrive and complain about the road not being open to Wonder Lake, the bears were still hanging around.

The first incident took place several hundred yards from the train station. A young woman from Holland and her male companion had arrived at the park by train, and were walking on the tracks to get to the youth hostel. The hostel was an unused Alaska Railroad car parked on a side track, a five minute walk from the train station. In a normal year, it was a very safe place to walk.

As the two followed the train tracks toward the hostel, they heard a noise in the bushes. Suddenly, a bear emerged and ran directly toward them. The woman turned and ran; her companion dove into the bushes. The bear, which was most likely chasing a moose, was diverted by the movement of the Dutch woman; since she was trying to run away, the bear concluded: "Prey." She tripped and fell. Almost instantly the bear was on her. Its teeth sank into her derriere, her thigh, and her foot.

The whole incident probably took place in less than five seconds. What happened next was that the Alaska Railroad train, from which the Dutch woman had just disembarked, got underway. The sound of its whistle blowing startled the bear. Abandoning its effort to gnaw on the woman's hind quarters, the bear immediately ran off, leaving her screaming beside the railroad tracks.

The victim did not need to be hospitalized. She sustained some puncture wounds on the back of her leg and her buttocks, as well as a sprained ankle. The bear's teeth had torn a hole in her jeans, which she proudly patched with a miniature Alaska flag. The next day she was seen lounging around in the hotel lobby, telling her story to many interested park visitors.

Her incident was unusual only in that it occurred so near civilization; in all other respects it was unremarkable. Anyone who ran from a bear was bound to get chased. She became more a celebrity than a casualty. The press might have only run a paragraph or two on page 16 about the incident, if it had not been followed by another, more serious, attack less than 24 hours later.

The victim of the second attack was also a young woman. This one, from Minnesota, was in Alaska visiting her sister, who worked for Alaska State Parks near Fairbanks. The mistake made by the Minnesota woman was not in running from a bear; it was in surprising one.

I was on duty, dispatching, the evening it happened. A station wagon pulled up in front of park headquarters. A college-age man jumped out of the vehicle and tore in through the front door.

"Quick!" he shouted. "She's been mauled by a bear!

Help!"

"Who? Where is she?" I ran to the door where he stood, out of breath.

"She's in the car. She's all bloody. Get help!"

"You stay right there with her," I said. I threw a first aid kit at him. "Stop the bleeding. Apply pressure to the wounds. I'll call the ambulance."

I called on the radio and found Clare down in the ambulance building, restocking bandages. She came up with the ambulance and began treating the mauled woman. Meanwhile, the resource management biologists, having heard the news, appeared and swarmed around the car in no time, all asking the question: "What happened?"

They continued to interview the woman there and on the long ride to the Fairbanks hospital, where she stayed for a week recuperating from the bear bites in her legs and buttocks. She too became a hero when the press got wind of the story; her picture was on the front page of the Fairbanks paper.

For all the hullabaloo, the story itself was predictable enough to be boring. She had been walking, alone and nearly silently, on a trail near the Savage campground 12 miles up the road from Park Headquarters, when she had stepped into the midst of a bear family.

To a mother bear, the cardinal sin was for a human to stand between her and her cubs. When the unfortunate woman saw that there were little bears to her right and a large one to her left, she knew she was in trouble. She tried to yell and wave her arms, but the sow bear attacked her anyway.

She tried to run to a tree. The mother bear, acting in defense of her triplet cubs, knocked the woman to the ground. After taking several bites on choice portions of the woman's anatomy, the bear retreated a few steps. The woman got up and again tried to run to the tree. The bear attacked again and took a few more bites.

Her screams reached the ears of a couple of men who were walking along the road, only a few yards away. The men burst through the bushes and diverted the bear's attention from the woman for a moment, long enough for her to get up and successfully climb a spindly spruce tree. Reunited with her cubs and frightened by the yells of the two men, the bear gathered up her cubs and took off. Her rescuers brought the victim in to park headquarters, where I encountered them in their station wagon.

The Alaska papers were full of bear stories for several days after word of the double bear maulings got out. The most entertaining of the half dozen articles which were written about the attacks began like this: "Bears. Big, grouchy, hungry brown bears. They've surrounded the hotel, the railway station, the youth hostel. They've been killing young moose in and around the campgrounds. And they've bitten two women. . . ." The tone of the *Anchorage Daily News* article reflected the hysteria voiced by many of the Denali park visitors.

Dutifully, park biologists hunted for the two suspect bears; however, since at least eight different bears had been reported in the park headquarters area, their chances of pinpointing the two which had attacked were slim. Consensus was that the bears in both situations had reacted in a very bear-like manner, doing what came naturally when they were startled and then fled from. Mostly, the hunt was a show put on for that outraged section of the public which always demanded the bears be destroyed after two women were "savagely" attacked in two days.

After an acceptable amount of time passed, the biologists issued a press release stating that they were unable to locate the suspect bears; however, the park was still suitable for human visitation. Just don't run away from a bear, the statement said. Respect them. They live on this land, not us. This ain't no zoo, lady.

Indeed, the bears themselves, by whatever means of communication they utilized, seemed to pass the message among themselves to keep their heads down. The tundra had finally shaken off the icy grip of winter, and the toothpick legs of moose calves had become sturdy. So the bears dematerialized from the civilized areas and reappeared where they were supposed to be, within view of a good 200 millimeter lens poked out the window of a shuttle bus.

The bear furor died down and the crowds increased as the summer solstice approached. Publicity received by the park surrounding the two bear incidents ultimately added fresh information to our endless speeches about bear awareness. The victims of the attacks became textbook cases about what not to do when a bear appears.

Into my ninth season as a parkie, I knew the speech well enough to recite it in my sleep. Never turn your back on a bear. I appreciated the addition of a couple of real stories with which to illustrate the moral graphically.

23

❖

The Search
In Sanctuary

$\mathbf{G}$reta was first reported over-
due by her friend Bryan, who lived in Healy. Bryan called the
park on a Thursday afternoon. I pulled out the form we used to
take down information on missing persons, and dutifully questioned Bryan about Greta's destination, her clothing, her outdoor survival skills, and her state of mind.

"She was supposed to be back last night," Bryan told me.
"When she didn't show up, we gave her another day, thinking
she might have simply changed her plans. It's not like her to
make a change in a backpacking itinerary, but we gave her the
benefit of the doubt."

"Where was she going and who was she with?" I asked mechanically. So far, I was not very concerned about the missing
woman.

"She was going up on Primrose Ridge. She was not with
anybody. She is an experienced backpacker; last summer she
taught classes in survival and outdoor skills. Greta is no novice
hiker, even though she's only 20 years old."

Bryan described Greta's blue Lowe backpack and state of the art camping and foul weather gear. He kept repeating that it was so unlike her not to show up at the appointed time.

"What was her state of mind when you last saw her?" It was a difficult question, very personal, but one I had to ask, in order to establish the level of concern the park would adopt in looking for her.

"Oh, no problem," Bryan said quickly. "Greta is an old friend of my wife's and mine. She came up to attend our wedding, which was last weekend. She had never been to Alaska before, and she was excited about her planned hike. She was so eager to see some of Alaska's backcountry."

After I finished taking information from Bryan and made a promise to call him back when the park had decided on what action to take, I called my friend and fellow ranger, Clare, on the radio and asked her to stop by the dispatch office. I related the information Bryan had given me to her when she arrived.

"I don't know," I said in conclusion. "Chances are that she will show up. It sounds like she knew what she was getting into, solo hiking. But still, all her outdoors experience was in California. This is Alaska at the end of August. Quite a difference from the Sierra Trail, where you know someone will show up to come to your aid within an hour or two. Maybe we had better check it out."

Clare hesitated. "I think so too. It seems strange that she is this late. Didn't you say she had reservations for the Friday train to Anchorage?"

"She did," I answered, "and if she is like Bryan described her, she wouldn't miss her train without a really good reason."

"Let me call Norm," Clare said. She dialed the number of her supervisor. After repeating an abbreviated version of the report, she listened for a minute.

"You don't think so?" she said into the phone. "I know, it probably isn't, but . . ." Another pause. "No, I think I should go. Really, if only because her friends are so concerned. If we find her right away, it will look really good for the park."

Clare listened awhile longer. Then she said to Norm, "Well, if you want to leave the decision up to me, I'm going. I'll get a couple of people and run up to the top of Primrose Ridge before dark. O.K. Bye."

I was already walking back to the other phone when Clare hung up hers. "Who do you want?" I asked her.

"Get Dave and Joe and Deb. Have them meet me in ten minutes at the rescue cache."

The four rangers assembled quickly and drove out to Primrose, just past the Savage River Campground, about 17 miles from Park Headquarters. Each of them carried a hand-held radio to call in their locations and, hopefully, the news that they had found Greta.

Meanwhile, I made some quick checks. I obtained from the backcountry desk the information off Greta's camping permit about her intended route. I also checked with the train and the airline on which she had been scheduled to depart, to make sure she hadn't already left the area. No one had a record of Greta as a passenger. Her pre-purchased tickets remained unused.

Clare and the other rangers climbed the steep slopes of Primrose Ridge and checked the Savage River Canyon. Finding no trace of the missing woman, they returned to Park Headquarters after dark. I called Bryan, told him of the unsuccessful hasty search the rangers had made, and asked him to come in and speak with them later in the evening. I also called Norm and my boss, the Chief Ranger, to brief them on the situation and request that they attend the late evening meeting also.

When everyone assembled, we exchanged what little information we had. Her hiking route had been from the Savage River up to the top of Primrose Ridge. Greta had then planned to traverse the ridge, camp the second night at Sanctuary River, then hike out to the road on the third day.

Dave, the backcountry ranger, said he was the one who had issued Greta her permit. "I spoke with her for quite a while about the trip. She seemed to know what she was doing. I gave her the usual spiel about bears, and she did take a bear-resistant food container with her. I also told her that passage through the Sanctuary River Canyon was difficult. She thought she could do it. But she seemed to be sensible about the whole thing; she said that if she encountered problems with that route, she would go around it and come back down the face of Primrose Ridge."

"What kind of weather forecast are we looking at?" asked the Chief Ranger.

"The weather service says it's going to get stormy," I said. "It's been foggy and raining a little this afternoon, with snow falling on the ridge tops. We are supposed to get some more snow by tomorrow, and temperatures in the 30s. Not too good. How was it up there today, Clare?"

"Like you said, snow. A couple inches about halfway up the ridge. More on top. Looks like winter is coming."

After more discussion, we decided on a plan. The following morning, at first light, eight teams of two would cover the entire area between the Savage and Sanctuary Rivers. Surely, we told each other, we would find Greta, perhaps injured or in a makeshift shelter, but alive. Besides the ground searchers, we planned to put up a helicopter, weather permitting, to search from the air for Greta's blue backpack, which would stand out against the background of gold and crimson tundra.

I was in the office dispatching for 12 hours straight the next day. The teams went out and checked all the likely routes without finding anything. Via radio, they reported their locations and areas searched; these I carefully recorded. The helicopter had been able to fly only two hours, due to the rain and lack of visibility; it, too, had been unable to locate Greta. At the end of the second day, I advised all the search parties to make camp and be ready to start searching again in the morning. Meanwhile, at the Chief Ranger's direction, I called several more rangers and instructed them to prepare to join the search in the morning.

On the third day, the weather improved. Although still cool, typical August weather, the clouds had lifted and visibility was greatly improved. The helicopter got out to the search area even before the new teams of searchers had assembled and been briefed.

Shortly after they began flying the Sanctuary River drainage, the spotter on the helicopter called on the radio.

"We've spotted the backpack," he said.

"Location?"

"In the middle of the Sanctuary River."

His response gave me the creeps. "Do you see the missing subject?" I asked.

"Negative, negative," the spotter said. "We will attempt to land near the river and investigate."

Other search teams, hearing the transmission, radioed that they were also proceeding to the Sanctuary River. I sat on the edge of my chair; it seemed to take forever for them to land the helicopter on a flat piece of ground and hike a half mile down to the river. Finally the spotter called me again.

"Dispatch, this is 232. We have recovered the blue Lowe backpack from the river. No sign of Greta. We will be searching the shoreline."

I had been to the Sanctuary River in the area near where the searchers had found the backpack. A typical Interior river, the Sanctuary's origin was a glacier in the Alaska Range. It flowed lazily across broad gravel beds in a braided channel for a number of miles before its icy waters reached the canyon. Although less traveled than its sister canyon, the Savage River Canyon to the east, Sanctuary Canyon was similar in appearance. The river cut through layers of Birch Creek Schist to form a steep, dark canyon through which travel was difficult. The water rushed over slick boulders and small waterfalls, increasing in velocity as it flowed north toward the Yukon River. The canyon was about two miles long. At its foot, the landscape opened up to a wide tundra-covered valley and the river, free of the confining walls of Birch Creek Schist, spread out into braided channels again and continued its leisurely journey north. The location of Greta's backpack was at the lower end of the canyon, about three miles from the park road.

Searchers gathered in the Sanctuary River area and spread out to look for clues. The backpack was flown in to park headquarters, and all the items inside of it were examined in hopes that a clue to Greta's whereabouts might be gleaned.

Among the items in the backpack was a diary. We used a hair drier to dry it out, after which the writing of the missing woman was readable. The last entry had been made on Monday, the second day of Greta's solo hike. She wrote of the beauty of the tundra at the height of its autumn display of gold and red. She commented on a bear she had viewed from a distance and some Dall sheep which she had approached and photographed.

Greta had written her last entry while stopping for lunch on the west end of Primrose Ridge, before she made the descent to the Sanctuary River. In her words there was no indication that she did not intend to follow her planned itinerary, no statement which could be construed as a reason for her disappearance. From her notes, she appeared to be a normal, well adjusted 20 year old woman having the time of her life on her first solo hike in Alaska's wilderness.

She was not much different from me, I could not help thinking. How many times had I gone on a day hike on Primrose Ridge or at Stony Hill or up the Toklat or Savage River, without leaving so much as a note stating my intended destination? I suspected that Greta had been falsely confident in her abilities as an outdoorswoman; yet I knew I held the same illusions she did. In the wilderness I had always felt safe, singing at the top of my lungs to ward off bears and stopping frequently to photograph the flowers and tundra with a close up lens.

Never during my own solo hikes had I considered what I would do if I became injured or got into serious trouble. I assumed that because I knew about the cause and symptoms of hypothermia, for example, I would be able to avoid succumbing to it. Because I understood that the bears had first claim to the land and I was the visitor, I did not think I could get into a situation of becoming a bear's prey. Despite lifelong awareness of the power of the wilderness, I had never seriously considered the consequences of solo hiking in the park. Being a resident of Denali, I had acquired an attitude of immunity to the natural hazards of Alaska and the outdoors. As I looked through her notes, I saw that Greta had possessed the same attitude: she was there to revel in it, not to ponder the dangers.

After three days of intensive ground and air searching, the fact that none of the searchers had found anything except the abandoned backpack alarmed the Chief Ranger. On the fourth day, he ordered more search teams into the field; the number of ground troops reached 60 people. He also requested the assistance of a volunteer search and rescue group out of Anchorage. Eight of their members were flown to the park, accompanied by two bloodhounds trained to track missing people. A C-130 plane was summoned to fly search patterns over the canyon; two helicopters were sent to the area as well.

The weather turned bad again. Aircraft could hardly see to fly in and out of the base camp established by the search teams above the Sanctuary river. I was playing air traffic controller as well as ranger dispatcher. Once the bloodhounds were able to get in, their handlers let them smell some of Greta's clothing, then set them loose on the bank of the river.

The dogs both followed a scent up river, into the canyon.

Several hundred yards into the canyon, the dogs either lost the scent or were physically unable to proceed further. The fact that both bloodhounds had initially located Greta's scent on the riverbank established that she had been there. Although the handlers dragged the dogs through the alder bushes and over the tundra for a mile in every direction from the river, the dogs were unable to pick up the scent anywhere else.

At noon on Sunday, a spotter on one of the helicopters reported that he saw a bear about a mile west of the Sanctuary River. The bear, he said, was feeding on something.

"Oh my God," I murmured to myself. Over the radio, I asked, "Can you fly over again and get a closer look?"

The helicopter did so, and reported back a little later, much to everyone's relief: "The bear is feeding on a caribou carcass."

Radio communications between the different search teams and me were poor. Our radio repeater was on the top of Mt. Healy; deep in the canyon at Sanctuary many of the searchers were unable to hit the repeater. Finally, one ranger was flown to the top of the west end of Primrose Ridge, almost directly above the canyon. From there she served the vital function of human repeater, linking the search command headquarters with the crews at the river. After two days she lost her voice, but nevertheless continued to croak into the radio repeating faithfully every word that was said.

At the end of the fourth day, all of us at headquarters met and brainstormed about possible locations for Greta. The atmosphere of that meeting was tense and desperate. I had been on 12 hour shifts for four days in a row; some of the others had been there 16 or 18 hours each day. We were all weary, bone tired and stressed out, running on an adrenaline that was becoming more and more difficult to summon as the search dragged on without results. Where was Greta? We were fresh out of answers. Finally, after checking in with the base camp at the Sanctuary River to assure that all the search teams were

present and in good physical shape, we went home, planning to
return at six the next morning.

That night I had a dream. I dreamed that Greta was alive.
She approached me slowly, without moving her legs, as if she
was floating. Her soft brown hair framed a young, pretty face.
Her eyes were bright and her legs, clad in hiking shorts and
knee socks, glowed with a summer tan. She moved close until
she was standing opposite me, and she put a slim but muscular
arm out to me. Her grip on my shoulder was firm, self assured.

"I'm all right," Greta said in a soft voice. Her smile
sparkled like a path of moonlight on the ocean. "Thank you for
searching for me. I am doing fine now and appreciate all the
effort you have made to find me. I'm feeling really good today."

I awoke with a jerk when my alarm went off. As I drove on
two inches of new snow through the darkness to the park, I was
unable to shake the memory of Greta in my dream. I had a
feeling of foreboding. I thought I could guess what had happened to the vibrant 20 year old woman who had marveled at
the colors of the tundra on Primrose Ridge.

The fifth day of the search was clear and cold. Again the
helicopters and the fixed wing plane flew up and down the
Sanctuary drainage, and again the search teams split up and
called in their locations to me via the human repeater on top of
the ridge.

At about 11:00 in the morning, I heard a broken transmission on the radio. I was certain I heard someone down in the
canyon say the word, "body." I called for silence over the air
and queried the ranger on the ridge: "Repeat, repeat last
transmission." The next words she spoke seemed deafening
against the hollow silence of the dispatch office. Rangers involved in the planning end of the search gathered at the door of
my office to listen. No one was looking at anyone else; all eyes
were glued to the speaker from which the human repeater's
voice was coming.

"The body has been located, repeat, body located," the ranger said.

"Where?" My voice was no louder than a whisper.

"The helicopter spotted it in the river, half a mile upstream from where the backpack was found. They are recovering the body now."

"Ten-four, copy that," I said, and went limp. All of a sudden, it was over. The intensity which had kept me alert, writing down every radio message, making phone calls, directing searchers, drained out of me.

I opened the window in the dispatch office. Cold autumn air blew in and hit my face like a slap. Tears were rolling down my cheeks. I could not stop them. My stomach felt as if I had swallowed a baseball. The body was found; the search was over. The finality of it felt like the cold air, stinging and real.

Later, I learned that they found Greta's body wedged underneath a large boulder in the Sanctuary River. The force of the water held her under; she had probably drowned quickly and had not felt much pain.

Theories were expounded about what had occurred in the final minutes of Greta's life. The consensus finally agreed upon by most of the searchers was a scenario like this:

The woman had descended Primrose Ridge and reached the river. With her backpack on, she had attempted to ford the thigh-deep water of the river. Because of her unfamiliarity with the technique of fording a glacial river, or perhaps because she simply lost her footing in the swift, icy water, Greta probably fell into the water, losing her backpack. She crawled back out of the river to the bank on the east side, leaving her pack where it lay.

Her next actions were most likely influenced by almost instantaneous onset of hypothermia. Rather than attempting to retrieve her pack with its survival gear and food, Greta had apparently decided she needed to get out to the road immediately.

Her mind, affected by the cold, might have been unable to reason that a three mile hike upriver through the canyon would have been a challenging route for a hiker in good condition, and it certainly was not a route she could complete in her present state, wet and cold.

So Greta went ahead into the unforgiving Birch Creek Schist of the canyon. Did she slip and fall into the swift waters of the river? Did she lose consciousness and lie for a while on a sharp granite boulder before gravity finally pushed her to a watery grave? No one would ever know for sure.

We rangers had all expended our best efforts to find Greta. Until the last moment, each of us secretly harbored a hope that she might have somehow survived. When her body was finally found and retrieved, we all finished up our paperwork and quietly went home.

I felt empathy for Greta because I knew that but for the grace of the Great Spirit, it could as well have been me who ended up tucked under a granite boulder in the Sanctuary River Canyon. But, as her mother later wrote in a thank you note to the Denali Park staff, there was some comfort in the fact that Greta died doing what she loved best.

"She loved the wilderness," the letter said. "If she had chosen it herself, she would not have wanted to die any other way. She died as she lived, with the natural world as her companion. We believe that she was happy to the end."

A more fitting epitaph, I thought, I could not have chosen for myself.

24

❖

Autumn

Even before Labor Day Weekend, a carpet of snow settled on the Denali Park road, so we had to close it during the holiday. As usual, the complaints about restricted access and the inconvenient quirks of the park weather patterns flooded in to the dispatch office telephone. The people insinuated that it was my fault personally that their trip had been "ruined" by the early snowfall.

It did no good to suggest that they search for some moose to photograph, or to point out the brilliance of color in a landscape of scarlet and gold foliage peeking out from beneath the new snow. They wanted to get to Wonder Lake, damn it, and why couldn't they just go out there and drive the road?

I could not help them. The lectures I automatically gave about how they were visiting the park on its own terms, etc., etc., lacked conviction. In my ninth year of working in national parks, I sensed the futility in trying to explain the seasons, the rhythm of the land, to its hurried visitors. After all that time, it still was difficult to express what I knew: we small humans were incapable of wielding our power on the power spots of the continent which had been designated national parks. Although people with vision had felt the power of these places sufficiently to declare them preserved, the very act of declaring a place a power spot, too sacred to bulldoze, attracted to it people who were incapable of acknowledging that power.

The mandate of the National Park Service, as set forth in the Antiquities Act of 1916, succinctly summarized the basic conflict. The Park Service's mission was to "preserve and protect for the enjoyment of future generations." I understood, from years of watching the people flock to the parks and listening to their unreasonable expectations for access, that "preserve and protect" was the polar opposite of "enjoyment." The Park Service was saddled with the chore of working at the same time toward those two opposite ends.

Unrestricted access meant destruction of the very quality the parks were created to keep intact. Yet without access to the parks, people could not discover the beauty within their boundaries. It was a knotty problem without a simple solution. Edward Abbey once proposed building a giant parking lot ten miles from each park. From there, he suggested, those who were willing to make the effort and endure the hardship could reach the park on its own terms. Those who refused or chose not to walk in could go to the Cinema Dome and watch movies about the park experience. The elitist attitude implied in Abbey's proposal did not appeal to me; surely the Park Service could be more flexible and understanding than that. But if the only alternative was an escalator down the Kaibab Trail or a tramway to Wonder Lake, I feared for the life of the parks.

Undaunted by the reality of an impossible mandate, the Park Service people, including myself, continued to stumble from one small conflict to the next, making apologies here for inconveniences and writing tickets over there for resource violations. We acted as if a resolution to the basic problem was forthcoming. If everybody who worked for the Park Service had been perfectly honest about it, though, we would all have had to

admit that no matter how many management plans we wrote and
no matter how many times we changed permit systems and road
quotas and backcountry zones, there was no way we could ever
devise a method to preserve the land in order for people to use
it.

The fact that the preservation/use problem presented an un-
solvable, existential dilemma never caused many Park Service
employees to quit their jobs and turn to, say, welding or bank
management. At least, not the permanent employees. As long as
they were guaranteed a permanent job, they stuck around for
years trying to unravel the unravelable knot. And meanwhile,
they reaped the benefits of living in the parks.

The seasonal employees, however, usually burned out after
a number of years of rangering, and went on to do other things.
Dedicated as I was to the parks, after a decade of putting my
heart and soul into preservation and education and use regula-
tion, only to be laid off at season's end, I began to question my
continued presence in the parks.

In my ninth year as a parkie, I cared a little less about
whether people knew if the mountain's true name was McKinley
or Denali. A weariness set in that rendered me less sympathetic
than I had been in the past when I fielded another complaint
from a tourist who was unable to secure a seat on the bus.

It was not that the parks had changed; the change was completely within me. In all the years of working and living and
playing in the most majestic spots in North America, I had been
searching for something. I looked for a purpose to my life; I
wanted to make a difference. I had by that time nine years'
worth of mementos which told me I had made some difference:
poems written on napkins, a couple of letters of appreciation
from park visitors whom I had assisted, clippings quoting me in
newspapers and magazines, and a certificate honoring my special achievement during the Colorado River high water emergency. I had received many verbal thank yous over the phone

and in person. But these things had never been enough for me; I wanted more. I wanted a card of gratitude from the parks themselves.

I spent all my time trying to make an impression on the parks. Though they did become a part of me, I finally had to acknowledge that they continued to exist whether I was there or not.

I could not exactly place my finger on the moment when my concern and empathy for the plight of the tourists changed to an attitude that they deserved what they got for trying to fight the forces of nature. But when it dawned on me that this attitude change had taken place, I knew that I had not much time left as a park employee.

I was burned out from the constant struggle to keep the people back behind the ropes. It did not help that I myself had stepped off the marked path in the parks a thousand times and my spirit had profited by doing so. Sometimes I wanted to just throw open the doors and let the people all pour in. I was tired to death of trying to stop the miners and the tour buses and the developers. My desire to see the parks remain untouched never diminished; but to continue fighting the advance of civilization into the farthest reaches of wilderness was exhausting. I no longer could find it in me to keep fighting. I was approaching the state of mind where blowing up Glen Canyon Dam appeared to be a good idea.

I wanted to see the wilderness assert itself, but I could not help it to do so. My days as a ranger were numbered as soon as I admitted that my patience was wearing thin. During my last year as a ranger, I committed the cardinal sin: I became cynical about the Park Service, and about all the lemmings trying to get into the wilderness. I knew they would never reach it. I could not assist them. I had already given as much as I had to give.

Getting to the wilderness was what I had been trying to do for nine years. When I found it, I was amazed at the simplicity of the answer. To sit in total silence on a mountain top, one only had to be right there in the moment. Running rivers and reaching precipices had nothing to do with goals. The goals, getting to the take out and reaching the peak, were anticlimactic. The real wilderness experience was in the process of getting there.

If I could be out there, lost in six million acres of tundra, and not be tempted to rearrange the flowers so that they might be more photogenic, I would truly be living in the moment. If I could let go of the panic which rose up in my chest when a bear came within a stone's throw of my tent, then I would truly be a part of the land. If I could resist the urge to stay on the trails and let go of any particular destination as a goal, then I could coexist with all the wilderness.

I was incapable of explaining wilderness to anyone during my last year as a ranger. I had amassed hundreds of stories about trips and adventures, but none of them was I able to share. The sum total of all my experiences was far too complex to be told at a campfire talk. There were not, in fact, any words I could use to bring my journey to life for others.

Fresh new rangers arrived the year I burned out. On their faces I saw the same expectant look that I must have worn when I began to work as a parkie. It was right, I knew, that they take over where I had to leave off. I hoped those who came behind me—or at least some of them—had half the adventures and learning experiences as myself. I wished for them to possess all of the energy I had expended over the years dealing with the tide of tourists, and all the joy I had gathered from those magic moments, like the one on the plateau above Government Draw on the hour of the solstice, when I had actually faced a caribou as an equal.

On a Wednesday in mid-September, the park road, temporarily cleared of snow, was reopened as far as Toklat to private vehicles. The Labor Day traffic had abated; the few that had stayed around patiently were rewarded with the opportunity to venture on a clear, cold morning out into a nearly deserted park. Frost nipped at branches of aspen still decked with golden, precariously clinging leaves. I had been laid off for the season the day before; I suspected that this might be the only day left for me to head out that gravel road one more time.

As I drove up the road toward the Savage River check station, I thought about how those leaves hung on to the aspen trees, as if to forestall the inevitable winter which lay ahead. We all knew it was coming; like the aspen, I was out to catch one of the last glorious curtain calls of the daylight season. Sooner or later, I knew I too would have to let go.

"Termination dust" signals the end of Alaska's daylight season.

The tundra was crimson, mottled with licks of yellow and orange. I crossed the low rise at the base of Primrose Ridge, which divided the Savage and Sanctuary rivers, and slowed as I drove over the wood bridge spanning the Sanctuary. I stopped in a turnout which overlooked the river's meandering route through the valley. The rushing water disappeared into the same rock canyon in which Greta had made her last stand.

I climbed up a cliff to reach a wonderfully inviting patch of blueberries, each as big as my fingernail. The navy blue fruits were easy to spot against a bright orange background of tiny leaves. Tinged with frost, they possessed a slightly crunchy texture and a juicy sweetness unmatched by anything I had ever purchased in a grocery store. I gathered several handfuls of the autumn bounty and ate them all, gazing without purpose at the Sanctuary drainage. From behind the mountains the sun poked up, strong in its light but weakening in its ability to warm the land.

It is useless to try to melt the frost, I wanted to tell the sun. But of course I could not tell the sun anything. I watched the glimmer of autumn flicker like a candle flame on the tundra foliage, and for once I did not shout at the sun. I accepted it, and with the acceptance came a profound sense of peace.

Continuing on my drive out the park road after eating my fill of blueberries, I saw a bull moose near the road at Teklanika. I knew that the moose were gathering strength for their annual fall rutting season. They could feel the chill in the air and were aware of the shortening of the days, despite the sunshine. The bull ate willow branches greedily, his great heavy antlers bumping against spruce tree trunks.

I drove over Sable Pass and up to Polychrome. There was a little bit of snow on the road at Polychrome. Although my tire tracks had easily cut back down to dirt, I knew the route would not improve; for eight more months, it would be a matter of addition. The accumulation of snow had begun.

From Polychrome Pass, the road descended for several miles in a steady downhill grade until it reached the crossing at Toklat River. I parked my truck at a wide spot near the river. Walking to the high bank above the gravel-lined braids of the Toklat River, I gazed at a vista which to me embodied the best of the wilderness: a slate-gray wild river flowed between two unnamed craggy peaks in the height of autumn's brilliant blaze of color.

Gradually, I became aware of the presence of bears. Down below me, in the river bed, I spied a female grizzly bear herding three cubs of the year. The mother moved with the effortlessness and grace I had come to admire in all grizzlies. Far from being clumsy, she seemed to flow from one to another gravel patch, stopping every few feet to scoop some soapberries from a bush to her mouth in one smooth movement. She moved slowly, without destination or goal.

The three cubs were engrossed in play. They leapt exuberantly across small ravines and played hide and seek in the brambles. The cubs, too, moved gracefully. Unencumbered, they were fully alive in the moment of a sunny autumn day. Whether winter was approaching was of no concern to the playful bundles of blonde fur; neither did they appear to be concerned about the number of buses scheduled to traverse the park road next year or whether they might become marked and hunted animals if they bit into the rear end of a visiting Dutch girl.

And none of the bears noticed me. The vision of the four bears romping on the river bar in the autumn sun brought tears to my eyes. There, in the heart of Denali, those bears were free to live out their lives in peace and with freedom. The Toklat River was their domain.

I was proud that I had spent so many years helping to keep it pristine for those bears. On the river bar I received, finally, the letter of appreciation written by the residents of Denali and the other parks at which I had lived. My letter was that picture: the sight of those new cubs frolicking on the river bar. The cubs had been born in Denali in the summer of 1985, my final year as a parkie.

It was not a reward I could boast about on my resume. No bands played. Nobody cheered for me. But as I watched the bears move up the river bed, I knew that it was enough.

Hours passed. Clouds rolled in from the west, and an icy wind ruffled the golden fur on the backs of the fat bears. Reluctantly, I returned to my truck late in the afternoon and drove back toward the park entrance.

It began to snow just as I reached the highway at the end of the park road. Holding in my heart the vision of the bears on the river, I turned south and left Denali behind.

Epilogue

While the controversy begun in the 1970s about alleviating overcrowding in Yosemite Valley continues, private enterprise has quietly begun to develop what used to be the fringe areas of Yosemite Park. In June, 1990, a 242-room luxury hotel was opened in Fish Camp, California. The tiny town on the southern edge of Yosemite Park, as I remember it from my childhood days, has evolved into a high-priced tourist mecca. I am not sure I would recognize Fish Camp today, and I am probably better off remembering what it was like when its population consisted of a mere 13 souls.

In Yellowstone, the fires of 1988 consumed a good portion of the park, setting off a raging battle over the wisdom of the long-standing "let it burn" policy adhered to by the Yellowstone Park resource management people. Since that summer, however, vegetation has started to grow back, and it appears that the scars of those fires will fade with time. Though the results of the fires are aesthetically shocking to the tourists, they may prove to be healthy for the forest in the end.

One of the Kantishna miners opened a huge new RV park at Denali Park in the summer of 1990. His act challenged the time-honored park regulations for road access. As a result, anyone with business in Kantishna may now compete with shuttle buses and wildlife for room on the narrow road. I expect that challenge will culminate in a court battle over the access issue in the park.

Meanwhile, last fall I went back to visit the Grand Canyon after an absence of more than five years. The vista was a little bit hazier; the viewpoints were a little bit more crowded; meals in the restaurants cost a little bit more, and the quality of the food certainly had not improved. But, once I got away from the rim and hiked down into the canyon, I saw that it had endured. Canyon wrens still whistled down the evening, and hidden springs still emerged from the Redwall to soothe my sore feet after a long day of hiking.

It is my hope that enjoyment of the national parks is not hindered by overuse. "Leave them as they are . . . " and go out there. Experience all they have to offer. Dare to step off the beaten paths, so that you too may discover places of power in the national parks.

Kathleen R. Kemsley
Sterling, Alaska
September 27, 1990